NEW EDITION

McDougal Littell

Math*Thematics*

Student Workbook

- Labsheets
- Practice and Applications
- Study Guides

BOOK 1

McDougal Littell
A DIVISION OF HOUGHTON MIFFLIN COMPANY
Evanston, Illinois • Boston • Dallas

Acknowledgments

Writers

The authors of *Math Thematics, Books 1–3*, wish to thank the following writers for their contributions to the *Student Workbooks* for the *Math Thematics* program: **Lyle Anderson, Mary Buck, Roslyn Denny, Jean Howard, Deb Johnson, Sallie Morse, Patrick Runkel, Thomas Sanders-Garrett, Bonnie Spence, Christine Tuckerman.**

Image Credits

Photography
Front Cover © Atlantech; **69** © Don Hammond/Design Pics/Corbis; **225** Bonnie Spence/McDougal Littell/Houghton Mifflin Co.

Illustration
All art by McDougal Littell/Houghton Mifflin Co.

THE STEM PROJECT *McDougal Littell Math Thematics®* is based on the field-test versions of The STEM Project curriculum. The STEM Project was supported in part by the

 NATIONAL SCIENCE FOUNDATION

under Grant No. ESI-0137682. Opinions expressed in *McDougal Littell Math Thematics®* are those of the authors and not necessarily those of the National Science Foundation.

ISBN-13: 978-0-547-00102-9
ISBN-10: 0-547-00102-9

3456789–0982–11 10 09

Book 1 Student Workbook Contents

About the Student Workbook

About the Student Workbook v

Labsheets, Practice and Applications, and Study Guides

Module 1: Patterns and Problem Solving   **1**

    Section 1 3
    Section 2 10
    Section 3 15
    Extended Exploration 20
    Section 4 21
    Section 5 27
    Sections 1–5 36
    Module Project 38

Module 2: Math Detectives   **39**

    Section 1 41
    Section 2 48
    Section 3 56
    Section 4 67
    Sections 1–4 76
    Extended Exploration 79
    Review and Assessment 81

Module 3: Mind Games   **82**

    Section 1 84
    Section 2 91
    Section 3 99
    Section 4 107
    Section 5 111
    Section 6 116
    Sections 1–6 121

Module 4: Statistical Safari   **123**

    Section 1 125
    Section 2 140
    Section 3 145
    Section 4 153
    Section 5 164
    Sections 1–5 175
    Module Project 178

Module 5: Creating Things 179

Section 1 181

Section 2 190

Section 3 195

Extended Exploration 201

Section 4 203

Section 5 208

Section 6 215

Sections 1–6 220

Review and Assessment 222

Module 6: Comparisons and Predictions 223

Section 1 225

Section 2 230

Section 3 235

Section 4 242

Section 5 246

Section 6 253

Sections 1–6 263

Module 7: Wonders of the World 265

Section 1 267

Section 2 276

Section 3 279

Section 4 284

Section 5 298

Sections 1–5 304

Module 8: MATH-Thematical Mix 307

Section 1 309

Section 2 314

Section 3 317

Section 4 322

Section 5 325

Section 6 332

Sections 1–6 336

About the Student Workbook

This Student Workbook contains worksheets for you to use along with your *Math Thematics, Book 1,* textbook. Your teacher will direct you in the use of these materials. The materials in this Workbook include:

Labsheets

These worksheets will be used with various Setting the Stage, Exploration, Key Concepts, Practice and Application Exercises, Module Project, and Review and Assessment sections in your textbook. The labsheets present data and extend the scope of the textbook material.

Practice and Applications

These additional practice pages provide extra exercises for each section in a module. Combined practice that covers the whole module is also included.

Study Guides

These Study Guide pages, available for each section in a module, feature key concepts, worked-out examples, and exercises to help you review material and study for quizzes and tests.

Name _____   Problem _____

Teacher Assessment Scales

For use with Module 1

 ☆ *The star indicates that you excelled in some way.*

Problem Solving

❶   ❷   ❸   ❹   ❺ ➡

❶ You did not understand the problem well enough to get started or you did not show any work.

❸ You understood the problem well enough to make a plan and to work toward a solution.

❺ You made a plan, you used it to solve the problem, and you verified your solution.

Mathematical Language

❶   ❷   ❸   ❹   ❺ ➡

❶ You did not use any mathematical vocabulary or symbols, or you did not use them correctly, or your use was not appropriate.

❸ You used appropriate mathematical language, but the way it was used was not always correct or other terms and symbols were needed.

❺ You used mathematical language that was correct and appropriate to make your meaning clear.

Representations

❶   ❷   ❸   ❹   ❺ ➡

❶ You did not use any representations such as equations, tables, graphs, or diagrams to help solve the problem or explain your solution.

❸ You made appropriate representations to help solve the problem or help you explain your solution, but they were not always correct or other representations were needed.

❺ You used appropriate and correct representations to solve the problem or explain your solution.

Connections

❶   ❷   ❸   ❹   ❺ ➡

❶ You attempted or solved the problem and then stopped.

❸ You found patterns and used them to extend the solution to other cases, or you recognized that this problem relates to other problems, mathematical ideas, or applications.

❺ You extended the ideas in the solution to the general case, or you showed how this problem relates to other problems, mathematical ideas, or applications.

Presentation

❶   ❷   ❸   ❹   ❺ ➡

❶ The presentation of your solution and reasoning is unclear to others.

❸ The presentation of your solution and reasoning is clear in most places, but others may have trouble understanding parts of it.

❺ The presentation of your solution and reasoning is clear and can be understood by others.

Content Used: _____   **Computational Errors:**   Yes ☐   No ☐

Notes on Errors: _____

Name _____   Problem _____

Student Self-Assessment Scales

For use with Module 1

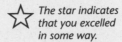 *If your score is in the shaded area, explain why on the back of this sheet and stop.*

☆ *The star indicates that you excelled in some way.*

 ## Problem Solving

❶   ❷   ❸   ❹   ❺

❶ I did not understand the problem well enough to get started or I did not show any work.

❷ I understood the problem well enough to make a plan and to work toward a solution.

❺ I made a plan, I used it to solve the problem, and I verified my solution.

 ## Mathematical Language

❶   ❷   ❸   ❹   ❺

❶ I did not use any mathematical vocabulary or symbols, or I did not use them correctly, or my use was not appropriate.

❷ I used appropriate mathematical language, but the way it was used was not always correct or other terms and symbols were needed.

❺ I used mathematical language that was correct and appropriate to make my meaning clear.

 ## Representations

❶   ❷   ❸   ❹   ❺

❶ I did not use any representations such as equations, tables, graphs, or diagrams to help solve the problem or explain my solution.

❷ I made appropriate representations to help solve the problem or help me explain my solution, but they were not always correct or other representations were needed.

❺ I used appropriate and correct representations to solve the problem or explain my solution.

 ## Connections

❶   ❷   ❸   ❹   ❺

❶ I attempted or solved the problem and then stopped.

❸ I found patterns and used them to extend the solution to other cases, or I recognized that this problem relates to other problems, mathematical ideas, or applications.

❺ I extended the ideas in the solution to the general case, or I showed how this problem relates to other problems, mathematical ideas, or applications.

 ## Presentation

❶   ❷   ❸   ❹   ❺

❶ The presentation of my solution and reasoning is unclear to others.

❸ The presentation of my solution and reasoning is clear in most places, but others may have trouble understanding parts of it.

❺ The presentation of my solution and reasoning is clear and can be understood by others.

Name _____   Date _____

A Dicey Problem (Use with the *Setting the Stage* on page 2.)

Directions Cut out the 3 operation squares at the bottom of the page.
Then read the rules below and play the game.

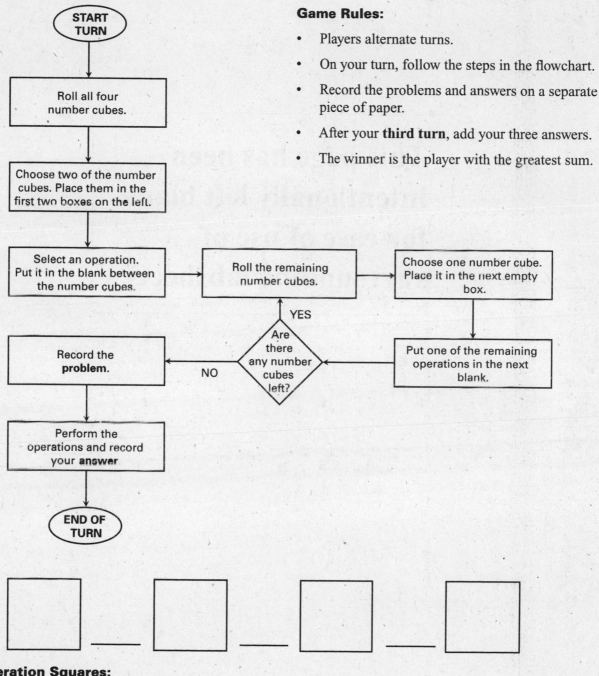

Game Rules:

- Players alternate turns.

- On your turn, follow the steps in the flowchart.

- Record the problems and answers on a separate piece of paper.

- After your **third turn**, add your three answers.

- The winner is the player with the greatest sum.

Operation Squares:

Math Thematics, Book 1
Student Workbook   **3**

This page has been
intentionally left blank
for ease of use of
surrounding labsheets.

Name _____ Date _____

The Great Arithmetic Race (Use with Questions 28 and 29 on page 9.)

Directions With your group, decide which role each of you will play in the game.

- **Player 1** You will use only mental math to find each answer.

- **Player 2** You will use paper and pencil to find each answer. Even if you know the answer, you must write out the entire problem and answer.

- **Player 3** You will use a calculator to find each answer. Even if you know the answer, you must enter the entire problem on your calculator.

- **Record Keeper.** Your job is to keep track of who answers the problem correctly and the order in which players answer. You may want to have the players raise their hands when they have an answer.

Now players 1, 2, and 3 will race to answer arithmetic problems called out by the teacher. The record keeper will record which computational method was the quickest for each problem.

	Mental Math		Paper and Pencil		Calculator	
	Correct?	1st, 2nd, 3rd	Correct?	1st, 2nd, 3rd	Correct?	1st, 2nd, 3rd
Problem #1						
Problem #2						
Problem #3						
Problem #4						
Problem #5						
Problem #6						
Problem #7						
Problem #8						
Problem #9						
Problem #10						

MODULE 1 Practice and Applications
For use with Section 1

For use with Exploration 1

1. Describe the order in which operations are performed to get the answers shown.

   a. $4 \cdot 9 - 7 = 29$
   b. $32 - 4 \cdot 3 = 20$
   c. $25 \div 5 + 9 = 14$
   d. $16 - 2 \cdot 3 + 8 = 18$

2. Find the value of each expression.

   a. $6 \cdot 8 + 5$
   b. $45 - 5 \cdot 7$
   c. $36 \div 6 + 2$
   d. $20 + 2 \cdot 8 - 3$
   e. $(4 + 8) \div 2 + 5$
   f. $9 + 72 \div 8$
   g. $3 + (10 - 6) \cdot 5$
   h. $35 - (12 + 8) + 4$
   i. $24 \div 6 \cdot (5 + 7)$
   j. $(18 - 9) \cdot 3 - 7$

3. Shelby bought 4 sets of baseball cards. There were 8 cards in each set. She gave 5 cards to her brother and 7 cards to her sister. How many cards did Shelby have left?

For use with Exploration 2

4. Estimate each sum or difference. If possible, decide whether the estimate is *greater than* or *less than* the exact answer.

   a. $153 + 79$
   b. $629 - 86$
   c. $12,132 + 4290$
   d. $384 + 176 + 206$
   e. $17,725 - 5321$
   f. $5161 - 2836$
   g. $48 + 65 + 88$
   h. $633 - 321$

5. Estimate each product. If possible, decide whether the estimate is *greater than* or *less than* the exact product.

   a. $17 \cdot 38$
   b. $42 \cdot 319$
   c. $98 \cdot 63$
   d. $384 \cdot 122$
   e. $2163 \cdot 426$
   f. $192 \cdot 14$
   g. $315 \cdot 6$
   h. $28 \cdot 17$

(continued)

Practice and Applications
For use with Section 1

6. Carla has $10 to spend at the supermarket on fruits and vegetables. The fruits and vegetables are sold by price per pound. If Carla wants to estimate to be sure that she has enough money to pay for the food, should her estimate for each weight and price be *greater than* or *less than* the actual price? Explain.

7. A caterer must determine the total number of shrimp that he will need for a large party. He thinks that 12 shrimp per person will be enough. About how many shrimp will he need for a party of 133 people? Is the estimate *greater than* or *less than* the actual number that he will need? Why might the caterer prefer the estimate to the exact answer?

8. Ralph must buy fabric to reupholster some furniture. He needs 38 yards of fabric for each sofa that he reupholsters. About how many yards of fabric will he need to reupholster 22 sofas? Is the estimate *greater than* or *less than* the exact answer? Do you think that Ralph would prefer his estimate to be greater than or less than the exact answer? Explain.

For use with Exploration 3

9. Use compatible numbers to find each sum by mental math.

   a. $70 + 63 + 30$

   b. $32 + 27 + 28 + 13$

   c. $84 + 22 + 98 + 16$

   d. $146 + 11 + 34 + 129$

   e. $65 + 25 + 42$

   f. $170 + 28 + 52 + 30$

10. Use compatible numbers to find each product by mental math.

   a. $3 \cdot 5 \cdot 4$

   b. $7 \cdot 5 \cdot 4 \cdot 5$

   c. $25 \cdot 8 \cdot 4$

   d. $4 \cdot 5 \cdot 25$

   e. $30 \cdot 2 \cdot 9$

   f. $20 \cdot 5 \cdot 8 \cdot 3$

Study Guide
For use with Section 1

The Science of Patterns   Operations, Estimation, and Mental Math

GOAL   **LEARN HOW TO:** • follow the order of operations
• estimate by rounding
• decide when to use an estimate
• use compatible numbers for mental math
• decide when to use mental math, paper and pencil, or a calculator

AS YOU: • look for patterns in number sentences
• look at everyday situations

An **expression** can contain numbers, operation symbols, and variables. For example, the dot between two numbers is a symbol for multiplication.

Exploration 1: Order of Operations

Order of Operations		
		$40 + (2 + 3) \cdot 7 - 14$
First	Calculate what is inside parentheses.	$= 40 + (2 + 3) \cdot 7 - 14$
		$= 40 + \quad 5 \quad \cdot 7 - 14$
Next	Perform multiplication and division in order from left to right.	$= 40 + 5 \cdot 7 - 14$
		$= 40 + \ 35 \ - 14$
Then	Perform addition and subtraction in order from left to right.	$= 40 + 35 - 14$
		$= \quad 75 \quad - 14$
		$= \qquad 61$

Exploration 2: Estimating With Rounding

When you do not need to know an exact answer, you can sometimes **estimate** an answer. **Rounding** is one method that is used to estimate sums, differences, products, and quotients. For example, to estimate the sum $198 + 72 + 34$, round to the nearest ten as $200 + 70 + 30 = 300$.

Exploration 3: Using Mental Math

When you need an exact answer, mental math may work. Look for **compatible numbers**, numbers that have sums and products that are easy to find and compute with.

Example

Look for partial sums that end in 0.   Look for partial products that end in 0.

$3 + 12 + 14 + 5$ $2 \cdot 5 \cdot 5 \cdot 21 \cdot 2$

$20 \rightarrow 20 + 14 = 34$ $100 \rightarrow 100 \cdot 21 = 2100$

Math Thematics, Book 1
Student Workbook

Study Guide: Practice & Application Exercises

For use with Section 1

Exploration 1

For Exercises 1–3, find the value of each expression.

1. $24 + 9 \cdot 4 \div 3$ 　　　　**2.** $5 \cdot 6 \div 2 + 8 \div 4$ 　　　　**3.** $6 + 2 \cdot (5 - 2) + 8$

4. To prepare for a canoe race, Paul rowed 2 hours one morning and 3 hours each of the next 5 mornings. Mort rowed 2 hours in the morning and 3 hours in the afternoon each day for 5 days.

    a. Write an expression to describe each boy's preparation time.

    b. Which boy had more preparation time? Explain.

Exploration 2

Estimate each answer. If possible, decide whether the estimate is _greater than_ or _less than_ the exact answer.

5. $98 + 63$ 　　　　**6.** $47 \cdot 890$ 　　　　**7.** $1139 \cdot 23$

8. $47 - 39$ 　　　　**9.** $99 \cdot 67$ 　　　　**10.** $\$15.98 + \$23.75$

11. $2956 \cdot 311$ 　　　　**12.** $103 + 191 + 99$ 　　　　**13.** $11 \cdot 71$

14. $\$68,256 - \$19,989$ 　　　　**15.** $321 \cdot 8$ 　　　　**16.** $12,977 + 1,104$

Exploration 3

Use compatible numbers to find each answer by mental math.

17. $4 \cdot 12 \cdot 15$ 　　　　**18.** $16 + 81 + 19 + 24$ 　　　　**19.** $50 \cdot 90 \cdot 4$

20. $3 + 17 + 21 + 19$ 　　　　**21.** $4 \cdot 5 \cdot 17 \cdot 5$ 　　　　**22.** $25 + 16 + 24 + 15$

23. $25 \cdot 2 \cdot 6 \cdot 4$ 　　　　**24.** $10 + 29 + 140 + 11$ 　　　　**25.** $20 \cdot 3 \cdot 30 \cdot 5$

26. $32 + 15 + 18$ 　　　　**27.** $6 \cdot 5 \cdot 25 \cdot 8$ 　　　　**28.** $77 + 46 + 13 + 14$

Explain how to use compatible numbers to estimate.

29. $416 \cdot 91$ 　　　　**30.** $78 \div 21$ 　　　　**31.** $1189 \cdot 237$

Name _____   Date _____

Practice and Applications

For use with Section 2

For use with Exploration 1

1. Look for a pattern and give the next term. Describe the rule you used.

   a. ◯, ⊖, ⊕, ⊛, ___?___

   b. ◇, ◇◇, ◇◇◇, ___?___

   c. △, ▽, △, ▽, ___?___

2. Look for a pattern and replace each ___?___ with the correct term. Describe the rule you used for each sequence.

   a. 1, 0.1, 0.01, 0.001, ___?___, ___?___

   b. 2, 40, 800, 16,000, ___?___, ___?___

   c. 1, $\frac{1}{4}$, $\frac{1}{9}$, $\frac{1}{16}$, ___?___, ___?___

   d. $\frac{1}{2}$, $\frac{1}{4}$, $\frac{1}{6}$, $\frac{1}{8}$, ___?___, ___?___

3. What is the next term in each sequence? What is its term number?

   a. 9, 18, 27, 36, 45, 54, …

   b. 6, 60, 600, 6000, …

   c. $\frac{1}{2}$, $\frac{2}{3}$, $\frac{3}{4}$, $\frac{4}{5}$, $\frac{5}{6}$, $\frac{6}{7}$, …

   d. 1, 2, 4, 8, 16, 32, 64, 128, …

4. In the thirteenth century, an Italian mathematician named Fibonacci studied the sequence 1, 1, 2, 3, 5, 8, 13, 21, … . This sequence often occurs in nature and is called the Fibonacci sequence. Describe a rule for the sequence, and then find the next three terms.

(continued)

Math Thematics, Book 1
Student Workbook

Name _____   Date _____

Practice and Applications
For use with Section 2

For use with Exploration 2

5. a. Extend the pattern below to include the next two shapes.

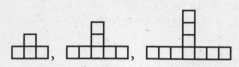

b. What rule did you use to extend the pattern?

6. For each sequence, first copy and complete the table. Then write an equation for the rule for the sequence, and use your rule to find the 20th term.

a.

Term number	1	2	3	4	?	?	?	?
Term	50	100	150	200	?	?	?	?

b.

Term number	7	8	9	10	?	?	?	?
Term	140	160	180	200	?	?	?	?

c.

Term number	1	2	3	4	?	?	?	?
Term	10	12	14	16	?	?	?	?

d.

Term number	1	2	3	4	?	?	?	?
Term	99	98	97	96	?	?	?	?

e.

Term number	1	2	3	4	?	?	?	?
Term	0	2	6	12	?	?	?	?

7. A designer is creating a triangular pattern for a mosaic. Each square represents a colored tile in the mosaic. Suppose he continues the pattern to include the next three terms. How many squares will be in the base of the last triangular shape? How many pieces of colored tile will he need to make the shape?

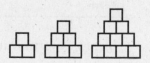

Name _____   Date _____

Study Guide

For use with Section 2

Shapely Numbers   Patterns and Sequences

GOAL   **LEARN HOW TO:** • find a rule to extend a pattern
• make a table to organize your work
• write an equation to find the terms of a sequence
• make predictions

AS YOU: • explore patterns using pattern blocks
• model sequences
• explore visual patterns

Exploration 1: Extending Patterns

Rule for a Pattern

A **rule** tells how to create or extend a pattern.

Example
Describe a rule for the pattern at the right. 
Sample Response
A rule for this pattern is to repeat .

Sequences

A **sequence** is an ordered list of numbers or objects.

4, 9, 14, 19, 24, ...

Each number or object of a sequence is a **term**.

14 is the third term of the sequence above.

The **term number** tells the order or position of the term in a sequence.

In the sequence above, the term number for the term 14 is 3.

A table can help you see how the term numbers and terms of a sequence are related.

Term number	1	2	3	4	5
Term	4	9	14	19	24

When you describe how to create or extend a sequence, you are giving a **rule** for the sequence.

<u>rule:</u> (5 × term number) − 1 = term
or
Start with 4 and add 5 to each
term to get the next term.

Name _____   Date _____

 **Study Guide**
For use with Section 2

Exploration 2: Analyzing Sequences

Variables and Expressions

A **variable** is a letter or symbol used to represent a quantity that is
unknown or can change. An expression can contain numbers, variables,
and operations. To **evaluate an expression** with one or more variables,
substitute a number for each variable and then carry out the operations.

> **Example**
>
> To evaluate the expression $15 + 7 \cdot x$ when $x = 6$, substitute the 6 for x and then follow
> the order of operations.
>
> $15 + 7 \cdot x = 15 + 7 \cdot 6$ ← Replace x with 6.
>
> $\qquad\qquad = 15 + 42 = 57$

Equations

An **equation** is a mathematical sentence
that uses the symbol "=" to show
that two expressions have the same value.

$100 \div 25 = 9 - 5$ is an equation.

You can write an equation to represent the rule for a sequence.

> **Example**
>
> Write an equation for the rule for the sequence 4, 9, 14, 19, 24, ….
> Use the equation to predict the 30th term of the sequence.
>
> ■ **Sample Response** ■
>
> Let $t =$ the term. Let $n =$ the term number.
>
> The term is 1 less than 5 times the number.
>
> $t = 5n - 1$
> $ = 5 \cdot 30 - 1$ ← For the 30th term, $n = 30$.
> $ = 150 - 1$
> $ = 149$ ← The 30th term is 149.

Study Guide: Practice & Application Exercises
For use with Section 2

Exploration 1

In Exercises 1 and 2, describe the rule for each pattern.

1. ▢▢ ▢▢ ▢▢ ▢▢ ▢▢ ▢▢

2. ABBCCCDDDD

3. If the pattern in Exercise 2 continues through the letter G, how many characters will have been used in the pattern?

4. Which of the numbers below shows a pattern of digits that is related to the visual pattern shown at the right? Explain your answer.

⊢ T ⊣ ⊢ T ⊣

   A. 222...   **B.** 242424...   **C.** 241241241...   **D.** 241524152415...

Exploration 2

In Exercises 5 and 6, look for a pattern and replace each ___?___ with the correct term. Describe the rule you used for each sequence.

5. 9, 15, 21, 27, __?__, __?__, __?__, __?__, 57

6. 101, 90, 79, 68, __?__, __?__, __?__, __?__, 13

7. **a.** Copy and complete the table.

Term number	1	2	3	4	?	?	?	?
Term	3	5	7	9	?	?	?	?

   b. How are the term numbers and terms related?

   c. Write an equation that can be used to find any term of the number sequence from its term number. Be sure to identify what each variable in the equation represents.

   d. Use your equation to find the 20th term of the number sequence.

8. Repeat parts (a)–(d) of Exercise 7 for the table below.

Term number	1	2	3	4	?	?	?	?
Term	8	16	24	32	?	?	?	?

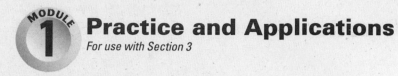

Practice and Applications
For use with Section 3

For use with Exploration 1

1. For each problem below, describe the problem you need to solve. State the important information in the problem. Do not solve the problems now.

    a. A long distance phone company offers two different rates. For the first service, you can call long distance at any time of the day for $0.15 per minute. For the second service, calls made during peak hours cost $0.30 per minute while calls made during off-peak hours cost $0.10 per minute. If you usually call between 45 and 50 minutes during off peak hours and 10 minutes during peak hours, which service should you choose?

    b. Janice has 3 winter hats (yellow, pink, purple), 4 pairs of mittens (green, red, black, blue), and two pairs of boots (black and blue). She must wear a hat, a pair of mittens, and a pair of boots to go sledding. How many different combinations of sledding clothes does Janice have?

For use with Exploration 2

2. Choose one or more strategies and describe how you could use the strategy to solve the problems in Exercise 1. Do not solve the problems now.

3. Tell whether the problem contains *too much* or *not enough* information. Identify any extra or missing information.

    a. Franco read 8 more mystery books than science fiction books this month. He also read 4 books about animals. How many books did Franco read altogether this month?

    b. Tickets to the movie theater are $3.75 for children under 12 and $6.50 for adults. What is the total cost of 8 adult tickets?

For use with Exploration 3

4. Solve the problems in Exercise 1.

5. Tricia is at the library. It takes her 10 minutes to walk home from the library, 15 minutes to get ready for soccer practice, and 10 minutes to walk to the park for practice. If Tricia has soccer practice at 5:00 P.M., by what time should she leave the library to be on time?

Math Thematics, Book 1

Study Guide
For use with Section 3

What's the Plan?   A Problem Solving Approach

GOAL **LEARN HOW TO:** • develop an understanding of a problem
• make a plan to solve a problem
• use several problem solving strategies
• carry out a plan and look back

AS YOU: • play and think about the *Card Swappers* game
• complete the 4-step approach to solve the *Card Swappers* problem

Exploration 1: Understand the Problem

To understand a problem, you should:

• Read the problem carefully, probably several times.
• Restate the problem in your own words.
• Identify the important information in the problem.

Example

A food stand at a shopping mall has three specials.   Below are the individual prices.

Special	Menu	Price
No. 1	Soup, 2 Salads, Pretzel, Drink	$6.00
No. 2	Salad, Pretzel, Drink	$4.00
No. 3	Salad, Drink	$3.00

Soup	$1.00
Salad	$2.00
Drink	$1.00
Pretzel	$2.00

Which special saves the most money?

Sample Response

Step 1 State the problem you need to solve.

Which special saves the most money?

Step 2 State the important information.

the price of each special
the price of each individual item

Step 3 Identify any information missing.

whether there are options for portion size

Name _____   Date _____

Study Guide
For use with Section 3

Exploration 2: Make a Plan

To make a plan, you may try one or more problem solving strategies.

- Look for a pattern
- Make an organized list
- Make a table
- Try a simpler problem
- Use logical reasoning
- Act it out
- Work backward
- Guess and check
- Make a picture or diagram

Exploration 3: Carry Out the Plan and Look Back

As you try to solve the problem using your plan, you may need to try different strategies.

Examine your result to check that:
- You have answered the question being asked.
- Your solution seems reasonable.
- Your work is accurate.

Ask yourself if you can:
- Find another method of solution and compare the results.
- Remember other problems with similar solutions.
- Generalize your solution to any situation.

Study Guide: Practice & Application Exercises
For use with Section 3

Exploration 1

For Exercises 1–8, do parts (a)–(c). Do not solve the problems.

a. Describe the problem you need to solve.

b. State the important information in the problem.

c. Identify any information missing from the problem.

1. Tenisha's little brother just learned to count. While at the playground one day, he told her he had counted the feet of all the pigeons and all the cats, and that there were a total of 38 feet. If there were twelve pigeons and cats altogether, how many cats were there?

2. In the diagram a large square is divided into nine smaller squares. Find the total number of squares of all sizes contained in the diagram.

3. Joe has one penny, one nickel, and one dime. How many different amounts of money can he make by taking one, two, or three of the coins?

4. Al runs the elevator in a building. He took Ms. Jacob up 6 floors from the middle floor, where she lives. Then Al went down 5 floors, where he picked up Sally. He took her down 10 floors to the first-floor lobby. What is the number of the floor where Ms. Jacob lives?

5. Kevin has $75.00. He bought a pair of pants for $24.95 and three shirts for $12.00 each. He wants to buy a pair of shorts for $14.95. Does he have enough money left?

6. Allison is growing a tomato plant. After four weeks, the plant was 12 inches tall. By the fifth week, the plant grew to 15 inches tall. By the sixth week, it was 18 inches tall. If the tomato plant continues to grow at this rate, how tall will it be in 10 weeks?

7. David is at the post office. He walks three blocks north to the barber shop. Then he walks five blocks east to the fruit stand. After that, he walks two blocks south to the grocery store. Then he walks 12 blocks west and arrives home. How far away is David's house from the post office?

8. Becca has several tasks to do on Saturday morning. She has to practice piano for 45 minutes. Then she has to spend 30 minutes cleaning her room. She also has to return a book to the library, which is a 20-minute bike ride from her house. Once home, she needs 20 minutes to change clothes and get ready for lunch with her aunt. If lunch is at noon, what time does Becca need to begin her tasks?

(continued)

Study Guide: Practice & Application Exercises

For use with Section 3

Exploration 2

9. Explain how you could use the guess and check strategy to solve the problem in Exercise 1.

10. Solve the problem in Exercise 2 by solving a simpler problem. Determine the number of different-sized squares separately.

11. Solve the problem in Exercise 3 by making an organized list.

12. Solve the problem in Exercise 4 by working backward.

13. Solve the problem in Exercise 5 by using logical reasoning.

14. Solve the problem in Exercise 6 by looking for a pattern.

15. Solve the problem in Exercise 7 by making a picture or diagram.

16. Solve the problem in Exercise 8 and describe any strategies you used.

Exploration 3

17. Carry out parts (a)–(c) below for this problem.

Find the sum of the first 25 odd numbers: $1 + 3 + 5 + 7 + \cdots$.

a. Solve the problem.

b. Describe the plan you used.

c. Look back:

- Did you answer the question asked in the problem?
- Does your solution seem reasonable? Explain.
- How can you check your work? Explain.
- Is the problem similar to other problems you have solved? If so, how is it similar?
- Can you generalize your solution to the sum of any number of consecutive odd numbers beginning with 1?

18. Is there another method you could have used to solve Exercise 17? Explain.

Name _____ Date _____

EXTENDED EXPLORATION LABSHEET E²

Geese Galore (Use with Extended Exploration on page 38.)

Math Thematics, Book 1
Student Workbook

Name _____Susu_____   Date _September_

Relating the Part to the Whole (Use with Question 5 on page 41.)

Directions: Use pattern blocks to complete the table.

Part	Whole	Fraction
red trapezoid	yellow hexagon	1 red trapezoid is $\frac{1}{2}$ of a yellow hexagon.
green triangle	blue rhombus	1 green triangle is __$\frac{1}{2}$__ of a blue rhombus.
green triangle	yellow hexagon	1 green triangle is __1/2__ of a yellow hexagon.
5 green triangles	yellow hexagon	5 green triangles are __5/6__ of a yellow hexagon.
green triangle	red trapezoid	1 green triangle is __1/3__ of a red trapezoid.
2 green triangles	red trapezoid	2 green triangles are __2/3__ of a red trapezoid.
blue rhombus	yellow hexagon	1 blue rhombus is __1/3__ of a yellow hexagon.
2 blue rhombuses	yellow hexagon	2 blue rhombuses are __2/5__ of a yellow hexagon.

Fractions of Shapes (Use with Question 5 on page 41.)

Directions Divide each shape into equal-sized parts and shade the parts
so that the shaded portion represents the given fraction.

$\frac{1}{2}$

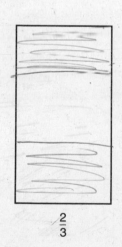

$\frac{2}{3}$

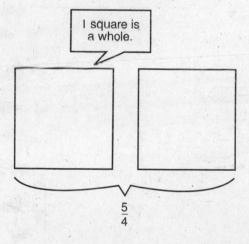

I square is a whole.

$\frac{5}{4}$

Math Thematics, Book 1
Student Workbook   **21**

MODULE 1   **LABSHEET** **4B**

Cover Each Shape (Use with Question 6 on page 41.)

Directions for each shape:

• Use pattern blocks of a single color to cover the shape. Use the fewest number of blocks possible.

• Trace around each block to show your solution.

• Cover the given fraction of the shape. Then shade the part of the shape you covered.

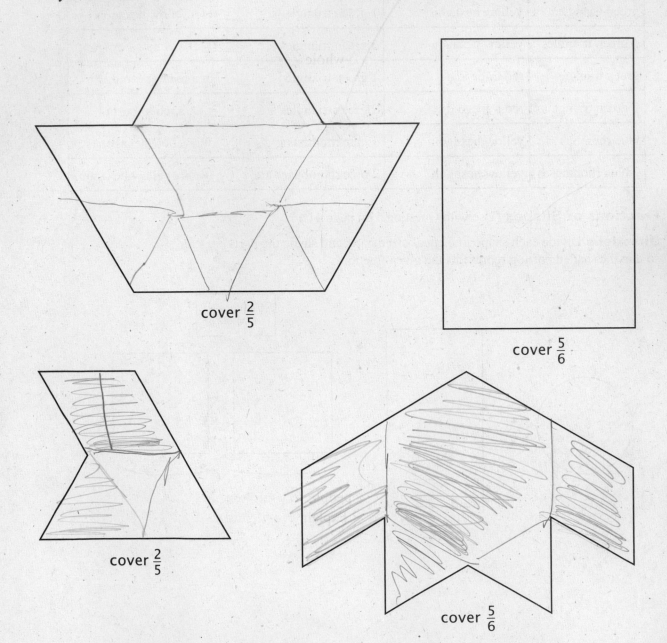

cover $\frac{2}{5}$

cover $\frac{5}{6}$

cover $\frac{2}{5}$

cover $\frac{5}{6}$

Name _____ Date _____

Practice and Applications

For use with Section 4

For use with Exploration 1

1. Write a fraction for the shaded part of each figure.

a.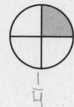

$\frac{1}{4}$

b.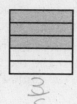

$\frac{3}{5}$

c.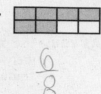

$\frac{6}{8}$

2. △ represents the whole. Write each part to whole relationship as a fraction and as a mixed number.

a.

$1\frac{3}{}$

b.

$2\frac{1}{4}$

c.

$1\frac{2}{4}$

For use with Exploration 2

3. Rewrite each fraction as a mixed number.

a. $\frac{11}{4}$ **b.** $\frac{7}{5}$ **c.** $\frac{19}{6}$

d. $\frac{13}{8}$ **e.** $\frac{11}{3}$ **f.** $\frac{35}{8}$

4. Rewrite each mixed number as a fraction.

a. $1\frac{7}{12}$ **b.** $2\frac{5}{6}$ **c.** $8\frac{1}{2}$

d. $5\frac{1}{3}$ **e.** $2\frac{3}{8}$ **f.** $1\frac{4}{5}$

5. Write each quotient as a mixed number.

a. $28 \div 3$ **b.** $39 \div 5$ **c.** $84 \div 10$

6. Suppose you are sharing 9 dollars among 4 people. Which form of $9 \div 4$ would you use to describe each share? Explain your choice.

A. 2 R1 **B.** 2.25 **C.** $2\frac{1}{4}$

Name _____ Date _____

 **Study Guide**
For use with Section 4

From Coins to Kites   Fractions and Mixed Numbers

GOAL   **LEARN HOW TO:** • write a fraction and a mixed number
• write a fraction greater than 1 as a
mixed number and vice versa

AS YOU: • use pattern blocks to explore the relationship
between part of a design and the whole design
• trade pattern blocks in the game *Flex Your Hex*

Exploration 1: Fractional Parts

Fractions

A **fraction** is a number that tells how a part of an object or part of a set
compares to the whole. The **numerator**, at the top of the fraction, tells
how many parts to consider. The **denominator**, at the bottom, tells how
many equal-sized parts the whole is divided into.

> **Example**
>
> The fraction $\frac{2}{3}$ is used to indicate that 2 of the 3 equal-sized parts
> of the whole triangle are shaded.

Mixed Numbers

When a fraction represents a part that is more than a whole, it can also be
written as a **mixed number**, the sum of a whole number and a nonzero
fraction less than one.

$$1\frac{5}{8}$$

whole-number part   fraction part

> **Example**
>
> If [ ] represents the whole, then [   ]
> [   ] can be represented by either the fraction $\frac{5}{4}$ or the mixed number $1\frac{1}{4}$.

 **Study Guide**
For use with Section 4

Exploration 2: Mixed Numbers

Fractions Greater Than 1

Fractions to Mixed Numbers

You can write fractions greater than 1 as mixed numbers by using division.

$$\frac{13}{8} = 8\overline{)13}\;^{1\;R5} = 1\frac{5}{8}$$

Mixed Numbers to Fractions

You can write a mixed number as a fraction greater than 1 by rewriting the whole number as a fraction and then combining it with the fraction part that is already there.

$$1\frac{5}{8} = \frac{8}{8} + \frac{5}{8} = \frac{13}{8}$$

Quotients as Mixed Numbers

The remainder in a division problem can be written over the divisor to form the fraction part of a mixed number.

$$13 \div 8 \rightarrow 8\overline{)13}\;^{1\;R5} = 1\frac{5}{8}$$

Name _____ Date _____

Study Guide: Practice & Application Exercises
For use with Section 4

Exploration 1

1. a. A study hall has 60 seats. The shaded portion of each circle below shows the fraction of the seats that are used for each of the first 3 periods. What are the fractions?

Period 1 Period 2 Period 3

b. Make an observation about the manner in which the study hall is used for all 3 periods.

2. a. What fraction of the figure is shaded?

b. What fraction of the figure is not shaded?

c. What is the sum of the fractions in parts (a) and (b)? Why?

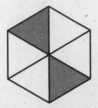

3. If each heart shape represents a whole, what is the part to whole relationship represented by the figure at the right? Write the relationship as a fraction and as a mixed number.

Exploration 2

Rewrite each fraction as a mixed number.

4. $\frac{15}{2}$ **5.** $\frac{23}{4}$ **6.** $\frac{143}{10}$ **7.** $\frac{120}{11}$

Rewrite each mixed number as a fraction.

8. $3\frac{2}{5}$ **9.** $1\frac{7}{16}$ **10.** $30\frac{5}{7}$ **11.** $10\frac{10}{13}$

Visual Thinking Copy the number line. Mark and label a point on the line where each fraction or mixed number would lie.

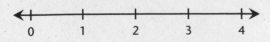

12. $\frac{9}{8}$ **13.** $3\frac{3}{8}$ **14.** $\frac{16}{8}$ **15.** $\frac{26}{16}$

MODULE 1   **LABSHEET** **5A**

Hexagon Section (Use with Question 3 on page 54.)

Directions Follow the steps in your book for covering the hexagon with pattern blocks. You will need blue rhombuses and green triangles from your pattern block set.

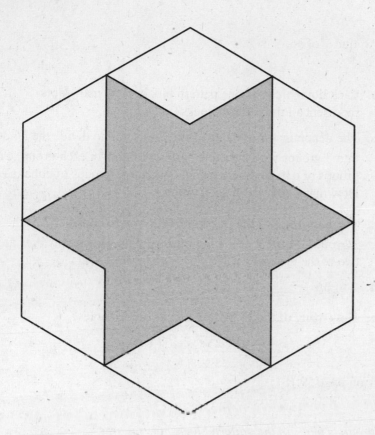

MODULE 1   **LABSHEET** 5B

Dot Grid 1 (Use with Question 20 on page 59.)

A class using 36 pattern blocks predicts that $\frac{2}{3}$ of the pattern blocks are triangles.

Directions Complete parts (a)–(d) to find $\frac{2}{3}$ of 36.

○ ○ ○ ○ ○ ○   **a.** Each dot represents one pattern block. How many dots
                        represent all the pattern blocks?

○ ○ ○ ○ ○ ○   **b.** The denominator of the fraction $\frac{2}{3}$ tells you to divide the 36 dots
                        into 3 groups with the same number of dots in each group. Circle
○ ○ ○ ○ ○ ○   groups of dots to divide the 36 dots into 3 groups of equal size.
                        How many dots are in each group?

○ ○ ○ ○ ○ ○   **c.** The numerator of the fraction $\frac{2}{3}$ tells you to consider 2 of the
                        3 groups. Shade 2 of the 3 groups of dots. How many dots are in
○ ○ ○ ○ ○ ○   two of the groups?

○ ○ ○ ○ ○ ○   **d.** $\frac{2}{3}$ of 36 = _____

                        e. How many of the 36 pattern blocks are triangles?

....

Dot Grid 2 (Use with Question 21 on page 59.)

A class using 24 pattern blocks predicts that $\frac{3}{4}$ of the pattern blocks are squares.

Directions Complete parts (a) and (b) to find $\frac{3}{4}$ of 24.

○ ○ ○ ○ ○ ○   **a.** Circle groups of dots to divide the 24 dots into 4 groups with
                        the same number of dots in each group. Then shade $\frac{3}{4}$ of 24.

○ ○ ○ ○ ○ ○   **b.** $\frac{3}{4}$ of 24 = _____

○ ○ ○ ○ ○ ○   **c.** How many of the 24 pattern blocks are squares?

○ ○ ○ ○ ○ ○

Math Thematics, Book 1   Copyright © McDougal Littell/Houghton Mifflin Company.
Student Workbook

Practice and Applications
For use with Section 5

For use with Exploration 1

1. Rectangular windows of the same size are divided into different panes of glass. The shaded area shows where each window is covered with a curtain.

A	B	C	D

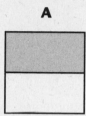 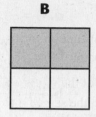 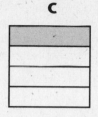 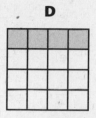

    a. What fraction of each window is covered?

    b. Which of the fractions in part (a) are equivalent?

2. Write two equivalent fractions that tell what part of each figure is shaded.

    a.   **b.** 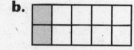   **c.**

    d. 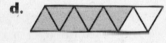   **e.**   **f.**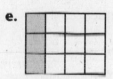

    g. 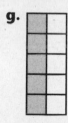   **h.**   **i.**

3. A circular glass window is divided into 8 equal panels. One half of the panels are tinted. What fraction, in eighths, is equivalent to the fraction of tinted panels in the glass window?

(continued)

Practice and Applications
For use with Section 5

For use with Exploration 2

4. Copy and complete the equivalent fractions.

a. $\dfrac{3}{4} = \dfrac{3 \cdot 2}{4 \cdot 2} = \dfrac{6}{?}$

b. $\dfrac{2}{3} = \dfrac{2 \cdot ?}{3 \cdot ?} = \dfrac{?}{12}$

c. $\dfrac{5}{6} = \dfrac{5 \cdot ?}{6 \cdot ?} = \dfrac{?}{12}$

d. $\dfrac{1}{2} = \dfrac{? \cdot ?}{? \cdot ?} = \dfrac{?}{16}$

e. $\dfrac{4}{8} = \dfrac{4 \div 4}{8 \div 4} = \dfrac{1}{?}$

f. $\dfrac{8}{20} = \dfrac{8 \div ?}{20 \div ?} = \dfrac{?}{5}$

g. $\dfrac{6}{24} = \dfrac{6 \div ?}{24 \div ?} = \dfrac{?}{4}$

h. $\dfrac{12}{18} = \dfrac{? \div ?}{? \div ?} = \dfrac{?}{3}$

5. Complete each pair of equivalent fractions.

a. $\dfrac{3}{5} = \dfrac{?}{15}$

b. $\dfrac{4}{9} = \dfrac{8}{?}$

c. $\dfrac{5}{8} = \dfrac{?}{32}$

d. $\dfrac{2}{3} = \dfrac{?}{18}$

e. $\dfrac{7}{8} = \dfrac{14}{?}$

f. $\dfrac{3}{4} = \dfrac{?}{36}$

g. $\dfrac{16}{36} = \dfrac{?}{9}$

h. $\dfrac{14}{21} = \dfrac{2}{?}$

i. $\dfrac{8}{32} = \dfrac{?}{16}$

j. $\dfrac{9}{27} = \dfrac{?}{3}$

k. $\dfrac{18}{30} = \dfrac{3}{?}$

l. $\dfrac{16}{20} = \dfrac{?}{5}$

6. Find the next three terms in each sequence.

a. $\dfrac{1}{4}, \dfrac{2}{8}, \dfrac{3}{12}, \dfrac{4}{16}, \cdots$

b. $\dfrac{2}{5}, \dfrac{4}{10}, \dfrac{6}{15}, \dfrac{8}{20}, \cdots$

c. $\dfrac{1}{2}, \dfrac{3}{6}, \dfrac{9}{18}, \dfrac{27}{54}, \cdots$

7. Choose the fractions in each list that are in lowest terms.

a. $\dfrac{6}{24}, \dfrac{5}{24}, \dfrac{4}{24}$

b. $\dfrac{4}{6}, \dfrac{8}{10}, \dfrac{6}{7}$

c. $\dfrac{3}{9}, \dfrac{3}{5}, \dfrac{3}{12}$

8. Write each fraction in lowest terms.

a. $\dfrac{16}{28}$

b. $\dfrac{15}{25}$

c. $\dfrac{8}{24}$

d. $\dfrac{12}{48}$

e. $\dfrac{18}{48}$

f. $\dfrac{16}{40}$

9. A screen is comprised of three large panels. The large panels are separated into smaller panels. Write three equivalent fractions for the center of the screen.

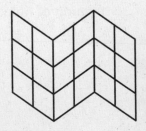

(continued)

Math Thematics, Book 1
Student Workbook

Name _____   Date _____

 Practice and Applications
For use with Section 5

For use with Exploration 3

10. Use mental math to find each value.

    a. $\frac{2}{3}$ of 9   **b.** $\frac{4}{5}$ of 20   **c.** $\frac{3}{8}$ of 16

    d. $\frac{3}{4}$ of 28   **e.** $\frac{2}{9}$ of 36   **f.** $\frac{2}{3}$ of 18

    g. $\frac{2}{5}$ of 15   **h.** $\frac{3}{7}$ of 21   **i.** $\frac{3}{8}$ of 40

    j. $\frac{2}{3}$ of 24   **k.** $\frac{4}{9}$ of 45   **l.** $\frac{5}{6}$ of 12

11. a. If $\frac{5}{8}$ of 24 marbles are clear, how many marbles are clear?

    b. How many striped marbles are there in a set of 35 marbles that is $\frac{2}{5}$ striped?

12. Eleven of the students in Mr. Fisher's class are girls. When Mrs. Jackson's class joins Mr. Fisher's class, there are a total of 45 students. In both classes combined, $\frac{3}{5}$ of the students are girls. How many students in Mrs. Jackson's class are girls?

13. Use compatible numbers to estimate.

    a. $\frac{1}{5}$ of 26   **b.** $\frac{3}{4}$ of 17   **c.** $\frac{2}{3}$ of 61

    d. $\frac{1}{6}$ of 35   **e.** $\frac{3}{7}$ of 20   **f.** $\frac{1}{3}$ of 29

    g. $\frac{2}{9}$ of 19   **h.** $\frac{1}{4}$ of 41   **i.** $\frac{2}{5}$ of 16

    j. $\frac{5}{6}$ of 31   **k.** $\frac{1}{8}$ of 25   **l.** $\frac{3}{5}$ of 44

Study Guide
For use with Section 5

The Same or Different?   Equivalent Fractions

GOAL   **LEARN HOW TO:** • recognize equivalent fractions
• find equivalent fractions
• write a fraction in lowest terms
• find a fraction of a whole number

AS YOU: • explore arrangements of floor tiles
• use pattern blocks to make floor designs
• make predictions from a sample of pattern blocks

Exploration 1: Recognizing Equivalent Fractions

Different fractions that name the same portion of a whole are
equivalent fractions.

Example

A regular polygon has equal sides and angles.
The first regular hexagon shown at the right is
divided into 6 congruent, or even, parts, 2 of which
are shaded.

The second regular hexagon is congruent to the first.

It shows that $\frac{1}{3}$ of the hexagon is congruent to the

shaded part of the first hexagon. This shows that $\frac{2}{6}$ and $\frac{1}{3}$

are equivalent fractions.

Exploration 2: Finding Equivalents

To find a fraction that is equivalent to a given
fraction, use either of these methods:

Multiply the numerator and denominator of the
given fraction by the same nonzero whole number.

$$\frac{3}{8} = \frac{3 \cdot 2}{8 \cdot 2} = \frac{6}{16}$$

So, $\frac{3}{8}$ is equivalent to $\frac{6}{16}$.

or

Divide the numerator and denominator of the
given fraction by the same nonzero whole number.

$$\frac{25}{50} = \frac{25 \div 25}{50 \div 25} = \frac{1}{2}$$

So, $\frac{25}{50}$ is equivalent to $\frac{1}{2}$.

Math Thematics, Book 1
Student Workbook

32

Name _____   Date _____

 **Study Guide**
For use with Section 5

Lowest Terms

When 1 is the only whole number that divides both the numerator and denominator evenly, the fraction is said to be in **lowest terms**.

The fraction $\frac{3}{8}$ is in lowest terms.

Exploration 3: Fractions of Whole Numbers

Finding a Fraction of a Whole

A **sample** is part of a whole set of objects being studied. The whole set is called the **population**. If you know how many objects are in a population and what fractional part of that population a sample represents, you can determine how many objects are in the sample.

Example

Suppose $\frac{3}{5}$ of the 30 fish in an aquarium are guppies. How many of the fish are guppies?

Sample Response

Separate the 30 fish into 5 equal-sized groups.
→ There are 6 fish in each group.

Find the number of fish in 3 of these groups.
→ There are 3(6), or 18 fish in 3 groups.

So, $\frac{3}{5}$ of 30 is 18. There are 18 guppies in the aquarium.

Name _____   Date _____

 Study Guide: Practice & Application Exercises
For use with Section 5

Exploration 1

For Exercises 1–6, write two equivalent fractions that tell what part of each figure is shaded.

1.   2.   3.

4. 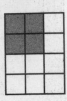   5.   6.

7. Copy and shade the three figures so that they model equivalent fractions. Write the fractions.

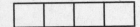 

Exploration 2

Complete each pair of equivalent fractions.

8. $\dfrac{3}{5} = \dfrac{?}{20}$ 9. $\dfrac{7}{11} = \dfrac{?}{55}$ 10. $\dfrac{5}{8} = \dfrac{45}{?}$

Divide the numerator and denominator of each fraction by 4. Write the result. Is the result in lowest terms? If not, tell how you can find an equivalent fraction in lowest terms.

11. $\dfrac{4}{8}$ 12. $\dfrac{56}{84}$ 13. $\dfrac{60}{180}$

In Exercises 14–19, write each fraction in lowest terms.

14. $\dfrac{45}{60}$ 15. $\dfrac{36}{72}$ 16. $\dfrac{45}{125}$

17. $\dfrac{35}{50}$ 18. $\dfrac{12}{42}$ 19. $\dfrac{80}{120}$

20. Find the next three terms of the sequence $\dfrac{1}{1 \cdot 2}, \dfrac{1}{2 \cdot 3}, \dfrac{1}{3 \cdot 4}, \cdots$

(continued)

Math Thematics, Book 1
Student Workbook

Name _____   Date _____

Study Guide: Practice & Application Exercises
For use with Section 5

Exploration 3

Use mental math to find each value.

21. $\frac{2}{3}$ of 21   **22.** $\frac{3}{4}$ of 24   **23.** $\frac{5}{16}$ of 48   **24.** $\frac{7}{10}$ of 1000

Use compatible numbers to estimate.

25. $\frac{2}{5}$ of 27   **26.** $\frac{5}{7}$ of 29   **27.** $\frac{4}{9}$ of 87   **28.** $\frac{3}{5}$ of 9800

Food Inspection A supermarket purchased a mixture consisting of 4 types of nuts. An inspector examined a sample of the mixture to determine the extent of the variety. Use the table of results for Exercises 29 and 30.

Type of nut	Number of grams in sample
almonds	200
peanuts	800
pecans	400
walnuts	600

29. What fraction of the sample is each type of nut? Write each fraction in lowest terms.

   a. almonds   **b.** peanuts   **c.** pecans   **d.** walnuts

30. In all, there were 50 kilograms of the mixture of nuts. Use your answer to Exercise 29 to estimate the number of kilograms of each type of nut in the mixture.

31. If $\frac{2}{5}$ of the 35 fruits in a basket are oranges, how many are oranges?

32. If $\frac{3}{8}$ of the 24 animals in a pet shop are cats, how many are cats?

33. If $\frac{4}{7}$ of the 14 paints in a paint set are watercolor, how many are watercolor?

34. How many roses are there in a bouquet of 36 flowers that is $\frac{3}{4}$ roses?

35. About how many trout are there in a pond of 891 fish that is $\frac{1}{9}$ trout?

36. Fifteen of the coins in Jillian's purse are pennies. She removes all of the coins from her purse and puts them into her piggy bank. There are now a total of 75 coins in her piggy bank. Two-thirds of the coins in the piggy bank are pennies. How many pennies were there in the piggy bank before Jillian added the coins from her purse?

Name _____   Date _____

Practice and Applications

For use after Sections 1–5

For use with Section 1

1. Find the value of each expression.

   a. $8 \cdot 5 - 4$ **b.** $16 + 4 \cdot 6$

   c. $(3 + 9) \div 3 + 9$ **d.** $100 - 40 \div 2$

2. Estimate each sum or difference. Decide whether the estimate is *greater than* or *less than* the exact answer.

   a. $278 + 81$ **b.** $731 - 92$

   c. $17{,}256 + 3350$ **d.** $12{,}942 - 8210$

3. Use compatible numbers to find each product by mental math.

   a. $4 \cdot 7 \cdot 5$ **b.** $5 \cdot 3 \cdot 4 \cdot 5$

   c. $20 \cdot 9 \cdot 5$ **d.** $4 \cdot 6 \cdot 25$

For use with Section 2

4. Look for a pattern and replace each ___?___ with the correct term. Describe the rule you used.

   a. $4, 0.4, 0.04, 0.004,$ __?__ , __?__   **b.** $\frac{1}{3}, \frac{1}{5}, \frac{1}{7}, \frac{1}{9},$ __?__ , __?__

5. What is the next term in each sequence? What is its term number?

   a. $7, 14, 21, 28, 35, \ldots$ **b.** $3, 9, 27, 81, \ldots$

6. Complete the table. Then write an equation for the rule for the sequence, and use your equation to find the 20th term.

Term number	1	2	3	4	?	?	?	?
Term	30	60	90	120	?	?	?	?

For use with Section 3

7. Dylan has 2 pairs of shorts (black and blue), 3 pairs of socks (black, white, blue), and 3 jerseys (yellow, green, and blue). He wears a pair of shorts, a pair of socks, and a jersey to soccer practice. How many different combinations of soccer clothes does Dylan have?

(continued)

Practice and Applications
For use after Sections 1–5

For use with Section 4

8. Rewrite each fraction as a mixed number.

    a. $\dfrac{10}{3}$ **b.** $\dfrac{9}{4}$ **c.** $\dfrac{29}{8}$

    d. $\dfrac{12}{7}$ **e.** $\dfrac{15}{2}$ **f.** $\dfrac{17}{6}$

9. Rewrite each mixed number as a fraction.

    a. $1\dfrac{5}{6}$ **b.** $3\dfrac{2}{9}$ **c.** $5\dfrac{1}{2}$

    d. $8\dfrac{3}{4}$ **e.** $2\dfrac{4}{5}$ **f.** $1\dfrac{5}{12}$

10. Write each quotient as a mixed number.

    a. $26 \div 4$ **b.** $43 \div 7$ **c.** $79 \div 11$

11. Suppose you are dividing 5 cups of cereal among 3 bowls. Which fraction or mixed number describes the amount of cereal in each bowl?

    A. 1 R2   **B.** 3.5   **C.** $1\dfrac{2}{3}$

For use with Section 5

12. Complete each pair of equivalent fractions.

    a. $\dfrac{2}{3} = \dfrac{?}{9}$ **b.** $\dfrac{3}{8} = \dfrac{15}{?}$ **c.** $\dfrac{5}{9} = \dfrac{?}{18}$

    d. $\dfrac{4}{5} = \dfrac{?}{20}$ **e.** $\dfrac{2}{7} = \dfrac{6}{?}$ **f.** $\dfrac{7}{12} = \dfrac{?}{36}$

13. Write each fraction in lowest terms.

    a. $\dfrac{12}{30}$ **b.** $\dfrac{18}{27}$ **c.** $\dfrac{6}{32}$

    d. $\dfrac{15}{45}$ **e.** $\dfrac{16}{32}$ **f.** $\dfrac{20}{35}$

14. Use mental math to find each value.

    a. $\dfrac{3}{5}$ of 30   **b.** $\dfrac{5}{8}$ of 56   **c.** $\dfrac{7}{9}$ of 36

MODULE 1   **PROJECT LABSHEET** Ⓐ

30 Pennies in a Row

The Situation

There were thirty pennies in a row. A nickel replaced the second penny and every second penny after it. Next, a dime replaced the third coin and every third coin after it. Then, a quarter replaced the fourth coin, and every fourth coin after it. Finally, a fifty-cent piece replaced the fifth coin, and every fifth coin after it.

The Problem

Suppose each sixth coin is now replaced with a silver dollar. What is the value of the thirty coins?

Something to Think About

- What pennies were never touched and why?
- What positions were changed more than once and why?

Name _____   Problem _____

Teacher Assessment Scales
For use with Module 2

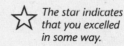
The star indicates that you excelled in some way.

 Problem Solving

①   ②   ③   ④   ⑤

You did not understand the problem well enough to get started or you did not show any work.

You understood the problem well enough to make a plan and to work toward a solution.

You made a plan, you used it to solve the problem, and you verified your solution.

 Mathematical Language

①   ②   ③   ④   ⑤

You did not use any mathematical vocabulary or symbols, or you did not use them correctly, or your use was not appropriate.

You used appropriate mathematical language, but the way it was used was not always correct or other terms and symbols were needed.

You used mathematical language that was correct and appropriate to make your meaning clear.

 Representations

①   ②   ③   ④   ⑤

You did not use any representations such as equations, tables, graphs, or diagrams to help solve the problem or explain your solution.

You made appropriate representations to help solve the problem or help you explain your solution, but they were not always correct or other representations were needed.

You used appropriate and correct representations to solve the problem or explain your solution.

 Connections

①   ②   ③   ④   ⑤

You attempted or solved the problem and then stopped.

You found patterns and used them to extend the solution to other cases, or you recognized that this problem relates to other problems, mathematical ideas, or applications.

You extended the ideas in the solution to the general case, or you showed how this problem relates to other problems, mathematical ideas, or applications.

 Presentation

①   ②   ③   ④   ⑤

The presentation of your solution and reasoning is unclear to others.

The presentation of your solution and reasoning is clear in most places, but others may have trouble understanding parts of it.

The presentation of your solution and reasoning is clear and can be understood by others.

Content Used: _____   **Computational Errors:**   Yes ☐ No ☐

Notes on Errors: _____

_____

Student Self-Assessment Scales

For use with Module 2

⬛ *If your score is in the shaded area, explain why on the back of this sheet and stop.*

⭐ *The star indicates that you excelled in some way.*

 Problem Solving

❶   ❷   ❸   ❹   ❺

I did not understand the problem well enough to get started or I did not show any work.

I understood the problem well enough to make a plan and to work toward a solution.

I made a plan, I used it to solve the problem, and I verified my solution.

 Mathematical Language

❶   ❷   ❸   ❹   ❺

I did not use any mathematical vocabulary or symbols, or I did not use them correctly, or my use was not appropriate.

I used appropriate mathematical language, but the way it was used was not always correct or other terms and symbols were needed.

I used mathematical language that was correct and appropriate to make my meaning clear.

 Representations

❶   ❷   ❸   ❹   ❺

I did not use any representations such as equations, tables, graphs, or diagrams to help solve the problem or explain my solution.

I made appropriate representations to help solve the problem or help me explain my solution, but they were not always correct or other representations were needed.

I used appropriate and correct representations to solve the problem or explain my solution.

 Connections

❶   ❷   ❸   ❹   ❺

I attempted or solved the problem and then stopped.

I found patterns and used them to extend the solution to other cases, or I recognized that this problem relates to other problems, mathematical ideas, or applications.

I extended the ideas in the solution to the general case, or I showed how this problem relates to other problems, mathematical ideas, or applications.

 Presentation

❶   ❷   ❸   ❹   ❺

The presentation of my solution and reasoning is unclear to others.

The presentation of my solution and reasoning is clear in most places, but others may have trouble understanding parts of it.

The presentation of my solution and reasoning is clear and can be understood by others.

Name _____   Date _____

Coin Toss Tally Table (Use with Questions 3–12 on pages 75 and 76.)

Group	Heads tally	Total heads	Total heads / Total tosses	Tails tally	Total tails	Total tails / Total tosses
Example of 20 tosses	‖‖‖ ‖‖‖ ‖‖	12	$\frac{12}{20}$	‖‖‖ ‖‖‖	8	$\frac{8}{20}$
Our 20 tosses						

MODULE 2

Never a Six (Use with Questions 15 and 16 on page 77 and Question 19(b) on page 78.)

Directions You will need a number cube. Work with a partner. Follow the game rules in your book to play one game of *Never a Six*. To keep track of your score, record the results of each of your turns in the table.

Turn	Player 1			Player 2		
	Numbers rolled	Total points rolled	Total score	Numbers rolled	Total points rolled	Total score
1						
2						
3						
4						
5						
6						
7						
8						
9						
10						
11						
12						
13						
14						
15						

Name _____   Date _____

 **Practice and Applications**
For use with Section 1

For use with Exploration 1

1. a. Some students took turns tossing a coin. They recorded their results in a table. Explain how the numbers in the "Experimental probability of heads" column were calculated.

Number of tosses	Number of heads	Experimental probability of heads
500	208	$\frac{208}{500} = \frac{52}{125}$
800	424	$\frac{424}{800} = \frac{53}{100}$

b. How many tails did the students get in 800 tosses? What is the experimental probability of tails?

2.

Outcome	Total
A	14
B	11
C	19
D	16

a. What is the experimental probability that the spinner stops on D?

b. What is the experimental probability that the spinner stops on A, B, or C?

3. a. A number cube was rolled 30 times. On 7 of the rolls, the outcome was 2. What is the experimental probability of rolling 2?

b. On how many rolls was the outcome not 2? What is the experimental probability of not rolling 2?

c. Suppose the number cube is thrown 100 times. Based on the experimental probabilities you found, about how many times do you expect to roll a 2? not roll a 2?

(continued)

2 Practice and Applications

For use with Section 1

For use with Exploration 2

4. Find the theoretical probability of each event.

   a. The spinner stops on 3.

   b. The spinner stops on 1.

   c. The spinner stops on an even number.

   d. The spinner stops on 5.

   e. Were any of the events in parts (a)–(d) impossible? If so, which ones?

5. Suppose you pick a card, without looking, from the number cards numbered 1 through 10.

   a. List the possible outcomes for picking an even numbered card.

   b. What is the theoretical probability of picking an even numbered card?

   c. What is the theoretical probability of picking a card greater than or equal to 5? less than 5?

   d. Plot your answers from parts (b) and (c) on a number line.

6. Is the event a *certain event* or an *impossible event*?

   a. A whale will speak English today.

   b. Water will evaporate today.

7. Ron has a bag of crayons. There are 2 red, 3 green, 4 blue, 1 yellow, 1 black, 2 brown, 1 orange, and 3 purple crayons in the bag. All of the crayons are the same size. Ron selects one crayon without looking. What is the theoretical probability that Ron selects a green crayon? What colors have the same probability of being selected as green?

Name _____ Date _____

 **Study Guide**
For use with Section 1

Detecting Outcomes   Probability

GOAL **LEARN HOW TO:** • find experimental and theoretical probabilities
• determine if outcomes are equally likely
• use probabilities to make predictions
• identify impossible and certain events
• plot probabilities on a number line

AS YOU: • perform coin toss and number cube experiments

Exploration 1: Experimental Probability

Outcomes of an Experiment

An **experiment** is an activity whose results can be observed and recorded.
Each result of an experiment is called an **outcome**.

> **Example**
>
> Kim and Hal conducted an experiment in which there were 10 balls placed in a bag.
> Five of the balls were shaded and five were unshaded.
>
> Without looking, Hal selected a ball from the
> bag and Kim recorded whether the ball was
> shaded or unshaded. Hal replaced the ball and
> selected again. They did this 100 times in all.
> Their results are shown in the table.
>
> | Outcome | Number of times |
> | --- | --- |
> | shaded | 53 |
> | unshaded | 47 |

Probability

A **probability** is a number from 0 through 1 that tells you how likely
something is to happen. An **experimental probability** is found by
repeating an experiment a number of times and observing the outcomes.

$$\text{experimental probability of an outcome} = \frac{\text{number of times the outcome occurred}}{\text{number of times the experiment was repeated}}$$

> **Example**
>
> Kim and Hal's table shows that a shaded ball was drawn in 53 of the 100 selections.
> So $\frac{53}{100}$ is the experimental probability of selecting a shaded ball and $\frac{47}{100}$ is the
> experimental probability of selecting an unshaded ball.

Outcomes with the same chance of occurring are **equally likely**. The
possible outcomes of the experiment above are equally likely.

Study Guide
For use with Section 1

Exploration 2: Theoretical Probability

Events

A **set** is any collection of objects. An **event** is a set of outcomes for a particular experiment.

Kim and Hal did another experiment using the same 10 balls. When a ball was selected, they recorded the number of the ball before placing it back in the bag. In this experiment, one event is *selecting a ball with an even number*. This event includes the five outcomes *select the 2, select the 4, select the 6, select the 8,* and *select the 10*.

Theoretical Probability

When you can determine the probability of an event without doing an experiment, it is called a **theoretical probability**. You can find a theoretical probability most easily when all the possible outcomes are equally likely.

$$\text{theoretical probability of an outcome} = \frac{\text{number of outcomes in the event}}{\text{total number of possible outcomes}}$$

Example

For the 10 numbered balls that Kim and Hal are using, what is the theoretical probability that Hal will select a ball with a number that is

a. even?   **b.** less than 11?   **c.** greater than 10?

▬ Sample Response ▬

a. probability of a ball with an even number: $\dfrac{5}{10}$ ← even outcomes: 2, 4, 6, 8, 10
← all possible outcomes: 1, 2, 3, …, 10

b. probability of a ball with a number $< 11 : \dfrac{10}{10}$ or 1 ← This event is *certain* to happen.

c. probability of a ball with a number $> 10 : \dfrac{0}{10}$ or 0 ← This event is *impossible*.

An event that cannot happen is an **impossible event**. Impossible events have a probability of 0. An event that must happen is a **certain event**. Certain events have a probability of 1. All other events have a probability between 0 and 1.

You can plot probabilities on a number line by labeling two points on the line as 0 and 1, and then dividing the space between these two points into equal parts.

Name _____   Date _____

 MODULE 2 **Study Guide: Practice & Application Exercises**
For use with Section 1

Exploration 1

The 20 slips of paper shown at the right are placed in a bag. Selections are made without looking.

1. What are the possible outcomes when you

    a. draw one slip of paper from the bag?

    b. draw two slips of paper from the bag at the same time?

2. When selecting a slip of paper, are the outcomes equally likely? Explain.

The table shows the results achieved while conducting an experiment with a standard deck of cards four times. In the experiment, one card was drawn from the deck without looking and then replaced before drawing another card. A standard deck of cards contains 26 red cards and 26 black cards.

Number of draws	Number of red cards	Experimental probability of red
25	16	$\frac{16}{25}$
50	22	$\frac{22}{50} = \frac{11}{25}$
100	47	$\frac{47}{100}$
200	104	$\frac{104}{200} = \frac{13}{25}$

3. Explain how the numbers in the *Experimental probability of red* column were calculated.

4. In the fourth running of the experiment, 104 red cards were drawn in 200 draws.

    a. How many black cards were drawn?

    b. What is the experimental probability of *black*?

5. a. For a standard deck of cards, are the outcomes *red* and *black* equally likely? Explain.

    b. Do the data in the table support your answer to part (a)?

Exploration 2

Each of the days of the week is written on a separate slip of paper and the papers are placed in a box. Without looking, Jessica draws a slip of paper from the box.

6. Determine the theoretical probability that Jessica draws a day that

    a. begins with T   **b.** has 6 letters   **c.** ends in y   **d.** begins with Q

7. Are the outcomes from Exercise 6 equally likely? Why or why not?

8. Plot your answers for Exercise 6 on a number line.

9. Which outcome from Exercise 6 is a certain event? an impossible event?

MODULE 2 **LABSHEET** **2A**

Team 1's Explanation (Use with Question 24 on page 92.)

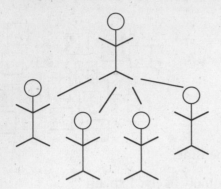

Each person has to shake 4 hands.
There are 5 people.

$$5 \cdot 4 = 20$$
20 handshakes

The problem was like the World Cup problem. So we worked it the same.

....

Directions Mark Team 1's score on the scales below.

 Problem Solving

❶　　❷　　❸　　❹　　❺

You did not understand
the problem well enough
to get started or you did
not show any work.

You understood the problem
well enough to make a plan
and to work toward a solution.

You made a plan, you used it to
solve the problem, and you verified
your solution.

 Representations

❶　　❷　　❸　　❹　　❺

You did not use any representations
such as equations, tables, graphs,
or diagrams to help solve the
problem or explain your solution.

You made appropriate representations to help solve the problem or
help you explain your solution, but
they were not always correct or
other representations were needed.

You used appropriate and correct
representations to solve the problem
or explain your solution.

 Connections

❶　　❷　　❸　　❹　　❺

You attempted or solved the
problem and then stopped.

You found patterns and used them to
extend the solution to other cases,
or you recognized that this problem
relates to other problems, mathematical ideas, or applications.

You extended the ideas in the
solution to the general case, or you
showed how this problem relates
to other problems, mathematical
ideas, or applications.

Name _____   Date _____

Team 2's Explanation (Use with Question 24 on page 92.)

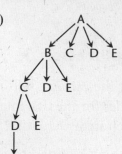

Person A shakes 4 hands.

Person B shakes 3 more hands.

Person C shakes 2 more hands.

Person D shakes 1 more hand.

Person E has no more hands to shake.

$4 + 3 + 2 + 1 = 10$

10 handshakes

This problem is like the string art problem because each person is like a peg and the pattern is the same. Five people have a total of 10 handshakes just like five pegs have a total of 10 linkups.

....

Directions Mark Team 2's score on the scales below.

 Problem Solving

1   **2**   **3**   **4**   **5**

You did not understand   You understood the problem   You made a plan, you used it to
the problem well enough   well enough to make a plan   solve the problem, and you verified
to get started or you did   and to work toward a solution.   your solution.
not show any work.

 Representations

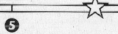

1   **2**   **3**   **4**   **5**

You did not use any representations   You made appropriate representa-   You used appropriate and correct
such as equations, tables, graphs,   tions to help solve the problem or representations to solve the problem
or diagrams to help solve the   help you explain your solution, but or explain your solution.
problem or explain your solution.   they were not always correct or
                                       other representations were needed.

 Connections

1   **2**   **3**   **4**   **5**

You attempted or solved the   You found patterns and used them to   You extended the ideas in the
problem and then stopped.   extend the solution to other cases,   solution to the general case, or you
                                 or you recognized that this problem   showed how this problem relates
                                 relates to other problems, mathe-   to other problems, mathematical
                                 matical ideas, or applications.   ideas, or applications.

Name _____ Date _____

For use with Exploration 1

1. A crafts booth at the carnival sells masks for $4 and hats for $3 each. If sales for the day totaled $60 for 18 items, how many of each item were sold?

The table shows how Manuel solved the above problem.

a. Do you think Manuel understood the problem? Explain.

b. Do you think Manuel used a plan to solve the problem?

c. Do you think he looked back?

d. Manuel gave himself a "5" on the problem solving scale. Do you agree with his scoring?

First guess:
10 hats ⇒ $30
8 masks ⇒ $32
Total $62
$62 > $60

The first guess is too high.
Try more hats and fewer masks.
12 hats ⇒ $36
6 masks ⇒ $24
Total $60
12 hats and 6 masks were sold.

Check total number of items:
12 hats + 6 masks = 18 items
Check total sales:
(12 × $3) + (6 × $4) = $60

For use with Exploration 2

2. Explain why each drawing is or is not an appropriate and correct solution to the problem: Draw a segment that divides a trapezoid into two triangles.

a.    **b.** 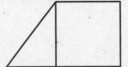   **c.**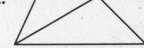

3. Sandra, Carlos, Rita, and Bill are on the baseball team. Each has a different position: catcher, pitcher, shortstop, and outfielder. Bill is neither shortstop nor catcher. A boy holds the position of outfielder. The name of the shortstop has four letters. Carlos holds a position that begins with the same letter as his name.

a. Which student is the pitcher?

b. Use the representations scale shown on page 87 of your book. What score would you give your solution to part (a)? Why?

4. Carla is *x* years old. Juan is 2 years older than Carla. Tony is 3 years younger than Juan, and Anita is 1 year older than Carla.

a. If Tony is 10 years old, how old are Carla, Juan, and Anita?

b. Use the representations scale shown on page 87 of your book. What score would you give your solution to part (a)? Why?

(continued)

Math Thematics, Book 1
Student Workbook

Practice and Applications

For use with Section 2

For use with Exploration 3

5. Solve each problem. Explain your solution and how it is related to another problem, mathematical idea, or application. Score your solution using the connections scale shown on page 87 of your book.

a. Kent has a 64-in. long piece of ribbon. After how many cuts will he have a 2-in. piece of ribbon if he successively cuts one piece of the ribbon in half?

b. Use the clues below to find the mystery number.

- The number is between 0 and 100.

- If you start with 4 and keep counting by 4's, the number will be on your list.

- The sum of the digits in the number is 9.

- The number does not contain 6 as a digit.

c. At a farmer's market, watermelons cost $4 each and honeydew melons cost $3 each. If Monica buys 8 melons for $29, how many watermelons does she buy?

d. At the annual library book sale, paperbacks cost $2 each and hardcover books cost $6 each. If $220 was earned by the sale of 58 books, how many paperback books were sold?

e. The temperature on Monday was 62°F. The next day the temperature fell 8 degrees. The day after that it fell 6 degrees. On the next two days, the temperature rose 2 degrees each day. What was the temperature on Friday?

f. A number is between 0 and 150. It can be evenly divided by 14 and the sum of its digits is 4. Find the number.

Name _____ Date _____

Detecting the Score   Assessment Scales

GOAL **LEARN HOW TO:** • use the problem solving scale
• apply different problem solving strategies
• use the representations scale
• extend solutions to the general case
• use the connections scale

AS YOU: • apply the 4-step approach to solve the *World Cup Problem*
• assess your group's solution
• work as a team to solve the *Handshake Problem*
• look for connections among problems you have solved

Exploration 1: The Problem Solving Scale

This scale, shown on page 87 of your book, can be used to assess how well
you follow the 4-step approach to problem solving.

Example

To determine the sum of the first 20 counting numbers, you plan to solve simpler
problems. First you find several sums and look for a pattern.

Your results are shown below.

$$1 \qquad\qquad = 1 = 1 \times 2 \div 2$$
$$1 + 2 \qquad\quad = 3 = 2 \times 3 \div 2$$
$$1 + 2 + 3 \quad\;\; = 6 = 3 \times 4 \div 2$$
$$1 + 2 + 3 + 4 = 10 = 4 \times 5 \div 2$$

You extend the pattern to find the sum of
the first 20 counting numbers.

$$1 + 2 + 3 + \cdots + 20 = 20 \times 21 \div 2 = 210$$

You use a calculator to verify your results.
You score a "5" on the problem solving
scale since you made a plan, used it to
solve the problem, and verified your result.

Exploration 2: The Representations Scale

Representations, such as equations, diagrams, tables, and graphs, can be
used to help you solve problems and explain your solutions. This scale,
shown on page 89 of your book, can be used to assess how well you use
representations to solve a problem.

Name _____ Date _____

Study Guide
For use with Section 2

Example (continued)

To determine the chances of getting exactly 2 heads in 3 tosses of a coin, Gavin drew the diagram shown. What score would you give Gavin on the representations scale?

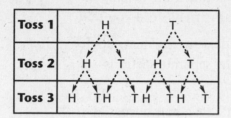

There are 3 ways to get exactly 2 heads.

I would give Gavin a 4. The diagram appropriately represents the situation and he has solved the problem. To better explain his solution, Gavin should state that he is using H for Heads and T for Tails. Additionally, Gavin should specify that the 3 ways of getting exactly 2 heads in 3 tosses are HHT, HTH, and THH.

Exploration 3: The Connections Scale

Connections are made by identifying patterns and extending them to other cases, or by relating a problem to other problems, mathematical ideas, or applications. It is sometimes possible to tell how a solution can apply to any case of that nature, the **general case**.

Example

To extend the solution of the problem in the Example from Exploration 1 to the general case, you write a rule for finding the sum of the first n counting numbers.

sum of the first n counting numbers $= n \times (n + 1) \div 2$

You score a "5" on the connections scale since you were able to extend the ideas in the solution to the general case.

Example

To extend the solution of the problem in the Example from Exploration 2 to the general case, you could write a rule for finding the possible outcomes of a coin toss.

1 toss = 2 possible outcomes

2 tosses = 4 possible outcomes

3 tosses = 8 possible outcomes

number of possible outcomes after n tosses = 2 multiplied by itself n times

You would score a "5" on the connections scale since you were able to extend the ideas in the solution to the general case.

Study Guide: Practice & Application Exercises

For use with Section 2

Exploration 1

For Exercises 1 and 2, solve each problem and score your solution using the problem solving scale on page 87 of your book.

1. You told each of your friends a secret. They each told 3 other people. Altogether, 29 people knew the secret. How many friends did you tell?

2. **Geometry Connection** A triangle is placed inside a circle. The triangle may or may not touch the circle. Into how many separate sections can the triangle divide the interior of the circle?

3. Of the 26 students in Mr. Fayad's class today, 19 ate a hamburger at lunch and 17 ate a slice of pizza. Thirteen students ate both.

   a. How many students ate only a hamburger?

   b. How many students ate only a slice of pizza?

   c. How many students ate neither a hamburger nor a slice of pizza?

   d. How can you verify your answers to parts (a)–(c)?

Exploration 2

4. To determine all of the options available to her at a conference, Ms. Lui studied the table shown below and then made the organized list at the right. Conference participants are required to choose one of the breakfast times and they must stay at each activity for the entire half-hour time period.

1MTA	2JTA	3JMA
1MFA	2JFA	3JFA
1FTA	2WTA	3WMA
1FFA	2WFA	3WFA

First number = Breakfast
Second letter = 1st activity
Third letter = 2nd activity
Fourth letter = Assembly

Time	Activity Choices (Choose One)		
8:00 A.M.	Breakfast 1	Jogging	Weight Room
8:30 A.M.	Breakfast 2	Makeup Seminar	Free Time
9:00 A.M.	Breakfast 3	Tennis Lesson	Free Time
9:30 A.M.	Assembly	Assembly	Assembly

What score would you give Ms. Lui using the representations scale?

(continued)

Study Guide: Practice & Application Exercises

For use with Section 2

Exploration 3

5. a. Find the sum of the first 25 even numbers: $2 + 4 + 6 + \cdots + 48 + 50$.

   b. How can you find the sum of n consecutive even numbers beginning with 2?

   c. Use the connections scale on page 90 of your book. What score would you give your solution to part (b)? Why?

6. a. Write the next two terms of the sequence 1, 3, 4, 7, 11, ...

   b. Write a general rule for finding any term of this sequence.

   c. Use the connections scale on page 90 of your book. What score would you give your solution to part (b)? Why?

7. a. Find the sum of the first 25 odd numbers: $1 + 3 + 5 + \cdots + 47 + 49$.

   b. Write a general rule for finding the sum of n consecutive odd numbers beginning with 1.

   c. Use the connections scale on page 90 of your book. What score would you give your solution to part (b)? Why?

8. Every Friday, Tyree makes $5 for mowing the lawn and watching his little brother. Every Saturday, he spends $3 on magazines. On Sundays, he makes $2 for washing the dishes and cleaning his room.

   a. How much money does Tyree have at the end of a weekend?

   b. How much money would he have after 4 weekends? after n weekends?

   c. Use the connections scale on page 90 of your book. What score would you give your solution to parts (a) and (b)? Why?

MODULE 2   **LABSHEET** **3A**

I Describe, You Draw Game Cards (Use with *Setting the Stage* on page 97.)

See your teacher for the game cards to use for this activity.

MODULE 2 | **LABSHEET** **3B**

Sticks of Different Sizes (Use with Questions 13 and 14 on page 102.)

Directions Cut out each stick.

This page has been
intentionally left blank
for ease of use of
surrounding labsheets.

Name _____   Date _____

Sides of a Triangle (Use with Questions 14 and 15 on page 102.)

Directions Try to form a triangle with each stick combination. For each triangle you form:

- Make a sketch and classify it as *scalene, isosceles,* or *equilateral*.
- Record the lengths of its sides in the appropriate columns.
- If you were not able to form a triangle, write *not possible*.

Stick combination	Sketch of triangle	Type of triangle	Length of the longest side	Length of the two other sides
3 in. 4 in. 5 in.		scalene	5 in.	3 in., 4 in.
2 in. 2 in. 5 in.				
3 in. 5 in. 5 in.				
6 in. 6 in. 6 in.				
2 in. 3 in. 4 in.				
2 in. 3 in. 6 in.				
3 in. 5 in. 8 in.				
5 in. 5 in. 8 in.				
4 in. 4 in. 8 in.				

Angles in a Triangle (Use with Questions 20 and 21 on pages 104 and 105.)

Triangle	Acute angles	Right angles	Obtuse angles	Type of triangle
A / B C (triangle)	∠A, ∠C	∠B	(none)	right
D E F (triangle)				
G I H (triangle)				
J K L (triangle)				
M O N (triangle)				
P Q R (triangle)				

Practice and Applications

For use with Section 3

For use with Exploration 1

1. Name each figure.

a.

b. C

c. C D

d. C D

2. A designer is using the figure below to design a window.

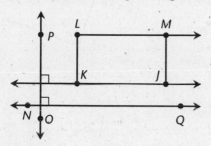

a. Name four line segments.   **b.** Name a ray.   **c.** Name a line.

d. Name a set of parallel lines.   **e.** Name a set of perpendicular lines.

For use with Exploration 2

3. Refer to the triangles below. Measure the sides if necessary.

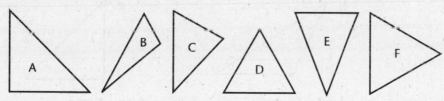

a. Which triangles are equilateral?

b. Which triangles are isosceles?

c. Which triangles are scalene?

4. Carol wants to make a triangular vegetable garden. She wants one side of the triangular garden to be 8 ft long and another side to be 14 ft long. Tell whether each length *can* or *cannot* be the third side of the triangle.

a. 7 ft   **b.** 5 ft   **c.** 15 ft

(continued)

Practice and Applications

For use with Section 3

For use with Exploration 3

5. Classify the angle as *right*, *acute*, *obtuse*, or *straight*.

a.    b.    c.

d.    e.    f.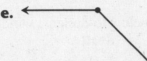

6. Classify each triangle as *right*, *acute*, or *obtuse*.

a.   b.    c.

7. Give two names for each triangle. Classify each according to the measures of its angles and the lengths of its sides.

a.   b. 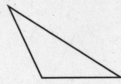   c.

d.   e. 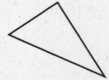   f.

8. Carl makes a triangle out of a square piece of paper by cutting the paper from one corner to the opposite corner. Two sides of the triangle are the same length. Classify the triangle according to the measures of its angles and the lengths of its sides.

Name _____ Date _____

Study Guide
For use with Section 3

Language Clues   Lines, Angles, and Triangles

GOAL   **LEARN HOW TO:** • name basic geometric figures
• classify triangles
• determine when triangles can be formed
• identify types of angles
• use the mathematical language scale

AS YOU: • describe and draw figures
• explore geometric figures around you

Exploration 1: Geometric Language

Basic Geometric Figures

Name of figure	Model	Symbol	Read as:
point	•P	P	point P
ray	← • ——— •	$\overrightarrow{QP}$	ray QP
	P Q		
line	← • ——— • →	$\overleftrightarrow{PQ}$ or $\overleftrightarrow{QP}$	line PQ or line QP
	P Q		
segment	• ——— •	$\overline{PQ}$ or $\overline{QP}$	segment PQ or segment QP
	P Q		

A **plane** is a flat surface that goes on forever in all directions. Two lines in a plane are **parallel** if they don't *intersect*, or meet. Two lines that intersect at a right angle are **perpendicular**.

Exploration 2: Sides of a Triangle

Classifying Triangles by Sides

An **equilateral triangle** has three sides of equal length. Figure 1 is equilateral. An **isosceles triangle** has two or more sides of equal length. Figure 2 is isosceles. All equilateral triangles are also isosceles. A **scalene triangle** has no sides of equal length. Figure 3 is scalene.

Figure 1   **Figure 2**   **Figure 3**

equilateral   **isosceles**   **scalene**

Triangle Side Lengths

You can form a triangle using three segments only if the sum of the lengths of any two of the segments is greater than the length of the other segment.

For example, segments of lengths 3 cm, 4 cm, and 7 cm will not form a triangle since 3 + 4 is not greater than 7. However, segments of lengths 3 cm, 4 cm, and 6 cm will form a triangle.

Study Guide
For use with Section 3

Exploration 3: Angles of a Triangle

Naming and Describing Angles

An **angle** is formed by two rays that have a common endpoint, called the **vertex of an angle**.

The angle at the right can be called ∠YXZ, ∠ZXY, or ∠X. When using three letters, the middle letter must be the vertex.

The measure of an angle refers to the size of the opening between the two rays of the angle. Angles are measured in units called **degrees**. The symbol for degree is °. For example, the measure of ∠YXZ is 40°.

| The measure of a **right angle** is exactly 90°. | The measure of an **acute angle** is between 0° and 90°. | The measure of an **obtuse angle** is between 90° and 180°. | The measure of a **straight angle** is exactly 180°. |

Classifying Triangles by Angles

An **acute triangle** has three acute angles. Figure 4 is acute. A **right triangle** has one right angle. Figure 5 is right. An **obtuse triangle** has one obtuse angle. Figure 6 is obtuse.

Figure 4   Figure 5   Figure 6

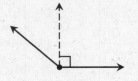 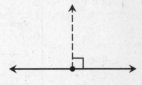

acute   right   obtuse

Mathematical Language Scale

Assess your use of mathematical language to be sure it is correct.

Example

Use the Assessment Scale for mathematical language shown on pages 87 and 105 of your book to score the description below.

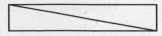

This is a rectangle with a segment that starts from the upper left corner and goes to the lower right corner.

Sample Response

The terms were used correctly and the description is clear, but the upper left corner is not necessarily the starting point. Also, the triangles should be mentioned. "This is a rectangle with a segment that connects the upper left corner to the lower right corner, dividing the rectangle into two right triangles."

Math Thematics, Book 1
Student Workbook

Name _____ Date _____

Study Guide: Practice & Application Exercises
For use with Section 3

Exploration 1

For Exercises 1–4, use the diagram.

1. Name the ray that passes through point Y.

2. Name a segment that is part of $\overrightarrow{PB}$.

3. Name the acute angle and the obtuse angle.

4. Name all the angles that have vertex P.

For Exercises 5–6, use the diagram.

5. Name all the sets of parallel lines.

6. Name all the sets of perpendicular lines.

Exploration 2

Classify each triangle according to its sides.

7. a triangle with side lengths 5 cm, 12 cm, and 14 cm

8. a triangle with side lengths 16 mm, 24 mm, and 16 mm

Tell whether the given lengths can form a triangle. Justify your answer.

9. 6 cm, 8 cm, 10 cm   10. 5 in., 7 in., 12 in.   11. 9 m, 15 m, 4 m

Exploration 3

In Exercises 12 and 13, use the diagram.

12. Name the angle in three ways.

13. Classify the angle.

In Exercises 14 and 15, sketch the triangle if possible.

14. a triangle that is both right and isosceles

15. a triangle that is both obtuse and equilateral

16. **Challenge** A triangle with side lengths 5 cm, 12 cm, and 13 cm is a right triangle. What kind of triangle is formed when the lengths are

    a. 5 cm, 12 cm, and 14 cm?   **b.** 5 cm, 12 cm, and 11 cm?

17. Tom wrote this description for the diagram shown. "This is a square with two segments that meet inside the square." Use the mathematical language scale to assess Tom's description.

This page has been intentionally left blank for ease of use of surrounding labsheets.

MODULE 2   **LABSHEET 4A**

Shape Cards (Use with Questions 3–5 and 9–14 on pages 113–115.)

This page has been intentionally left blank for ease of use of surrounding labsheets.

MODULE 2   **LABSHEET** (4B)

Sea Star (Use with Questions 16–18 on pages 116 and 117.)

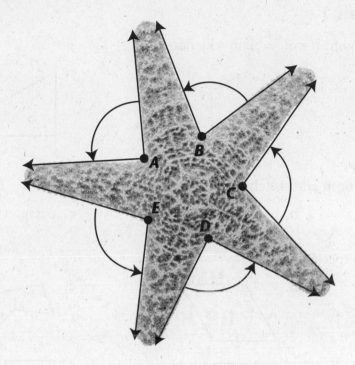

Angle	Acute, Right, or Obtuse	Estimated Measure (degrees)	Actual Measure (degrees)
∠A			
∠B			
∠C			
∠D			
∠E			

Name _____ Date _____

For use with Exploration 1

1. Is the figure a regular polygon? If not, explain why not.

a.
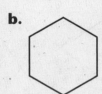

b.
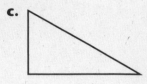

c.

2. Write a definition of each term and sketch two examples.

   a. triangle   **b.** hexagon   **c.** octagon

3. Name each polygon. Be as specific as possible.

a.
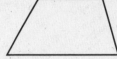

b.
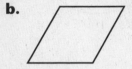

c.
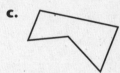

d.
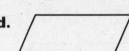

e.

f.

4. Sketch an example of each quadrilateral.

   a. a parallelogram that is not a rectangle   **b.** a quadrilateral that is not a parallelogram

5. A designer uses the template shown below to create rectangles, trapezoids, parallelograms, and triangles to use in her designs. Identify at least one of each figure from her template.

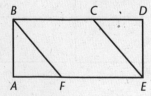

(continued)

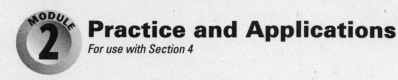

Practice and Applications
For use with Section 4

For use with Exploration 2

6. Trace each angle and extend the rays. Then find each angle's measure.

   a.

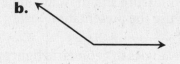   **b.**

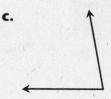   **c.**

7. Use a protractor to draw an angle with each measure.

    a. 24°   **b.** 136°   **c.** 82°

    d. 47°   **e.** 169°   **f.** 64°

For use with Exploration 3

8. Use your solution to Exercise 7 to answer part (a).

    a. Explain to a classmate how to use a protractor to draw angles.

    b. Use the presentation scale shown on page 118 of your book to score your solution to part (a).

9. Look back at your solution to the *World Cup Problem* on page 86 of your book.

    a. Prepare a team presentation for the *World Cup Problem*.

    b. Use the presentation scale to score your presentation.

Study Guide
For use with Section 4

Detecting Shapes   Polygons and Angles

GOAL **LEARN HOW TO:** • classify and sort polygons
• measure and draw an angle using a protractor
• use the presentation scale

AS YOU: • explore geometric shapes
• examine angles in geometric figures
• assess how well you present solutions

Exploration 1: Naming Polygons

Polygons

A **polygon** is a closed plane figure made from segments, called sides, that do not cross. *Poly* means *many* and *gon* means *angles*.

Each endpoint of a side is a **vertex**. (The plural is *vertices*.) A polygon can be named by listing the vertices in consecutive order.

A polygon can be classified by the number of sides it has as shown in the table below.

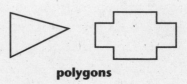
polygons

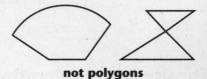
not polygons

Number of sides	Name of polygon	Example
3	triangle	
4	quadrilateral	
5	pentagon	
6	hexagon	
8	octagon	
10	decagon	

Regular Polygons

A **regular polygon** has all angles the same measure and all sides the same length. The four polygons at the right are regular.

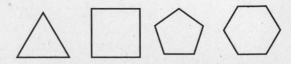

Math Thematics, Book 1
Student Workbook

Name _____   Date _____

Study Guide
For use with Section 4

Quadrilaterals

Quadrilaterals can be classified by their number
of pairs of parallel sides. A **trapezoid** is a
quadrilateral with exactly one pair of parallel sides.
A **parallelogram** is a quadrilateral with two pairs
of parallel sides. A **rhombus** is a parallelogram
with all sides the same length.

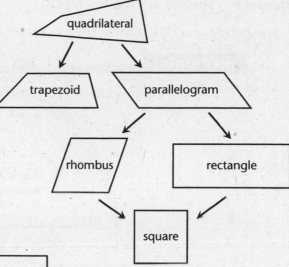

Venn Diagrams

You can use a **Venn diagram** to show how sets
are related. The diagram above can be shown
using a Venn diagram.

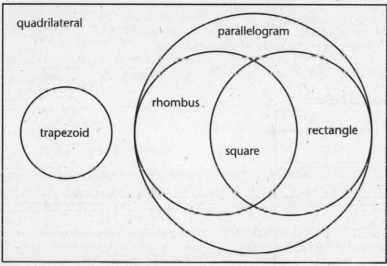

Exploration 2: Measuring Angles

The measure of an angle is the amount of rotation measured in degrees.

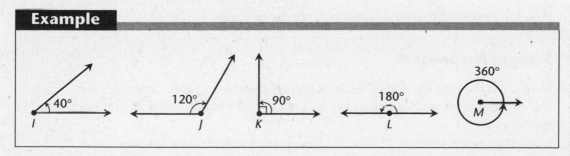

Name _____   Date _____

Measuring Angles with a Protractor

A **protractor** is an instrument used to measure and draw angles.

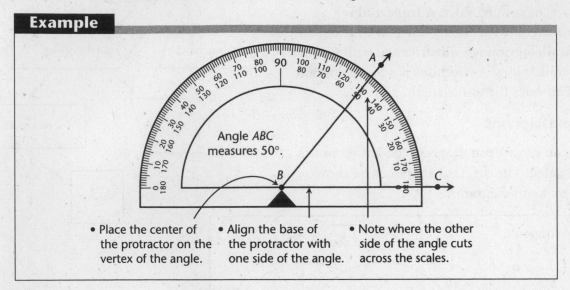

> **Example**
>
> Angle *ABC* measures 50°.
>
> • Place the center of the protractor on the vertex of the angle.
> • Align the base of the protractor with one side of the angle.
> • Note where the other side of the angle cuts across the scales.

Exploration 3: The Presentation Scale

This scale helps you assess how well you present your solutions.

 Presentation

①　　②　　③　　④　　⑤

| ① The presentation of your solution and reasoning is unclear to others. | ③ The presentation of your solution and reasoning is clear in most places, but others may have trouble understanding parts of it. | ⑤ The presentation of your solution and reasoning is clear and can be understood by others. |

> **Example**
>
> Complete the exercise below. Then use the presentation scale to score your answer.
>
> Which types of quadrilaterals are always regular polygons? Explain.

> ▌ **Sample Response** ▐
>
> A square is the only quadrilateral that is regular. Regular polygons have sides and angles of equal measure. A square has 4 sides of equal measure and 4 angles that each measure 90°.
>
> I would score my solution a "4" on the presentation scale because the solution is organized and could be clearly understood by others. However, the solution does not explain why other quadrilaterals are *not* regular.

MODULE 2

Study Guide: Practice & Application Exercises
For use with Section 4

Exploration 1

For Exercises 1–3, name each polygon. Be as specific as possible.

1.   **2.**   **3.**

4. Which of the figures in Exercises 1–3 are regular polygons? If a figure is not a regular polygon, explain why not.

5. a. Draw a trapezoid whose nonparallel sides are the same length.

   b. What name would you give to the figure in part (a)? Explain how you came to choose this name.

6. Use the Venn diagram shown.

   a. Which foods are Kate's favorites?

   b. Which foods are favorites of both Emily and Kate?

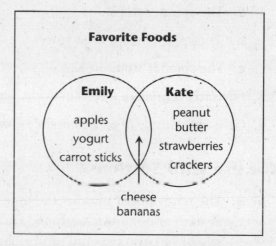

Exploration 2

7. Trace each angle and extend the rays. Then measure each angle.

   a.   **b.**   **c.**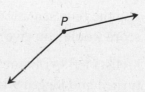

8. Use a protractor to draw an angle with each measure.

   a. 103°   **b.** 19°   **c.** 78°

Exploration 3

9. Explain why the presentation of your solution to a problem is important.

Math Thematics, Book 1
Student Workbook

Practice and Applications

For use after Sections 1–4

For use with Section 1

1. a. A number cube was rolled 60 times. On 8 of the rolls, the outcome was 1. What is the experimental probability of rolling 1?

   b. On how many rolls was the outcome not 1? What is the experimental probability of not rolling 1?

   c. Suppose the number cube is rolled 100 times. Based on the experimental probabilities you found, about how many times do you expect to roll a 1? not roll a 1?

Use the spinner for Exercises 2–4.

2. Find the theoretical probability of each event.

   a. The spinner stops on C.

   b. The spinner stops on a vowel.

   c. The spinner stops on K.

3. Give an example of a certain event when spinning the spinner.

4. Give an example of an impossible event when spinning the spinner.

For use with Section 2

5. a. The refreshment stand at the little league field sells beverages for $1 each and sandwiches for $3 each. If $122 was earned on the sale of 74 beverages and sandwiches during one game, how many beverages were sold?

   b. Use the representations scale on page 87 of your book. What score would you give your solution to part (a)? Why?

6. a. Melissa left her home and jogged 12 blocks east. Then she turned and jogged 9 blocks west before she turned and jogged 16 blocks east again. She continued 8 more blocks east before turning to go 20 blocks west. How far and in what direction would Melissa have to go to return home?

   b. Use the problem solving scale on page 87 of your book. What score would you give your solution to part (a)? Why?

(continued)

Practice and Applications

MODULE 2

For use after Sections 1–4

For use with Section 3

7. Classify the angle as *right*, *acute*, *obtuse*, or *straight*.

a.

b.

c.

8. Give two names for each triangle. Classify each according to the measures of its angles and the lengths of its sides.

a.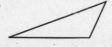

b.

c.

For use with Section 4

9. Name each polygon. Be as specific as possible.

a.

b.

c.

10. Use a protractor to draw an angle with each measure

    a. 38°

    b. 160°

    c. 73°

11. Use the Venn diagram shown.

    a. How many sports do both Dave and Lindsay play?

    b. Which sports does Dave play?

    c. Why is "running" outside of the sets?

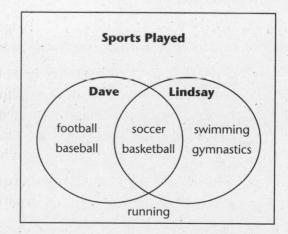

This page has been
intentionally left blank
for ease of use of
surrounding labsheets.

MODULE 2   **EXTENDED EXPLORATION LABSHEET**   E²

Pattern Blocks (Use with Extended Exploration on page 123.)

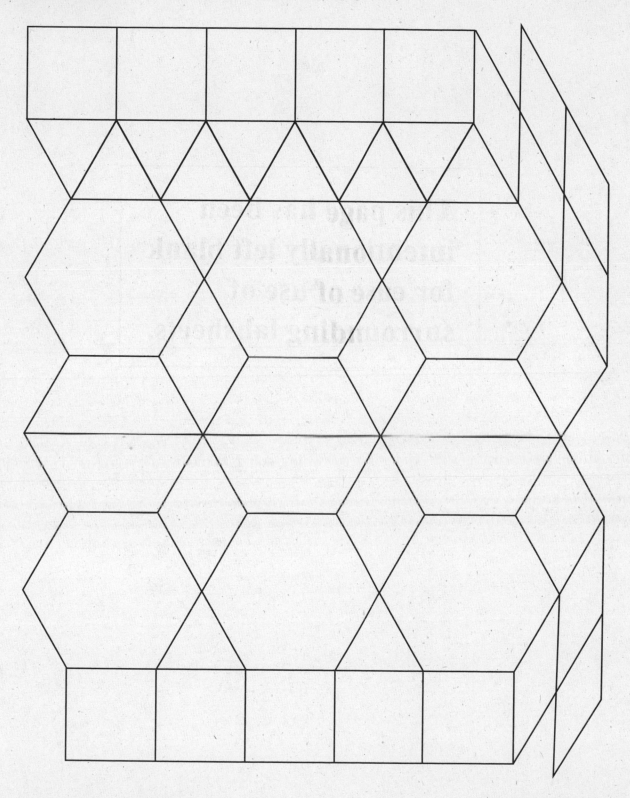

This page has been intentionally left blank for ease of use of surrounding labsheets.

Name _____   Date _____

MODULE 2   **REVIEW AND ASSESSMENT LABSHEET**

Identifying Quadrilaterals (Use with Exercise 20 on page 127.)

Directions Sketch the quadrilateral identified above each rectangle. You may use only the points on the rectangle.

Example

RECTANGLE

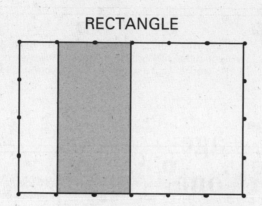

TRAPEZOID

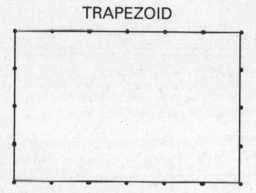

PARALLELOGRAM
with no right angles

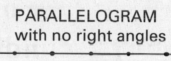

SQUARE

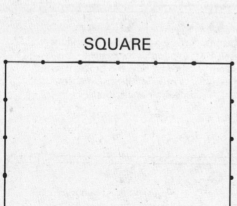

RHOMBUS
with no right angles

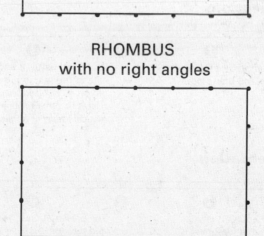

Name _____   Problem _____

 MODULE 3

Teacher Assessment Scales
For use with Module 3

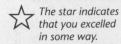 *The star indicates that you excelled in some way.*

 ## Problem Solving

❶   ❷   ❸   ❹   ❺

❶ You did not understand the problem well enough to get started or you did not show any work.

❸ You understood the problem well enough to make a plan and to work toward a solution.

❺ You made a plan, you used it to solve the problem, and you verified your solution.

 ## Mathematical Language

❶   ❷   ❸   ❹   ❺

❶ You did not use any mathematical vocabulary or symbols, or you did not use them correctly, or your use was not appropriate.

❸ You used appropriate mathematical language, but the way it was used was not always correct or other terms and symbols were needed.

❺ You used mathematical language that was correct and appropriate to make your meaning clear.

 ## Representations

❶   ❷   ❸   ❹   ❺

❶ You did not use any representations such as equations, tables, graphs, or diagrams to help solve the problem or explain your solution.

❸ You made appropriate representations to help solve the problem or help you explain your solution, but they were not always correct or other representations were needed.

❺ You used appropriate and correct representations to solve the problem or explain your solution.

 ## Connections

❶   ❷   ❸   ❹   ❺

❶ You attempted or solved the problem and then stopped.

❸ You found patterns and used them to extend the solution to other cases, or you recognized that this problem relates to other problems, mathematical ideas, or applications.

❺ You extended the ideas in the solution to the general case, or you showed how this problem relates to other problems, mathematical ideas, or applications.

 ## Presentation

❶   ❷   ❸   ❹   ❺

❶ The presentation of your solution and reasoning is unclear to others.

❸ The presentation of your solution and reasoning is clear in most places, but others may have trouble understanding parts of it.

❺ The presentation of your solution and reasoning is clear and can be understood by others.

Content Used: _____   **Computational Errors:**   Yes ☐   No ☐

Notes on Errors: _____

_____

Math Thematics, Book 1
Student Workbook

82

Name _____   Problem _____

 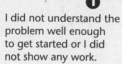

Student Self-Assessment Scales

For use with Module 3

If your score is in the shaded area, explain why on the back of this sheet and stop.

☆ The star indicates that you excelled in some way.

 Problem Solving

❶ — ❷ — ❸ — ❹ — ❺ — ☆→

❶ I did not understand the problem well enough to get started or I did not show any work.

❸ I understood the problem well enough to make a plan and to work toward a solution.

❺ I made a plan, I used it to solve the problem, and I verified my solution.

 Mathematical Language

❶ — ❷ — ❸ — ❹ — ❺ — ☆→

❶ I did not use any mathematical vocabulary or symbols, or I did not use them correctly, or my use was not appropriate.

❸ I used appropriate mathematical language, but the way it was used was not always correct or other terms and symbols were needed.

❺ I used mathematical language that was correct and appropriate to make my meaning clear.

Representations

❶ — ❷ — ❸ — ❹ — ❺ — ☆→

❶ I did not use any representations such as equations, tables, graphs, or diagrams to help solve the problem or explain my solution.

❸ I made appropriate representations to help solve the problem or help me explain my solution, but they were not always correct or other representations were needed.

❺ I used appropriate and correct representations to solve the problem or explain my solution.

 Connections

❶ — ❷ — ❸ — ❹ — ❺ — ☆→

❶ I attempted or solved the problem and then stopped.

❸ I found patterns and used them to extend the solution to other cases, or I recognized that this problem relates to other problems, mathematical ideas, or applications.

❺ I extended the ideas in the solution to the general case, or I showed how this problem relates to other problems, mathematical ideas, or applications.

 Presentation

❶ — ❷ — ❸ — ❹ — ❺ — ☆→

❶ The presentation of my solution and reasoning is unclear to others.

❸ The presentation of my solution and reasoning is clear in most places, but others may have trouble understanding parts of it.

❺ The presentation of my solution and reasoning is clear and can be understood by others.

MODULE 3   **LABSHEET** **1A**

Missing Values Table (Use with Question 8(a) on page 132.)

Directions Complete parts (a)–(c).

a. Fill in the missing words, fractions, or decimals for the values of the 9
    and the 8 in 25,436.98.

	Words	**Fraction**	**Decimal**
Value of the 9	nine tenths		
Value of the 8			0.08

b. Why do you think there is a 0 between the decimal point and the 8 in
    the decimal form of eight hundredths?

c. Why do you think there is a 0 to the left of the decimal point in the
    decimal form of eight hundredths?

....

Pattern Block Flat (Use with Question 8(b) on page 132.)

Directions Complete parts (a)–(d). The flat below represents one whole.

a. The decimals 0.9 and 0.08 can be added to get the decimal 0.98.
    Shade 0.98 of the Pattern Block Flat. Be sure to shade as many complete
    rods as possible.

b. How many complete rods did you shade?

c. How many extra squares did you shade?

d. 0.9 is read as nine tenths and 0.08 is read as eight hundredths. Use the part
    you shaded to explain why 0.98 is read as ninety-eight hundredths.

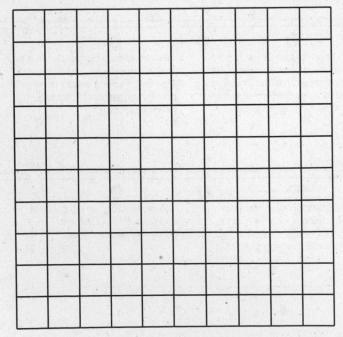

Math Thematics, Book 1
Student Workbook

MODULE 3   **LABSHEET** **1B**

Words to Fractions to Decimals Table (Use with Question 9 on page 132.)

Directions Represent each decimal number using as few base-ten blocks as possible. Then complete each row in the table.

Number in words	Sketch of base-ten blocks	Fraction	Decimal
one and eighteen hundredths	To save time, you can draw flats and rods without subdivisions.		1.18
		$\frac{4}{10}$	
one and three tenths			
one and three hundredths			
			0.34
			0.7

Math Thematics, Book 1
Student Workbook   **85**

Name _____ Date _____

Practice and Applications
For use with Section 1

For use with Exploration 1

1. Write the decimal, fraction, and word name for each picture below.

   a.    **b.** 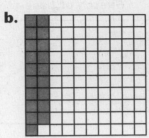   **c.**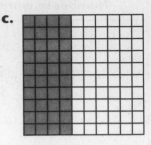

2. Write the place value of each underlined digit.

   a. 0.02<u>9</u>   **b.** 4.<u>5</u>21   **c.** 12.6<u>3</u>2

   d. 1<u>7</u>.266   **e.** 3.016<u>9</u>   **f.** 68.<u>4</u>08

3. Write each number as a decimal and as a fraction or a mixed number.

   a. eight tenths   **b.** one and twelve hundredths

   c. twenty-three thousandths   **d.** nine hundred and two tenths

4. Write each decimal in words.

   a. 7.3   **b.** 0.058   **c.** 242.06

   d. 1.009   **e.** 12.12   **f.** 5.75

5. Louis uses a metric ruler to measure his sister's height. She is 2.15 meters tall. How should Louis read his sister's height?

6. Using the least number of pennies, dimes, and one-dollar bills, how can you represent three and forty-eight hundredths?

(continued)

Name _____ Date _____

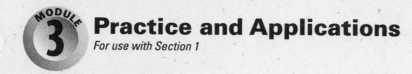

Practice and Applications
For use with Section 1

For use with Exploration 2

7. Compare each pair of decimals. Use <, >, or =.

a. 26.34 __?__ 26.341 **b.** 6.7 __?__ 6.700 **c.** 8.005 __?__ 8.050

d. 38.01 __?__ 38.006 **e.** 12 __?__ 5.997 **f.** 1.333 __?__ 1.3402

g. 0.1 __?__ 0.099 **h.** 4.055 __?__ 4.502 **i.** 0.02 __?__ 0.006

j. 0.6 __?__ 0.48 **k.** 0.455 __?__ 4.502 **l.** 0.20 __?__ 0.060

8. Order each list of numbers from least to greatest.

a. 4, 4.23, 4.05, 4.052 **b.** 2.8, 2.88, 2.088, 2.808

c. 70.03, 7.37, 70.7, 7.007 **d.** 426.3, 426, 4.26, 42.36, 43.26

e. 0.525, 0.552, 0.225, 0.252 **f.** 6.123, 6.321, 6.003, 6.023

g. 38.15, 3.815, 35.81, 3.18 **h.** 9.03, 9.003, 9.31, 9.013

9. An electronics store is having a contest. The salesperson with the greatest amount of sales for a month will win an all expense paid weekend at a ski resort. The person with the second greatest sales will win a lift ticket for the resort. Ms. Kelly's total sales for the month are $8269.99, Mr. Jermin's total sales are $6889.89, Mr. Walker's total sales are $8622.25, and Ms. Martin's total sales are $8926.11. Who will win the trip? Who will win the lift ticket?

10. Marla, Michael, Manny, and Mavis went shopping for some birthday gifts. Marla spent $26.05 for her gifts. Michael's gifts totaled $25.95. Mavis spent $25.99, while Manny's total for the gifts he bought was $26.00. Who spent the least amount of money? Who spent the greatest amount?

11. Rafik counted the amount of money in his coin bank and wrote down the total. The amount was more than $12 but less than $13. The next day, he added a penny to the bank. To show the new total, he had to change exactly two digits in the old total. What are the possible amounts he could have had in the bank before he put in the additional penny?

Name _____   Date _____

Quite a Collection   Understanding Decimals

GOAL   **LEARN HOW TO:** • read and write decimals
• compare and order decimals
AS YOU: • discover patterns using base-ten blocks

Exploration 1: Decimal Place Value

Decimal System

Our number system, based on tens, is called the **decimal system**.

The *decimal point* in a decimal number separates its whole-number part on the left from its fractional part on the right.

The **place values** on either side of the decimal point are similar, with the values to the right of the decimal point ending in *-ths*.

When reading or writing a decimal number, only the last place value is used to name the fractional part.

$$36.5$$
↑   ↑
whole-number part   fractional part

In 36.5, the digit 3 is in the *tens* place and the digit 5 is in the *tenths* place. The digit 6 is in the *ones* place.

While the decimal number 36.5 is read *thirty-six and five tenths*, the decimal number 36.55 is read *thirty-six and fifty-five hundredths*.

Example

Draw a place-value chart for the number 17,638.245 and then write it in words.

Sample Response

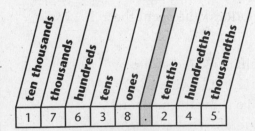

ten thousands	thousands	hundreds	tens	ones	.	tenths	hundredths	thousandths
1	7	6	3	8	.	2	4	5

In words, the number is:
seventeen thousand, six hundred thirty-eight and two hundred forty-five thousandths.

Notice the use of the word *and* where the decimal point occurs when writing a decimal number in words. When reading or writing a decimal number, only the decimal point is read as the word *and*.

Name _____ Date _____

Study Guide
For use with Section 1

Place values to the right of the decimal point can be written using words, fractions, or decimals.

Place value	tenths	hundredths	thousandths
In words	one tenth	one hundredth	one thousandth
As a fraction	$\frac{1}{10}$	$\frac{1}{100}$	$\frac{1}{1000}$
As a decimal	0.1	0.01	0.001

Place values in the decimal system are related to each other, as shown in the diagram below.

As you move one place to the *right*, the place value is *divided* by 10.

Tens are hundreds ÷ 10.   *Hundredths are tenths ÷ 10.*

Hundreds are tens × 10.   *Tenths are hundredths × 10.*

As you move one place to the *left*, the place value is *multiplied* by 10.

Exploration 2: Comparing Decimals

If two decimal numbers differ only by their fractional parts, you can determine which is greater by examining them in the following manner.

Begin the comparison by noting the number of decimal places in the two decimal numbers.

Compare 4.7 and 4.23.
4.7 has one decimal place.
4.23 has two decimal places.

If the number of decimal places is different, write an **equivalent decimal** (a decimal number that represents the same amount) for the one with fewer decimal places by adding zeros to the right end of it until it has the same number of decimal places as the other number.

Rewrite 4.7 as 4.70 so it also has two decimal places.

Now that they have the same number of decimal places, you can compare while ignoring the decimal point.

Compare 4.70 and 4.23. Since 470 > 423, then 4.70 > 4.23 and therefore 4.7 > 4.23.

Name _____   Date _____

Study Guide: Practice & Application Exercises
For use with Section 1

Exploration 1

One cubic inch is approximately 16.387 cubic centimeters. In the number 16.387, give the place value of each digit.

1. 1   **2.** 6   **3.** 3   **4.** 8   **5.** 7

Write each decimal in words and as a fraction or mixed number.

6. 0.35   **7.** 15.8   **8.** 358.09   **9.** 34.005

Write each number as a decimal.

10. $\frac{47}{100}$ **11.** $\frac{6}{100}$ **12.** twelve and eight tenths

13. $\frac{723}{10,000}$ **14.** one hundred eleven and eleven thousandths

15. Using only pennies, dimes, and one-dollar bills, how can you represent nine and four hundredths?

Exploration 2

Choose the correct answer. Explain your choice.

16. A decimal that is equivalent to 0.25 is ___?___.

    A. 0.205   **B.** 0.025   **C.** 0.2500   **D.** 0.2005

17. Of the following, the decimal that has the greatest value is ___?___.

    A. 0.7   **B.** 0.707   **C.** 0.077   **D.** 0.77

18. Of the following, the decimal that has the least value is ___?___.

    A. 0.003   **B.** 0.0003   **C.** 0.029   **D.** 0.0029

19. A number that is between 4.72 and 4.73 is ___?___.

    A. 4.7   **B.** 4.725   **C.** 4.736   **D.** 4.8

Compare each pair of decimals. Use >, <, or =.

20. 23.7 ___?___ 2.37   **21.** 0.7 ___?___ 0.700   **22.** 12.507 ___?___ 12.075

23. 0.04 ___?___ 0.3   **24.** 3.33 ___?___ 3.330   **25.** 15.89 ___?___ 15.892

26. 1.21 ___?___ 12.1   **27.** 0.9761 ___?___ 1   **28.** 1.023 ___?___ 1.103

Math Thematics, Book 1
Student Workbook

90

MODULE 3   **LABSHEET 2A**

Decimal Puzzle (Use with the *Setting the Stage* on page 138.)

Directions

- Cut out the puzzle pieces on Labsheet 2B. Then arrange the pieces in the rectangle below to make the sum shown.

- Add down the columns to check that your solution has the correct sum.

- If your solution does not equal 15.32, continue rearranging the puzzle pieces and re-adding until the sum is correct.

- Record the decimal numbers that make a sum of 15.32.

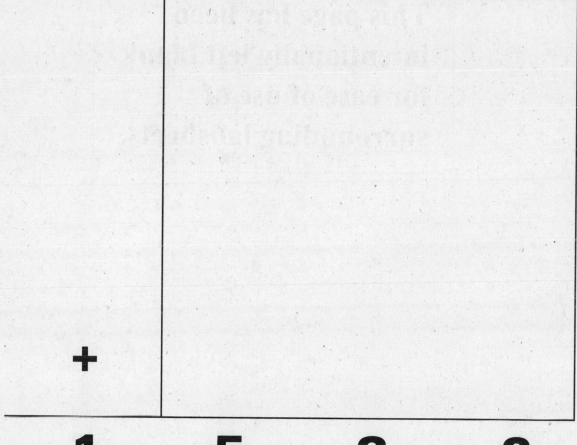

This page has been
intentionally left blank
for ease of use of
surrounding labsheets.

MODULE 3   LABSHEET **2B**

Decimal Puzzle (Use with Labsheet 2A to complete the *Setting the Stage* on page 138.)

Directions Cut out the puzzle pieces. Then follow the directions on Labsheet 2A.

```
. 5      7          1
```

```
0  .  0     9       6
```

```
3
4                   0
                    .
```

```
2  .  8     3 . 8
```

This page has been
intentionally left blank
for ease of use of
surrounding labsheets.

Practice and Applications

For use with Section 2

For use with Exploration 1

1. Find each sum.

a.   17.08
       + 3.7

b.   1.329
       + 25.62

c.   3.45
         15.32
       + 5.9

d. 1.4 + 26.72

e. 0.038 + 0.054

f. 35.7 + 32.91

g. 42.091 + 17.902

h. 11.03 + 0.45 + 9.2

i. 51 + 89.2 + 0.062

2. A tuna sandwich costs $3.25 and a turkey sandwich costs $2.75 at the deli. Orange juice costs $1.35 and apple juice costs $0.95. Alan decides to buy a turkey sandwich and a container of orange juice. His sister decides on the tuna sandwich and an apple juice. Who spends more, Alan or his sister? How much do they spend altogether?

For use with Exploration 2

3. Find each difference.

a.   7.4
       − 2.9

b.   62.55
       − 51.8

c.   36.006
       − 4.25

d. 6.9 − 3.127

e. 156.83 − 8.327

f. 0.07 − 0.024

g. 2.035 − 0.4

h. 42.4 − 0.009

i. 18 − 5.892

4. Find the missing terms in each sequence.

a. 0.1, 0.2, 0.4, 0.7, __?__, __?__, __?__, 2.9, …

b. 2.91, 2.81, 2.71, 2.61, __?__, __?__, __?__, 2.21, …

c. 3.1, 3.3, 3.7, 4.3, __?__, __?__, __?__, 8.7, …

d. 10, 9.99, 9.97, 9.94, 9.9, __?__, __?__, __?__, 9.64, …

5. There are 28.5 m of string on a spool. Denise cuts 12.6 m of string from the spool. Then she cuts off another 8.7 m of the string. How much string is left on the spool?

Study Guide
For use with Section 2

A Fitting Puzzle Decimal Addition and Subtraction

GOAL **LEARN HOW TO:** • add decimals
• subtract decimals

AS YOU: • model with base-ten blocks

Exploration 1: Adding Decimals

These are the basic shapes of the base-ten blocks.

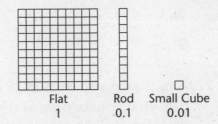

Flat   Rod   Small Cube
1   0.1   0.01

Example

To find the sum 1.46 + 0.67 using base-ten blocks, follow this procedure:

1. Use base-ten blocks to represent each decimal.

 1.46

0.67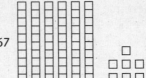

2. Group the small cubes together. If there are 10 or more, trade each group of 10 cubes for 1 rod.

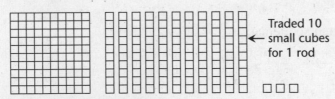

Traded 10
← small cubes
for 1 rod

3. Group the rods together. If there are 10 or more, trade each group of 10 rods for 1 flat.

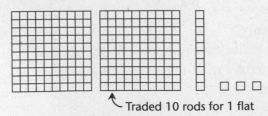

Traded 10 rods for 1 flat

4. If no more trading is possible, the remaining blocks represent the sum. In this model, the 2 flats, 1 rod, and 3 small cubes represent 2.13.

Math Thematics, Book 1
Student Workbook

 **Study Guide**
For use with Section 2

Exploration 2: Subtracting Decimals

The results of modeling addition and subtraction using base-ten blocks can be used to formulate a method for adding and subtracting decimals using paper and pencil.

	Addition	Subtraction
	Find the sum:	Find the difference:
	23.58 + 9.6	23.58 − 9.6

1. Line up the decimal points.

$$\begin{array}{r} 23.58 \\ +\ 9.6 \\ \hline \end{array}$$ $$\begin{array}{r} 23.58 \\ -\ 9.6 \\ \hline \end{array}$$

2. Insert zeros so that both numbers have the same number of decimal places.

$$\begin{array}{r} 23.58 \\ +\ 9.60 \\ \hline \end{array}$$ $$\begin{array}{r} 23.58 \\ -\ 9.60 \\ \hline \end{array}$$

3. Add or subtract as with whole numbers.

$$\begin{array}{r} 23.58 \\ +\ 9.60 \\ \hline 33\ 18 \end{array}$$ $$\begin{array}{r} 23.58 \\ -\ 9.60 \\ \hline 13\ 98 \end{array}$$

4. Place the decimal point in the final answer.

$$\begin{array}{r} 23.58 \\ +\ 9.60 \\ \hline 33.18 \end{array}$$ $$\begin{array}{r} 23.58 \\ -\ 9.60 \\ \hline 13.98 \end{array}$$

Example

After spending $14.37 and $18.52 on two gifts, Zoila wondered if she had enough money left to buy a pair of shoes that, with tax included, would cost $18.86. If Zoila had $50 when she began her shopping, does she have enough money left to pay for the shoes?

Sample Response

Add to find out how much Zoila has spent on the two gifts.

$$\begin{array}{r} \$14.37 \\ +\ 18.52 \\ \hline \$32.89 \end{array}$$

Subtract the sum above from the amount she had when she began shopping.

$$\begin{array}{r} \$50.00 \\ -\ 32.89 \\ \hline \$17.11 \end{array}$$

No, Zoila does not have enough money for the shoes.

Name _____   Date _____

Study Guide: Practice & Application Exercises

For use with Section 2

Exploration 1

Use base-ten blocks to find each sum.

1. $2.34 + 0.1$ **2.** $1.64 + 1.57$ **3.** $2.31 + 1.69 + 0.98$

For Exercises 4–9, find each sum without using a calculator.

4. $37.6 + 0.015$

5. $0.9 + 27.05 + 10$

6. $4.29 + 10.0037 + 3.378$

7. $0.005 + 9.3 + 1.107$

8. $x + 16.703$ where $x = 5.39$

9. $20.022 + y$ where $y = 2.99$

10. Estimation Sara Beth wants to buy an MP3 player for $199.95 and a television for $127.50. To find how much money she needs, excluding taxes, she used her calculator as shown below.

> [1] [9] [9] [.] [9] [5] [+] [1] [2] [.] [7] [5] [0] [=]   [212.70]

    a. Is Sara Beth's result reasonable? Explain.

    b. If the result is not reasonable, explain her error.

Exploration 2

Use base-ten blocks to find each difference.

11. $3.86 - 1.52$ **12.** $2.13 - 1.52$ **13.** $3.12 - 1.47$

For Exercises 14–19, find each difference without using a calculator.

14. $82.95 - 41.23$ **15.** $235.8 - 194.25$ **16.** $176.2 - 59.374$

17. $10 - 6.89$ **18.** $5.006 - x$ where $x = 4.06$ **19.** $y - 18.909$ where $y = 20.22$

20. Rosa is ordering lunch at a restaurant. She orders a garden salad for $2.75, a chicken sandwich for $5.89, and a glass of juice for $0.99. If she pays with a ten-dollar bill, how much change will Rosa receive?

21. Insurance On the declaration sheet for his auto insurance, Mr. Seymour noted that he was to be charged $751.14 for three types of coverage: bodily injury liability, property damage, and collision. If the premium (cost) for bodily injury liability was $351.52 and the premium for property damage was $162.48, how much was the premium for collision?

Math Thematics, Book 1
Student Workbook

Paper Clip Products (Use with the *Setting the Stage* on page 148, Question 3 on page 149, Question 14 on page 151, and Excrcise 28 on page 159.)

Directions You will need 2 paper clips and 10 each of two different-colored chips, Follow the game rules in the book to play *Paper Clip Products*.

Game Board

7	14	24	16	40
20	15	55	28	9
35	8	12	25	19
4	17	30	48	45
36	18	32	11	21

Factor List

2	3	4	5
6	7	8	9
10	11	12	13
14	15	16	17
18	19	20	21
22	23	24	25

MODULE 3   **LABSHEET 3B**

Divisibility Test for 3 (Use with Question 7 on page 150.)

Directions Follow the steps below to fill in the table. Then use the completed table to answer parts (a)–(d).

Step 1 Multiply the number in the first row by 3. Write the product in the second row.

Step 2 Add the digits of the product in the second row. Write the sum in the third row.

$3 \cdot 4 = 12$

Number	1	2	3	4	5	6	13	27	55	456	659	2260
Multiply by 3				12								
Sum of the digits				3								

The sum of the digits 1 and 2 is 3.
$1 + 2 = 3$

a. Are all the numbers in the second row divisible by 3? How do you know?

b. What do all the numbers in the third row have in common?

c. Use the pattern from part (b) to develop a test for divisibility by 3.

d. Choose several three-digit and four-digit numbers and use your test to check them for divisibility by 3. Use a calculator to check your results. Does your divisibility test seem to work?

MODULE 3 | **LABSHEET** **3C**

Prime Time (Use with Question 17 on page 152, and Questions 19 and 21 on page 153.)

Directions You will need a supply of paper clips and 15 each of two different-colored chips. Work with a partner. Follow the game rules in your book to play *Prime Time*.

Game Board

12	50	49	6	18
15	9	27	30	105
4	8	10	35	20
32	25	14	28	42
40	21	75	54	63
45	98	60	125	81

Factor List

2	3	5	7

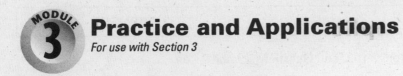

Practice and Applications
For use with Section 3

For use with Exploration 1

1. Without dividing, tell whether each number is divisible by 2, by 5, or by 10.

    a. 118   **b.** 225   **c.** 350

    d. 420   **e.** 371   **f.** 685

2. Test each number for divisibility by 3 and by 9.

    a. 138   **b.** 279   **c.** 608

    d. 189   **e.** 451   **f.** 342

3. Test each number for divisibility by 2, 3, 5, 9, and 10.

    a. 670   **b.** 240   **c.** 567

    d. 925   **e.** 414   **f.** 168

4. List all the factors of each number.

    a. 36   **b.** 20   **c.** 42

    d. 45   **e.** 29   **f.** 16

5. Find the greatest common factor of each set of numbers.

    a. 16 and 36   **b.** 20 and 45   **c.** 15 and 24

    d. 16, 20, and 30   **e.** 12 and 25   **f.** 9, 18, and 21

6. Mr. Gerald has $13.65. He wants to divide the money equally among his 3 grandchildren. Can he do this so that each child gets the same amount of money? Explain.

(continued)

Name _____ Date _____

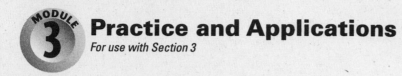

Practice and Applications
For use with Section 3

For use with Exploration 2

7. Tell whether each number is *prime* or *composite*.

    a. 33   **b.** 47   **c.** 153

    d. 19   **e.** 366   **f.** 95

8. Use a factor tree to find the prime factorization of 40.

For use with Exploration 3

9. Write the prime factorization of each number, using exponents for repeated factors.

    a. 30   **b.** 24   **c.** 57

    d. 98   **e.** 180   **f.** 200

10. Find the value of each expression.

    a. 3^4 **b.** 8^2 **c.** 4^4

    d. 8^3 **e.** 5^3 **f.** 2^4

11. Write each of the following as a single number raised to either the 2nd or 3rd power.

    a. 81   **b.** 27   **c.** 144

    d. 16   **e.** 49   **f.** 216

12. Replace each ___?___ with >, <, or =.

    a. 3^3 ___?___ 4^2 **b.** 2^5 ___?___ $5 \cdot 5$ **c.** 6^3 ___?___ $6 \cdot 6 \cdot 6$

13. One byte of memory stored in a computer is made up of 2^3 bits.

    a. In standard form, how many bits are in a byte?

    b. Writing the number using exponents, how many bits are in 2 bytes of memory? Explain.

Name _____ Date _____

 **Study Guide**
For use with Section 3

Paper Clip Products   Factors and Divisibility

GOAL **LEARN HOW TO:** • use divisibility tests
• find factors, including the greatest common factor
• recognize prime and composite numbers
• use a factor tree to find prime factors
• identify powers and write numbers using exponents

AS YOU: • develop game-playing strategies and investigate puzzles

Exploration 1: Testing for Divisibility

Divisibility Rules

When a number can be divided evenly by another number (no remainder), it is **divisible** by that number. You can tell whether a number is divisible by 2, by 3, by 5, by 9, or by 10 by applying the divisibility tests shown in the table.

A number is divisible by:	if:
2	the ones digit is 0, 2, 4, 6, or 8
3	the sum of the digits is divisible by 3
5	the ones digit is 0 or 5
9	the sum of the digits is divisible by 9
10	the ones digit is 0

Factors and Common Factors

When a whole number is divisible by a second whole number, the second number is a **factor** of the first.

When two numbers have the same factor, that factor is a *common factor* of both numbers.

The **greatest common factor (GCF)** of two or more numbers is the greatest number that is a factor of each number.

Since 20 is divisible by 2, 2 is a factor of 20.

Since $20 = \mathbf{2} \cdot 10$ and $12 = \mathbf{2} \cdot 6$, 2 is a common factor of 20 and 12.

Since $20 = \mathbf{4} \cdot 5$ and $12 = \mathbf{4} \cdot 3$, 4 is a common factor of 20 and 12.

The GCF of 20 and 12 is 4.

Example

Find the greatest common factor of 12 and 64.

Sample Response

List the factors of each number and circle the common factors.

factors of 12: (1), (2), 3, (4), 6, 12   factors of 64: (1), (2), (4), 8, 16, 32, 64

The GCF of 12 and 64 is 4.

Math Thematics, Book 1
Student Workbook

104

Name _____   Date _____

Study Guide
For use with Section 3

Exploration 2: Prime Factors

All whole numbers greater than 1 are either *prime* or *composite*. A **prime** number has exactly two factors, 1 and the number itself. A **composite** number has more than two factors.

The number 7 is a prime number.
The number 12 is a composite number.

Every composite number can be written as the product of prime factors. This product is the **prime factorization** of the number. Drawing a **factor tree** can help you find the prime factorization of a number.

> ### Example
>
> Use a factor tree to find the prime factorization of 50.
>
> 50
> 2   25
>   5   5
>
> The prime factorization of 50 is 2 • 5 • 5.

Exploration 3: Powers of Numbers

There is a short way to write an expression that repeats a factor.

$$4 \cdot 4 \cdot 4 = 4^3$$

The **exponent** 3 tells how many times the **base** 4 is used as a factor.

A number that can be written using an exponent and a base is a **power** of the base.

standard form
$$64 = 4 \cdot 4 \cdot 4 = 4^3 \rightarrow 64 \text{ is the 3rd power of 4.}$$

You can use exponents to write prime factorizations. The prime factorization of a number is the same, no matter how you begin.

> ### Example
>
> Use a factor tree to write the prime factorization of 36.
>
> 36   36
> 6   6   or   4   9
> 2 3 2 3   2 2 3 3
>
> The prime factorization of 36 is 2 • 2 • 3 • 3, or $2^2 \cdot 3^2$.

Name _____   Date _____

Study Guide: Practice & Application Exercises

For use with Section 3

Exploration 1

Test each number for divisibility by 2, 3, 5, 9, and 10.

1. 90   **2.** 150   **3.** 66   **4.** 225

For Exercises 5–8, list all the factors of each number. Then find the GCF of each set of numbers.

5. 55 and 77   **6.** 19 and 49   **7.** 20, 40, and 90   **8.** 18, 72, and 90

9. Copy and complete the Venn diagram at the right to illustrate all the common factors of 48 and 64.

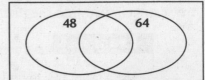

10. Use your completed Venn diagram from Exercise 9 to find the GCF of 48 and 64.

11. The factors of a number other than itself are called the proper divisors of the number. For example, the proper divisors of 12 are 1, 2, 3, 4, and 6. The number 12 can be written as a sum using only its proper divisors (once each) in exactly two ways, $1 + 2 + 3 + 6 = 12$ and $2 + 4 + 6 = 12$. Find the proper divisors of 24. Then find all the ways that 24 can be written as a sum using only its proper divisors.

Exploration 2

Tell whether each number is *prime* or *composite*.

12. 17   **13.** 39   **14.** 11   **15.** 101

Write the prime factorization of each number, using exponents for repeated factors.

16. 100   **17.** 288   **18.** 360   **19.** 540

20. All even numbers are composite except for the number 2.

     a. Explain why 2 is not a composite number.

     b. Explain why all other even numbers are composite.

Exploration 3

For Exercises 21–24, find the value of each expression.

21. 6^2 **22.** 2^6 **23.** 8^2 **24.** 5^3

25. Write the prime factorization of 2400 using exponents.

26. One number is chosen at random from the set of all the prime factors of 12. What is the probability that the number will be odd? Explain.

Sequence Tables for Multiples (Use with Question 7 on page 166.)

Directions Each table lists multiples of different numbers. For each table:

- Complete the heading to show the number used.

- Fill in the missing terms for each sequence.

- Write an expression for the general term of the sequence. Use the variable *n* for the term number. The first one has been done for you.

- Use your expression to find the 50th term.

a. Multiples of 5

Term Number	1	2	3	4	5	6	7	8	9	...	*n*
Term	5	10	15	20					45	...	5 • *n*

50th term = _____

b. Multiples of _____

Term Number	1	2	3	4	5	6	7	8	9	10	...	*n*
Term	13	26	39							130	...	__ • *n*

50th term = _____

c. Multiples of _____

Term Number	1	2	3	4	5	6	7	...	*n*
Term		16	24		40	48	56	...	

50th term = _____

d. Multiples of 9

Term Number	1	2	3	4	5	6	7	...	*n*
Term							63	...	

50th term = _____

Practice and Applications

For use with Section 4

For use with Exploration 1

1. List the first seven multiples of each number.

    a. 8   **b.** 30   **c.** 104

    d. 4   **e.** 10   **f.** 16

    g. 15   **h.** 27   **i.** 11

2. Suppose you withdraw only multiples of $10 from a bank teller machine. Which amount(s) can you not withdraw?

    A. $30   **B.** $50   **C.** $75   **D.** $90

3. Find the least common multiple of each set of numbers.

    a. 4 and 5   **b.** 3, 8, and 12   **c.** 18 and 10

    d. 15 and 25   **e.** 64 and 16   **f.** 12 and 20

    g. 34 and 85   **h.** 84 and 24   **i.** 39 and 33

4. For her English class, Mikenna must complete a novel every 4 weeks. For her science class, she has a project due every 8 weeks. Lastly, for her math class, she has a unit test every 6 weeks. If the school year is 36 weeks long, will Mikenna ever have to complete a novel and science project and take a unit test during the same week? Explain.

5. Ryan and Ben are jogging on a 400-meter track. They start from the same point and begin jogging at the same time. Ryan is jogging at a pace of 125 seconds per lap, and Ben is jogging at a pace of 100 seconds per lap. Both are jogging at a constant pace.

    a. After how many seconds will Ben and Ryan both be at their starting point?

    b. When they meet at the starting point, how many laps will each have jogged?

6. Short tours of the Lone Mine Cave leave every 15 minutes. Long tours of the cave leave every 40 minutes. If both tours start at 8 A.M., at what time will the tours leave together again?

Math Thematics, Book 1
Student Workbook

Name _____   Date _____

Study Guide
For use with Section 4

Pattern Play   Multiples

GOAL   **LEARN HOW TO:** • find multiples and least common multiples
AS YOU: • analyze the game *Pattern Tick-Tock*

Exploration 1: Multiples and Common Multiples

A **multiple** of a whole number is the product of that number and any nonzero whole number.

Since 4 • 3 = 12, 12 is a multiple of 3.

The multiples of a number form a sequence.

multiples of 2: 2, 4, 6, 8, 10, 12, …
multiples of 3: 3, 6, 9, 12, 15, 18, …

Two numbers may have common multiples.

Some common multiples of 2 and 3 are 6, 12, and 18.

The **least common multiple (LCM)** of two or more whole numbers is the least number that is a multiple of all the numbers.

The LCM of 2 and 3 is 6.

Example

Find the least common multiple of 8 and 12.

Sample Response

List the multiples of each number. Then circle the common multiples.

multiples of 8: 8, 16, ㉔, 32, 40, ㊽, …
multiples of 12: 12, ㉔, 36, ㊽, …
common multiples: 24, 48, …
The LCM of 8 and 12 is 24.

When you are trying to find the LCM of two numbers, you can stop listing the multiples of the second number as soon as you come upon the *first* common multiple.

multiples of 8: 8, 16, 24, 32, 40, 48, …
                          ↕
multiples of 12: 12, 24, …

Study Guide: Practice & Application Exercises

For use with Section 4

Exploration 1

List the first seven multiples of each number.

1. 9   **2.** 24   **3.** 75   **4.** 110

5. 12   **6.** 17   **7.** 200   **8.** 222

Find the least common multiple of each set of numbers.

9. 15 and 25   **10.** 120 and 144   **11.** 12, 24, and 36   **12.** 36, 72, and 120

13. 81 and 51   **14.** 38 and 112   **15.** 8, 10, and 48   **16.** 15, 90, and 110

17. Suppose you can withdraw only multiples of $30 from a bank teller machine. Which amounts can you withdraw?

     A. $60   **B.** $80   **C.** $130   **D.** $210

18. Lori is selling granola bars. She wants to choose a price that will allow people to pay with only dimes or with only quarters. What is the lowest price that Lori could charge so that she can collect either only dimes or only quarters for her granola bars?

19. a. Copy and complete the Venn diagram to show all the prime factors of 24 and 30, and those prime factors that are common factors. (Be sure to show each prime factor as many times as it occurs in the prime factorization of each number.)

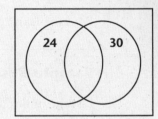

     b. Find the LCM of 24 and 30 by listing multiples.

     c. Explain how you could use your Venn diagram from part (a) to find the LCM of 24 and 30.

20. A traveling entertainment company has two Ferris wheels. One of them makes a complete rotation every 120 seconds, while the other makes a complete rotation every 144 seconds. If they start at the same time, how many *minutes* will it take before the wheels begin a new rotation together?

21. Eastbound trains leave Central Depot every 24 minutes and northbound trains leave every 42 minutes. If both an eastbound and a northbound train left at 6 P.M., when is the next time that two such trains will leave at the same time? Explain your process.

Name _____   Date _____

Practice and Applications
For use with Section 5

For use with Exploration 1

1. a. Find $\frac{3}{4}$ of 8.   **b.** Find $\frac{3}{8}$ of $\frac{1}{4}$.

2. Use common factors to write each fraction in lowest terms.

   a. $\frac{6}{15}$ **b.** $\frac{35}{45}$ **c.** $\frac{24}{36}$

   d. $\frac{9}{45}$ **e.** $\frac{14}{24}$ **f.** $\frac{12}{27}$

   g. $\frac{9}{18}$ **h.** $\frac{18}{20}$ **i.** $\frac{16}{28}$

   j. $\frac{7}{35}$ **k.** $\frac{16}{30}$ **l.** $\frac{33}{55}$

3. Find each product. Write each answer in lowest terms.

   a. $\frac{2}{5} \cdot \frac{1}{4}$ **b.** $\frac{4}{5} \cdot \frac{5}{12}$ **c.** $\frac{2}{3} \cdot \frac{9}{10}$

   d. $\frac{3}{5} \cdot \frac{5}{6}$ **e.** $\frac{1}{2} \cdot \frac{8}{9}$ **f.** $\frac{1}{8} \cdot \frac{1}{5}$

   g. $\frac{3}{8} \cdot \frac{4}{5}$ **h.** $\frac{10}{20} \cdot \frac{6}{8}$ **i.** $\frac{1}{10} \cdot \frac{2}{3}$

   j. $\frac{16}{25} \cdot \frac{5}{12}$ **k.** $\frac{7}{8} \cdot \frac{16}{21}$ **l.** $\frac{2}{3} \cdot \frac{4}{9}$

4. Brittany has $\frac{7}{8}$ of a yard of fabric. She uses $\frac{4}{5}$ of the fabric to make a
scarf. What fraction of a yard of fabric does Brittany use to make the
scarf? Is it more or less than $\frac{1}{2}$ yard?

5. Students who take music lessons make up about $\frac{3}{4}$ of a sixth grade class.

   a. About $\frac{1}{2}$ of the students take piano lessons. About what part of the
   class take piano lessons?

   b. About $\frac{5}{12}$ of the students take violin lessons. About what part of
   the class take violin lessons?

(continued)

Name _____   Date _____

Practice and Applications

For use with Section 5

For use with Exploration 2

6. Use the distributive property and mental math to find each product. Write each answer in lowest terms.

a. $2 \cdot 6\frac{1}{3}$ **b.** $4\frac{1}{4} \cdot 3$ **c.** $3\frac{1}{6} \cdot 6$

d. $3\frac{1}{8} \cdot 8$ **e.** $3\frac{1}{2} \cdot 4$ **f.** $10 \cdot 2\frac{1}{5}$

7. Find each product. Write each answer in lowest terms.

a. $6 \cdot 2\frac{1}{8}$ **b.** $3 \cdot 5\frac{3}{4}$ **c.** $2\frac{3}{5} \cdot 4$

d. $\frac{5}{7} \cdot \frac{2}{5}$ **e.** $3\frac{1}{2} \cdot \frac{4}{5}$ **f.** $\frac{5}{8} \cdot \frac{8}{5}$

g. $2\frac{1}{3} \cdot 4\frac{1}{2}$ **h.** $3\frac{1}{4} \cdot 2\frac{2}{5}$ **i.** $3\frac{1}{4} \cdot 4\frac{3}{8}$

8. Predict whether each product will be *greater than* or *less than* $6\frac{7}{8}$.

a. $1\frac{1}{2} \cdot 6\frac{7}{8}$ **b.** $\frac{5}{8} \cdot 6\frac{7}{8}$ **c.** $\frac{99}{100} \cdot 6\frac{7}{8}$

9. Shani is making muffins. Her recipe calls for the following ingredients:

Bran Muffins (*Serves 12*)	
1 cup water	$1\frac{1}{2}$ cups butter
$3\frac{1}{2}$ cups bran cereal	$1\frac{1}{3}$ cups sugar
$2\frac{1}{2}$ cups flour	2 eggs
$2\frac{1}{2}$ teaspoons baking soda	2 cups buttermilk

a. Shani only wants to make two servings of this recipe. What fraction of the recipe should Shani make?

b. Rewrite the muffin recipe to show how much of each ingredient Shani should use.

10. A recipe for chocolate pudding calls for $3\frac{1}{2}$ cups milk. How much milk would you need to make $2\frac{1}{2}$ times the original recipe?

Math Thematics, Book 1
112 Student Workbook

Study Guide
For use with Section 5

A Fair Share   Fraction and Mixed Number Multiplication

GOAL   **LEARN HOW TO:** • multiply fractions
                                     • use the distributive property
                                     • multiply mixed numbers

AS YOU: • use paper folding to solve the treasure puzzle
              • find the weight of coins in a treasure

Exploration 1: Fraction Multiplication

Multiplying Fractions

To multiply two fractions, follow these steps:

Multiply $\frac{5}{8} \cdot \frac{4}{3}$.

Step 1 Multiply the numerators of the fractions
to find the numerator of the product.

$$\frac{5}{8} \cdot \frac{4}{3} = \frac{5 \cdot 4}{} = \frac{20}{}$$

Step 2 Multiply the denominators of the fractions
to find the denominator of the product.

$$\frac{5}{8} \cdot \frac{4}{3} = \frac{5 \cdot 4}{8 \cdot 3} = \frac{20}{24}$$

Writing Fractions in Lowest Terms

Divide both the numerator and the denominator of a
fraction by a common factor to write an equivalent fraction.
At the right, the greatest common factor is used, resulting
in an equivalent fraction in lowest terms. Recall that a
fraction is in lowest terms when 1 is the only whole number
that will divide its numerator and denominator evenly.

$$\frac{20}{24} = \frac{20 \div 4}{24 \div 4} = \frac{5}{6}$$

If you have not used the greatest common factor, you
will have to continue dividing until the fraction is in
lowest terms.

$$\frac{20}{24} = \frac{20 \div 2}{24 \div 2} = \frac{10}{12}$$

$$\frac{10}{12} = \frac{10 \div 2}{12 \div 2} = \frac{5}{6}$$

Reducing Fractions Before Multiplying

When multiplying fractions, you may choose to divide a
numerator and a denominator (not necessarily in the same
fraction) by a common factor *before* you multiply.

Multiply $\frac{5}{8} \cdot \frac{4}{3}$.

Divide a numerator and a denominator by a
common factor.

Divide 8 by 4. $\rightarrow \dfrac{5}{\overset{}{\underset{2}{8}}} \cdot \dfrac{\overset{1}{4}}{3} \leftarrow$ Divide 4 by 4.

Using the reduced numbers, multiply the numerators
and multiply the denominators.

$$= \frac{5 \cdot 1}{2 \cdot 3} = \frac{5}{6}$$

Study Guide
For use with Section 5

Exploration 2: Multiplying Mixed Numbers

The Distributive Property

Recall that you use the **distributive property** to multiply a sum by a number. This property tells you to multiply the number by each term of the sum.

$$6 \cdot (5 + 2) = 6 \cdot 5 + 6 \cdot 2$$
$$= 30 + 12$$
$$= 42$$

Multiplying Mixed Numbers

To multiply a mixed number by a whole number, write the mixed number as a sum and apply the distributive property.

Example

Find $6 \cdot 5\frac{1}{2}$.

Sample Response

$6 \cdot 5\frac{1}{2} = 6 \cdot \left(5 + \frac{1}{2}\right)$ ← Rewrite as a sum.

$= (6 \cdot 5) + \left(6 \cdot \frac{1}{2}\right)$ ← Apply the distributive property.

$= 30 + 3$ ← Simplify.

$= 33$

To multiply two mixed numbers, first rewrite each of them as a fraction. Then multiply.

Example

Find $7\frac{1}{2} \cdot 1\frac{3}{4}$.

Sample Response

$7\frac{1}{2} \cdot 1\frac{3}{4} = \frac{15}{2} \cdot \frac{7}{4}$ ← Rewrite mixed numbers as fractions.

$= \frac{15 \cdot 7}{2 \cdot 4}$ ← Multiply numerators and denominators.

$= \frac{105}{8}$ ← Simplify.

$= 13\frac{1}{8}$ ← Rewrite fraction as mixed number.

Study Guide: Practice & Application Exercises

MODULE 3

For use with Section 5

Exploration 1

Use common factors to write each fraction in lowest terms.

1. $\frac{12}{36}$ 2. $\frac{14}{28}$ 3. $\frac{24}{72}$ 4. $\frac{144}{576}$

For Exercises 5–12, find each product. Write your answer in lowest terms.

5. $\frac{3}{4} \cdot \frac{1}{2}$ 6. $\frac{5}{7} \cdot \frac{2}{3}$ 7. $\frac{3}{8} \cdot \frac{7}{11}$ 8. $\frac{2}{5} \cdot \frac{3}{15}$

9. $\frac{5}{8} \cdot \frac{2}{3}$ 10. $\frac{3}{2} \cdot \frac{4}{9}$ 11. $\frac{4}{7} \cdot \frac{21}{8}$ 12. $\frac{6}{8} \cdot \frac{3}{12}$

13. **Writing** Explain how you would find the product $\frac{2}{3} \cdot 12$.

14. Mrs. Simmons has a recipe that makes 24 muffins. To make a smaller batch of muffins, she decides to use $\frac{5}{6}$ of each ingredient. After mixing the ingredients, Mrs. Simmons decides to bake only $\frac{1}{2}$ of the mixture she has prepared. How many muffins will she bake?

15. For use in a parking lot during the winter, the lot manager ordered $\frac{3}{4}$ of a ton of salt. Throughout the winter, $\frac{2}{3}$ of the supply was used. How many tons of salt were used?

Exploration 2

Mental Math Use the distributive property and mental math to find each product. Write each answer in lowest terms.

16. $8 \cdot 3\frac{1}{4}$ 17. $12 \cdot 5\frac{1}{2}$ 18. $6\frac{1}{3} \cdot 6$ 19. $10\frac{1}{5} \cdot 15$

Find each product. Write each answer in lowest terms.

20. $5\frac{3}{5} \cdot 1\frac{3}{10}$ 21. $7\frac{5}{8} \cdot 3\frac{2}{3}$ 22. $4\frac{4}{5} \cdot 7\frac{2}{3}$ 23. $3\frac{5}{6} \cdot 2\frac{7}{12}$

24. **Geometry** Mrs. Gold had her students use pipe cleaners to construct a cube and then dip it into a bubble solution to observe how the bubbles clung to the pipe cleaners. The recipe for bubble solution is 1 c dishwashing liquid, $\frac{1}{2}$ c glycerin, and 2 c water. This recipe makes enough solution for 2 groups working together. If Mrs. Gold wanted enough solution for 8 groups, how much glycerin did she need?

MODULE 3   **LABSHEET** 6A

Target Number (Use with *Setting the Stage* on page 184.)

Directions Work with a partner. Follow the game rules in your book to play *Target Number*. Place a sheet of paper over the table. To begin a game, slide the paper down to reveal the target number and the constant factor. Record the numbers you chose to multiply by and the resulting products. Start with Game 2, since a sample game for Game 1 is shown on page 184.

Game 1	Target Number = 226	Constant Factor = 13
Game 2	Target Number = 408	Constant Factor = 7
Game 3	Target Number = 845	Constant Factor = 38
Game 4	Target Number = 256	Constant Factor = 6
Game 5	Target Number = 942	Constant Factor = 64
Game 6	Target Number = 537	Constant Factor = 27
Game 7	Target Number = 351	Constant Factor = 19
Game 8	Target Number = 1031	Constant Factor = 8

MODULE 3   **LABSHEET** **6B**

Decimal Multiplication Grids (Use with Question 5 on page 186.)

Directions Shade each grid to model the given product. Then write each product in both fraction and decimal form.

Model 0.5 • 0.4.

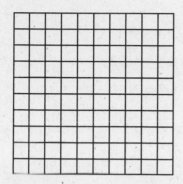

Model 0.3 • 0.3.

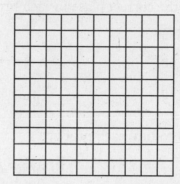

$\frac{5}{10} \cdot \frac{4}{10} =$ _____ 0.5 • 0.4 = _____ $\frac{3}{10} \cdot \frac{3}{10} =$ _____ 0.3 • 0.3 = _____

. . . .

Decimal and Fraction Products (Use with Questions 6, 7, and 9(b) on page 186.)

Directions Write each decimal multiplication problem as a fraction multiplication problem. Then find the fraction product and write it in decimal form.

> Written in fraction form, the whole number 4 is $\frac{4}{1}$

Decimal multiplication problem	Equivalent fraction problem	Fraction product	Decimal product
0.6 • 4	$\frac{6}{10} \cdot \frac{4}{1}$	$\frac{24}{10}$	2.4
0.3 • 0.2			
0.8 • 0.19			
0.05 • 0.07			
6 • 0.03			

Name _____   Date _____

Practice and Applications
For use with Section 6

For use with Exploration 1

1. Copy each problem. Then, without using a calculator, place the decimal point in the correct place in each product.

   a. 346 • 0.16 = 5536   **b.** 4.8 • 9.3 = 4464

   c. 59 • 2.15 = 12685   **d.** 2.34 • 0.8 = 1872

   e. 72 • 1.03 = 7416   **f.** 0.03 • 6.7 = 201

2. Use mental math to find each product.

   a. 0.1 • 78   **b.** 43.6 • 0.01   **c.** 382.5 • 0.01

   d. 5.07 • 0.01   **e.** 32.7 • 0.1   **f.** 0.01 • 39.2

3. Find each product without using a calculator. Then use estimation to check that your answer is reasonable.

   a. 0.4 • 0.17   **b.** 3.7 • 6.2   **c.** 4.6 • 0.9

   d. 0.08 • 0.01   **e.** 32.1 • 0.25   **f.** 1.92 • 0.53

   g. 412 • 1.18   **h.** 26.3 • 0.02   **i.** 1.8 • 3.02

4. A dietician orders fruit for cafeteria lunches. Apples cost $0.59 per pound this week. What is the total cost for an order of 215.8 pounds of apples?

For use with Exploration 2

5. Predict whether each product will be *greater than*, *less than*, or *equal to* the number in boldface. Explain how you know.

   a. 6.9 • 1.2   **b. 0.43** • 0.95   **c. 0.059** • 1

6. Isabelle has $184.56 in a savings account that earns 3% interest annually. At the end of one year, the bank will pay her 3% of the $184.56 she has in the account. Estimate 0.03 • $184.56 to choose the correct amount she will receive after one year.

   A. $553.68   **B.** $55.37   **C.** $5.54   **D.** $0.55

Name _____   Date _____

 **Study Guide**
For use with Section 6

Target Games   Decimal Multiplication

GOAL **LEARN HOW TO:** • multiply decimals
• estimate decimal products
• improve your estimating skills

AS YOU: • model decimal products on grids

Exploration 1: Multiplying Decimals

Decimal products can be modeled on a grid by shading a part of a part.

Example

Model the product 0.3 • 0.9 using a 10 × 10 grid.

Step 1 Lightly shade grids modeling 0.9 in a vertical direction.

Step 2 Lightly shade grids modeling 0.3 in a horizontal direction.

Result The region that is shaded twice models the product: 0.3 • 0.9 = 0.27

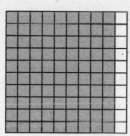      

Decimal multiplication is similar to whole number multiplication.

Example

To multiply 55.5 • 1.75, follow these steps:

Step 1 Multiply the numbers as whole numbers.   555 • 175 = 97125

Step 2 Place the decimal point in the product.   55.5 • 1.75 = 97.125

Use the sum of the number of the decimal places in the factors.

1 decimal place + 2 decimal places = 3 decimal places

Exploration 2: Estimating Decimal Products

You can use estimation to check that your answer is reasonable, especially to see if you have placed the decimal point correctly.

The product 55.5 • 1.75 in the Example above is about 55 • 2, or 110. So, the answer 97.125 is reasonable.

Name _____   Date _____

Study Guide: Practice & Application Exercises

MODULE 3

For use with Section 6

Exploration 1

Copy each problem. Then correctly place the decimal point.

1. $4.8 \cdot 5.1 = 2448$ **2.** $2.39 \cdot 7.6 = 18164$ **3.** $5.6 \cdot 0.9 = 504$

For Exercises 4–6, find each product without using a calculator. Then use estimation to check that your answer is reasonable.

4. $3.2 \cdot 0.99$ **5.** $12.8 \cdot 5.9$ **6.** $69.84 \cdot 11.9$

7. Use a calculator to multiply 27.8 by each decimal. Record the results and tell whether the product is less than or greater than 27.8.

    a. 0.25   **b.** 0.82   **c.** 1.04   **d.** 2.6

8. Find each product where $a = 0.02$ and $b = 1.7$.

    a. $0.16 \cdot a$ **b.** $9.06 \cdot b$ **c.** $a \cdot b$

9. Frank types other students' term papers on his word processor. He charges $1.75 per page. A page with a table counts as 1.5 pages. Lillian's term paper turned out to be 52 pages in all, with tables on 8 of the pages. How much does Lillian owe Frank?

Exploration 2

10. **Measurement** One inch is equivalent to about 2.54 cm. To find out how many centimeters there are in one yard, Carlos used the following key sequence on his calculator.

    `2 · 5 4 × 1 · 2 × 3 = 9.144`

    Is this answer reasonable? If not, what did Carlos do wrong?

11. **Energy** Where Jean lives, regular unleaded gasoline costs $2.869 per gallon. The tank in her car holds 14 gallons of gasoline.

    a. Choose the best estimate of the cost to fill the gas tank in Jean's car if the tank is completely empty.

        A. $0.042   **B.** $0.42   **C.** $4.20   **D.** $42.00

    b. For highway driving, Jean's car averages 32 miles per gallon. Use your answer from part (a) to estimate the cost of a trip of 1750 mi.

Math Thematics, Book 1
Student Workbook

Practice and Applications

For use after Sections 1–6

For use with Section 1

1. Write each decimal in words.

  a. 9.01　　　　　　**b.** 0.172　　　　　　**c.** 18.065

2. Replace each ___?___ with <, >, or =.

  a. 34.63 __?__ 34.603　　**b.** 7.25 __?__ 7.025　　**c.** 5.002 __?__ 5.020

  d. 82.01 __?__ 82.001　　**e.** 12.00 __?__ 12　　　**f.** 3.353 __?__ 33.55

  g. 0.03 __?__ 0.009　　　**h.** 4.721 __?__ 4.717　　**i.** 0.4 __?__ 0.400

For use with Section 2

3. Find each sum or difference without using a calculator.

  a. 2.9 + 14.68　　　　**b.** 0.057 + 0.138　　　**c.** 61.4 + 14.82

  d. 63.008 + 12.928　　**e.** 8.3 + 4.7 + 0.15　　**f.** 19.3 + 28 + 0.077

  g. 7.6 – 2.817　　　　**h.** 230.11 – 6.258　　　**i.** 0.08 – 0.018

  j. 4.029 – 0.5　　　　**k.** 63.7 – 0.002　　　　**l.** 25 – 4.992

4. Jamie, Jill, and Jesse want to combine their money to buy a gift for
their mother. Jamie has $12.98. Jill has $3.50 less than Jamie. Jesse has
$2.83 more than Jamie.

  a. How much money do Jill and Jesse each have?

  b. How much money do the three children have altogether?

  c. How much more money do they need to buy a $50 sweater?

For use with Section 3

5. Find the greatest common factor of each set of numbers.

  a. 15 and 21　　　　**b.** 24 and 30　　　　**c.** 14 and 42

6. Write the prime factorization of each number.

  a. 34　　　　　　**b.** 48　　　　　　**c.** 120

7. Find the value of each expression.

  a. 6^3　　　　　　**b.** 11^2　　　　　　**c.** 3^5

(continued)

Name _____ Date _____

Practice and Applications
For use after Sections 1–6

For use with Section 4

8. Local trains leave the station every 30 minutes. Express trains leave the station every 45 minutes. If a local train and an express train both left the station at 6 A.M., what time will another local and express train leave together?

9. Find the least common multiple of each set of numbers.

a. 24 and 14 **b.** 3, 6, and 27 **c.** 26 and 65

d. 36 and 9 **e.** 28 and 49 **f.** 2, 5, and 15

For use with Section 5

10. Find each product. Write your answer in lowest terms.

a. $\frac{3}{5} \cdot \frac{1}{6}$ **b.** $\frac{2}{7} \cdot \frac{5}{8}$ **c.** $\frac{5}{12} \cdot \frac{2}{9}$

d. $\frac{4}{5} \cdot \frac{5}{16}$ **e.** $\frac{6}{11} \cdot \frac{7}{18}$ **f.** $\frac{2}{3} \cdot \frac{9}{20}$

11. Find each product. Write each answer in lowest terms.

a. $4 \cdot 2\frac{1}{6}$ **b.** $5 \cdot 2\frac{1}{4}$ **c.** $6\frac{3}{4} \cdot 4$

d. $\frac{5}{7} \cdot \frac{7}{5}$ **e.** $2\frac{3}{5} \cdot 1\frac{3}{8}$ **f.** $1\frac{3}{4} \cdot \frac{2}{3}$

For use with Section 6

12. Use mental math to find each product.

a. $0.1 \cdot 93$ **b.** $72.1 \cdot 0.01$ **c.** $0.01 \cdot 428.6$

d. $0.1 \cdot 41$ **e.** $7.3 \cdot 0.01$ **f.** $0.01 \cdot 4.34$

13. Find each product without using a calculator. Then use estimation to check that your answer is reasonable.

a. $0.8 \cdot 0.12$ **b.** $6.9 \cdot 5.1$ **c.** $7.26 \cdot 0.9$

d. $0.2 \cdot 1.31$ **e.** $8.13 \cdot 0.5$ **f.** $4.7 \cdot 8.1$

Math Thematics, Book 1
Student Workbook
122

Name _____   Problem _____

Teacher Assessment Scales
For use with Module 4

☆ *The star indicates that you excelled in some way.*

 ## Problem Solving

❶   **❷**   **❸**   **❹**   **❺**

You did not understand the problem well enough to get started or you did not show any work.

You understood the problem well enough to make a plan and to work toward a solution.

You made a plan, you used it to solve the problem, and you verified your solution.

 ## Mathematical Language

❶   **❷**   **❸**   **❹**   **❺**

You did not use any mathematical vocabulary or symbols, or you did not use them correctly, or your use was not appropriate.

You used appropriate mathematical language, but the way it was used was not always correct or other terms and symbols were needed.

You used mathematical language that was correct and appropriate to make your meaning clear.

 ## Representations

❶   **❷**   **❸**   **❹**   **❺**

You did not use any representations such as equations, tables, graphs, or diagrams to help solve the problem or explain your solution.

You made appropriate representations to help solve the problem or help you explain your solution, but they were not always correct or other representations were needed.

You used appropriate and correct representations to solve the problem or explain your solution.

 ## Connections

❶   **❷**   **❸**   **❹**   **❺**

You attempted or solved the problem and then stopped.

You found patterns and used them to extend the solution to other cases, or you recognized that this problem relates to other problems, mathematical ideas, or applications.

You extended the ideas in the solution to the general case, or you showed how this problem relates to other problems, mathematical ideas, or applications.

 ## Presentation

❶   **❷**   **❸**   **❹**   **❺**

The presentation of your solution and reasoning is unclear to others.

The presentation of your solution and reasoning is clear in most places, but others may have trouble understanding parts of it.

The presentation of your solution and reasoning is clear and can be understood by others.

Content Used: _____

Computational Errors: Yes ☐   No ☐

Notes on Errors:

_____

Name _____   Problem _____

Student Self-Assessment Scales

MODULE 4

For use with Module 4

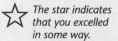 *If your score is in the shaded area, explain why on the back of this sheet and stop.*

☆ *The star indicates that you excelled in some way.*

 Problem Solving

①   **②**   **③**   **④**   **⑤**   ☆

I did not understand the problem well enough to get started or I did not show any work.

I understood the problem well enough to make a plan and to work toward a solution.

I made a plan, I used it to solve the problem, and I verified my solution.

 Mathematical Language

①   **②**   **③**   **④**   **⑤**   ☆

I did not use any mathematical vocabulary or symbols, or I did not use them correctly, or my use was not appropriate.

I used appropriate mathematical language, but the way it was used was not always correct or other terms and symbols were needed.

I used mathematical language that was correct and appropriate to make my meaning clear.

 Representations

①   **②**   **③**   **④**   **⑤**   ☆

I did not use any representations such as equations, tables, graphs, or diagrams to help solve the problem or explain my solution.

I made appropriate representations to help solve the problem or help me explain my solution, but they were not always correct or other representations were needed.

I used appropriate and correct representations to solve the problem or explain my solution.

 Connections

①   **②**   **③**   **④**   **⑤**   ☆

I attempted or solved the problem and then stopped.

I found patterns and used them to extend the solution to other cases, or I recognized that this problem relates to other problems, mathematical ideas, or applications.

I extended the ideas in the solution to the general case, or I showed how this problem relates to other problems, mathematical ideas, or applications.

 Presentation

①   **②**   **③**   **④**   **⑤**   ☆

The presentation of my solution and reasoning is unclear to others.

The presentation of my solution and reasoning is clear in most places, but others may have trouble understanding parts of it.

The presentation of my solution and reasoning is clear and can be understood by others.

Name _____ Date _____

Yellowstone Mammal Cards (Use with Question 3 on page 201.)

Directions Cut out the mammal cards. Then use them as directed in Exploration 1.

Bighorn Sheep	
Classification	mammal
Lifespan	about 13 yr
Approximate Head and Body Length	1.7 m
Approximate Mass	120 kg
Offspring per Birth	1–2
Habitat	land
Diet	herbivore

Bison	
Classification	mammal
Lifespan	about 20 yr
Approximate Head and Body Length	3.4 m
Approximate Mass	900 kg
Offspring per Birth	1
Habitat	land
Diet	herbivore

Dwarf Shrew	
Classification	mammal
Lifespan	about 2 yr
Approximate Head and Body Length	6 cm
Approximate Mass	3.2 g
Offspring per Birth	4–8
Habitat	land
Diet	herbivore

Black Bear	
Classification	mammal
Lifespan	about 20 yr
Approximate Head and Body Length	1.5 m
Approximate Mass	120 kg
Offspring per Birth	1–3
Habitat	land
Diet	omnivore

Bobcat	
Classification	mammal
Lifespan	about 12 yr
Approximate Head and Body Length	85 cm
Approximate Mass	9.2 kg
Offspring per Birth	2–4
Habitat	land
Diet	carnivore

Grizzly Bear	
Classification	mammal
Lifespan	about 25 yr
Approximate Head and Body Length	2.6 m
Approximate Mass	325 kg
Offspring per Birth	1–4
Habitat	land
Diet	omnivore

Coyote	
Classification	mammal
Lifespan	about 15 yr
Approximate Head and Body Length	95 cm
Approximate Mass	16 kg
Offspring per Birth	3–7
Habitat	land
Diet	carnivore

Deer Mouse	
Classification	mammal
Lifespan	about 3 yr
Approximate Head and Body Length	8 cm
Approximate Mass	24 g
Offspring per Birth	3–5
Habitat	land
Diet	herbivore

Little Brown Bat	
Classification	mammal
Lifespan	about 30 yr
Approximate Head and Body Length	8.6 cm
Approximate Mass	10 g
Offspring per Birth	1–2
Habitat	land
Diet	carnivore

This page has been
intentionally left blank
for ease of use of
surrounding labsheets.

Name _____   Date _____

Yellowstone Mammal Cards (Use with Question 3 on page 201.)

Directions Cut out the mammal cards. Then use them as directed in Exploration 1.

Gray Wolf	
Classification	mammal
Lifespan	about 16 yr
Approximate Head and Body Length	1.2 m
Approximate Mass	55 kg
Offspring per Birth	1–14
Habitat	land
Diet	carnivore

Northern Flying Squirrel	
Classification	mammal
Lifespan	about 4 yr
Approximate Head and Body Length	17 cm
Approximate Mass	140 g
Offspring per Birth	1–6
Habitat	land
Diet	omnivore

Pika	
Classification	mammal
Lifespan	about 6 yr
Approximate Head and Body Length	19.5 cm
Approximate Mass	150 g
Offspring per Birth	2–5
Habitat	land
Diet	herbivore

Least Chipmunk	
Classification	mammal
Lifespan	about 6 yr
Approximate Head and Body Length	20 cm
Approximate Mass	45 g
Offspring per Birth	2–6
Habitat	land
Diet	herbivore

Porcupine	
Classification	mammal
Lifespan	about 6 yr
Approximate Head and Body Length	75 cm
Approximate Mass	9.5 kg
Offspring per Birth	1
Habitat	land
Diet	herbivore

Red Squirrel	
Classification	mammal
Lifespan	about 5 yr
Approximate Head and Body Length	20 cm
Approximate Mass	220 g
Offspring per Birth	2–3
Habitat	land
Diet	herbivore

Marten	
Classification	mammal
Lifespan	about 8 yr
Approximate Head and Body Length	40 cm
Approximate Mass	1.1 kg
Offspring per Birth	1–5
Habitat	land
Diet	carnivore

Striped Skunk	
Classification	mammal
Lifespan	about 3 yr
Approximate Head and Body Length	68 cm
Approximate Mass	3.2 kg
Offspring per Birth	5–6
Habitat	land
Diet	omnivore

Water Vole	
Classification	mammal
Lifespan	about 1 yr
Approximate Head and Body Length	17 cm
Approximate Mass	25 g
Offspring per Birth	3–7
Habitat	land
Diet	herbivore

This page has been
intentionally left blank
for ease of use of
surrounding labsheets.

MODULE 4   **LABSHEET** **1C**

Sorting Grid (Use with Question 5 on page 202.)

Directions Sort the *Mammal Cards* into separate piles by placing the cards inside the correct rectangles.

	Mass in Kilograms ⬇	**Mass in Grams** ⬇
Length in Meters ➡	Set *C* Stack cards with **meter** and **kilogram** characteristics here.	Set *D* Stack cards with **meter** and **gram** characteristics here.
Length in Centimeters ➡	Set *E* Stack cards with **centimeter** and **kilogram** characteristics here.	Set *F* Stack cards with **centimeter** and **gram** characteristics here.

This page has been intentionally left blank for ease of use of surrounding labsheets.

Name _____   Date _____

Directions (Use with Question 8 on page 203.) Cut out the ruler along the edge of this page. Then use it to answer the following questions.

Adult Wolf Track
(Actual Size)

One centimeter (1 cm) is the same length as 10 millimeters (10 mm). The ruler is 25 cm in length.

1. 5 cm is the same length as _____ mm.

2. 80 mm is the same length as _____ cm.

3. What is the ruler's length in millimeters? _____ mm

Use the ruler to answer the following questions.

4. What are the length and width of the wolf track in centimeters (cm)? Length: _____   Width: _____

5. What are the length and width of the wolf track in millimeters (mm)? Length: _____   Width: _____

6. What are the length and width of the toe pad labeled A in millimeters? Length: _____   Width: _____

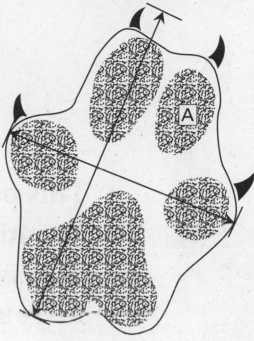

7. What is the body length of the Dwarf Shrew?
    _____ cm _____ mm

8. What is the shoulder height of the Dwarf Shrew?
    _____ cm _____ mm

Life-Size Drawing of a Dwarf Shrew

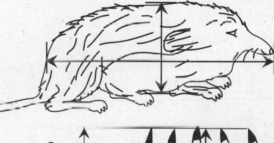

9. Use the dimensions shown to sketch a **life-size** copy of the grizzly bear track. Will the sketch fit on the back of this page?

10. Work in a group of four students.

    a. Tape your four 25-centimeter rulers end-to-end to form a one-meter ruler. Renumber the meter ruler in centimeters.

    b. How many centimeters are in a meter?

    c. How many millimeters are in a meter?

    d. What is the distance around the actual-size grizzly bear track you sketched in Question 9? (**Hint:** Find this distance by placing your meter ruler on edge and encircling the grizzly track.)

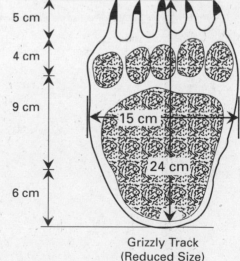

5 cm

4 cm

9 cm

15 cm

24 cm

6 cm

Grizzly Track
(Reduced Size)

This page has been
intentionally left blank
for ease of use of
surrounding labsheets.

MODULE 4 | **LABSHEET 1E**

Special Multipliers Multiplication Table
(Use with Question 22 on page 207.)

Directions Use your calculator to fill in the missing products in the table. Then use your table to answer the questions about multiplying decimals by the special multipliers 0.001, 0.01, 0.1, 1, 10, 100, and 1000.

•	0.001	0.01	0.1	1	10	100	1000
3		0.03			30		3000
0.6				0.6	6		600
4.9	0.0049		0.49			490	
0.002		0.00002					

a. What happens to a number when you multiply it by 1? by a special multiplier greater than 1? by a special multiplier less than 1?

b. Complete each statement below to describe what happens to the decimal point of a number when you multiply by each of the special multipliers.

- **1000**   When I multiply by 1000, the decimal point moves ___?___.

- **100**   When I multiply by 100, the decimal point moves ___?___.

- **10**   When I multiply by 10, the decimal point moves ___?___.

- **1**   When I multiply by 1, the decimal point ___?___.

- **0.1**   When I multiply by 0.1, the decimal point moves ___?___.

- **0.01**   When I multiply by 0.01, the decimal point moves ___?___.

- **0.001**   When I multiply by 0.001, the decimal point moves ___?___.

MODULE 4   LABSHEET **1F**

Metric Conversions (Use with Question 23 on page 207.)

Directions Use the table of prefix meanings to fill in the missing information
for the metric conversions.

Prefix	**kilo**	hecto	deka	**meter/gram**	deci	**centi**	**milli**
Meaning	1000	100	10	1	0.1 or $\frac{1}{10}$	0.01 or $\frac{1}{100}$	0.001 or $\frac{1}{1000}$

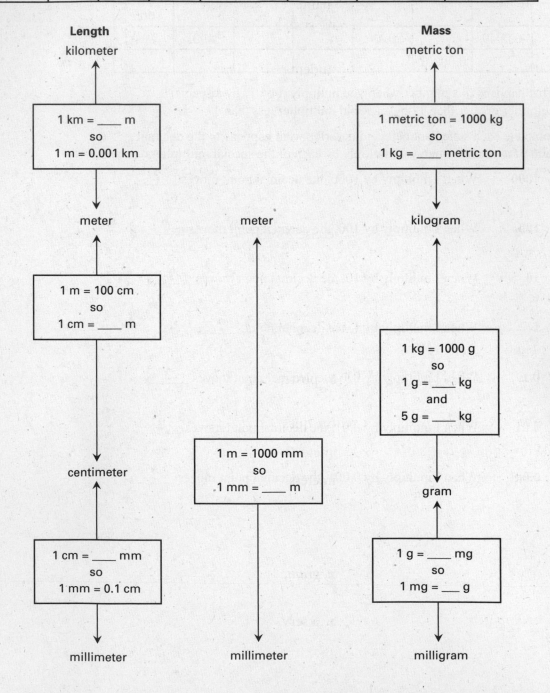

Length

kilometer

1 km = _____ m
so
1 m = 0.001 km

meter

1 m = 100 cm
so
1 cm = _____ m

centimeter

1 cm = _____ mm
so
1 mm = 0.1 cm

millimeter

meter

1 m = 1000 mm
so
1 mm = _____ m

millimeter

Mass

metric ton

1 metric ton = 1000 kg
so
1 kg = _____ metric ton

kilogram

1 kg = 1000 g
so
1 g = _____ kg
and
5 g = _____ kg

gram

1 g = _____ mg
so
1 mg = ___ g

milligram

Practice and Applications
For use with Section 1

For use with Exploration 1

1. Use the sorting grid to answer.

    a. How many girls' names are there? What are they?

    b. How many boys' names are there? What are they?

    c. What does the placement of the name "Spot" in the grid indicate? Who might have such a name?

	Names Used by Girls ⬇	Names Not Used by Girls ⬇
Names Used by Boys ➡	Dana, Taylor, Leslie	Frank, Herb, Ralph, Bob
Names Not Used by Boys ➡	Mary, Susan, Jane	Spot

2. Make a sorting grid showing what students have the kinds of pets indicated below.

Dogs	Cats	Both
Andrea	David	Harry
Jason	Helen	Jean
Kelly		
Stephanie		

3. Are any of the sets in the grid in Exercise 2 empty? If so, what does this mean?

For use with Exploration 2

4. Decide which metric unit (*millimeter*, *centimeter*, or *meter*) to use for the length of each object.

    a. bus   **b.** poster   **c.** paper clip

5. Use the drawing at right to answer the questions.

    a. How long is the goldfish in millimeters?

    b. How long is the goldfish in centimeters?

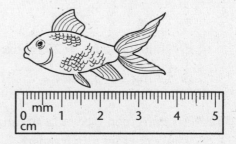

6. Decide which metric unit (*milligram*, *gram*, *kilogram*, or *metric ton*) to use for the mass of each object.

    a. an apple   **b.** a serving of salt   **c.** a bus

(continued)

Name _____ Date _____

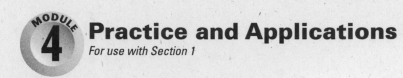

Practice and Applications
For use with Section 1

For use with Exploration 3

7. a. Name a bird whose mass could be measured in kilograms.

  b. Name a bird whose length is measured in millimeters.

8. Replace each ___?___ with the number that makes the statement true.

  a. 2 g = ___?___ mg   **b.** 2 m = ___?___ km

    10 g = ___?___ mg   58 m ___?___ km

  c. 2 metric tons = ___?___ kg

    6.2 metric tons = ___?___ kg

9. Find each product.

  a. 8 • 0.01   **b.** 7.3 • 0.01   **c.** 0.9 • 0.001

  d. 0.003 • 10   **e.** 0.29 • 100   **f.** 0.01 • 0.1

  g. 4.7 • 0.001   **h.** 0.093 • 10   **i.** 0.005 • 0.1

10. Replace each ___?___ with the number that makes the statement true.

  a. 4 km = ___?___ m   **b.** 7.1 m = ___?___ cm   **c.** 325 m = ___?___ km

  d. 6310 mm = ___?___ m **e.** 0.4 m = ___?___ mm   **f.** 52 cm = ___?___ mm

11. Replace each ___?___ with <, >, or =.

  a. 720 g ___?___ 7.2 kg   **b.** 6000 mg ___?___ 6 g

  c. 2000 kg ___?___ 0.25 metric tons   **d.** 4.9 kg ___?___ 4500 g

  e. 38 mg ___?___ 3.8 g   **f.** 9 metric tons ___?___ 900 kg

12. An evergreen tree is 12 m tall. A Bonsai tree is 18 cm tall. Which tree is taller? How much taller?

Study Guide
For use with Section 1

The Mammals of Yellowstone Sets and Metric Measurement

GOAL **LEARN HOW TO:** • sort data using a rectangular diagram
• estimate length and mass in metric units
• convert between metric units

AS YOU: • explore the characteristics of Yellowstone Park mammals
• measure everyday objects
• relate metric prefixes to place values

Exploration 1: Sorting Data

Empty Set

A set is a collection of objects. A set with no objects in it is called the **empty set**. You can use a rectangular diagram as a sorting grid to show how sets are related.

This sorting grid shows that of the 12 months of the year, there are 4 months whose names end in y and 3 months whose names begin with J. Two of the months have names that end in y and begin with J. No months begin with J and end with R.

	Months ending in Y ⬇	Months ending in R ⬇	Months ending in other letters ⬇
Months beginning with J ➡	January, July		June
Months beginning with other letters ➡	February, May	September, October, November, December	March, April, August

Exploration 2 : Metric Length and Mass

Metric Length

The *metric system* of measurement is a decimal system.

Metric units of length are based on the **meter (m)**. The names of the other units of length have been chosen to show how these units are related to a meter.

Name of unit	Prefix	Meaning	Relationship to a meter
millimeter (mm)	milli-	thousandth	1 mm = 0.001 m
centimeter (cm)	centi-	hundredth	1 cm = 0.01 m
kilometer (km)	kilo-	thousand	1 km = 1000 m

A **benchmark** is a comparison with a familiar measure. Benchmarks for the metric units of length are: 1 m is about the length of a baseball bat, 1 cm is about the width of a key on a telephone push pad, and 1 mm is about the thickness of a quarter.

Name _____   Date _____

Study Guide
For use with Section 1

Metric Mass

Metric units of mass are based on the **gram (g)**.
A benchmark for one gram is the mass of a
paper clip.

The table shows the commonly used units
of mass.

Name of unit	Relationship to a gram
milligram (mg)	1 mg = 0.001 g
kilogram (kg)	1 kg = 1000 g
metric ton	1 metric ton = 1,000,000 g

Exploration 3: Converting Metric Units

The prefixes used in the metric system are like place values. They show
how the other units of measure in the system are related to the basic unit.

Prefix	kilo-	hecto-	deka-	basic unit	deci-	centi-	milli-
Meaning	1000	100	10	1	0.1	0.01	0.001

To convert metric units, it is helpful to know how to multiply by special multipliers.

- To multiply by 10, 100, or 1000, move the decimal point to the right as many places as there are zeros in the multiplier.

$562.34 \times 100 = 562.34. = 56,234$

Move the decimal point 2 places to the right.

If there are not enough places to move the decimal point, add extra zeros to the right of the number in order to complete the movement.

34.72×1000
$= 34.720.$ ← Insert an extra 0 to the right in order to move the decimal point 3 places to the right.
$= 34,720$

- To multiply by 0.001, 0.01, or 0.1, move the decimal point to the left as many places as there are decimal places in the multiplier. If needed, insert zeros to the left of the original number.

16.79×0.001
$= .016.79$ ← Insert an extra 0 to the left, in order to move the decimal point 3 places to the left.
$= 0.01679$

Example

The main span of the Brooklyn Bridge is about 486 m. The main span of the old
London Bridge is about 2620 cm. Which bridge has the longer span?

Sample Response

To make a comparision, both lengths should be expressed in terms of the same unit.

Brooklyn Bridge: 486 m = 48,600 cm   London Bridge: 2620 cm

So the main span of the Brooklyn Bridge is longer than that of the London Bridge.

Study Guide: Practice & Application Exercises

For use with Section 1

Exploration 1

For Exercises 1 and 2, use the sorting grid at the right, which shows the number of freshmen who are taking a Spanish or a French class at a certain school.

Freshmen

	Taking Spanish ⬇	Not Taking Spanish ⬇
Taking French ➡	50	100
Not Taking French ➡	175	275

1. How many of the freshmen in the data group are taking

   a. a Spanish class but not a French class?

   b. a French class but not a Spanish class?

   c. both Spanish and French?

   d. neither Spanish nor French?

2. How many freshmen are in the data group?

Exploration 2

Decide which metric unit (*millimeter, centimeter, meter*, or *kilometer*) to use for the length of each item.

3. a length of carpeting

4. the distance covered on an auto trip

5. the thickness of a nickel

6. the length of a page in your textbook

Decide which metric unit (*milligram, gram, kilogram*, or *metric ton*) to use for the mass of each item.

7. yourself   8. a truck   9. a feather   10. a serving of cereal

Exploration 3

Find each product.

11. $456.13 \cdot 1000$ 12. $76.4 \cdot 0.1$ 13. $9.245 \cdot 0.001$

Replace each __?__ with the number that makes the statement true.

14. $3 \text{ g} = \underline{} \text{ mg}$

    $50 \text{ g} = \underline{} \text{ mg}$

15. $7 \text{ metric tons} = \underline{} \text{ kg}$

    $3.8 \text{ metric tons} = \underline{} \text{ kg}$

16. $5 \text{ m} = \underline{} \text{ km}$

    $46 \text{ m} = \underline{} \text{ km}$

17. $2132 \text{ mm} = \underline{} \text{ m}$

    $95 \text{ mm} = \underline{} \text{ m}$

Practice and Applications

For use with Section 2

For use with Exploration 1

Use the line plot for Exercises 1–4.

Time Students Spend Exercising in Mr. Tino's Class

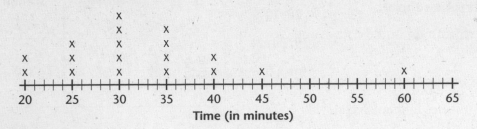

Time (in minutes)

1. What is the range of time students spend exercising in Mr. Tino's class?

2. How many students exercise more than 30 minutes?

3. How many students exercise at least 25 minutes?

4. What can you conclude about the amount of time students spend exercising in Mr. Tino's class?

5. The students in Ms. Samuel's class recorded their heights. The heights, in inches, are: 43, 47, 45, 43, 44, 46, 50, 43, 40, 45, 43, 41, 44, 45, 46.

   a. Find the range of the heights.

   b. Make a line plot for the data.

   c. Is there a height on your line plot that has more X's than any other? If so, which height?

   d. Is there a height on your line plot that has the same number of X's to the right of it as there are to the left of it? Explain.

   e. What do you notice about how the data are distributed in the line plot?

   f. Identify any clusters and gaps in the data.

(continued)

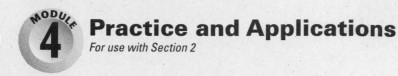

Practice and Applications

For use with Section 2

For use with Exploration 2

6. Find the mean, the median, and the mode(s) of each data set.

   a. length of 9 hummingbirds (in.): 4, 2, 5, 2, 3, 3, 4, 2, 2

   b. number of eggs of 8 turtles: 14, 16, 23, 8, 28, 12, 11, 16

   c. wingspan of 7 birds (in.): 34, 11, 16, 22, 19, 34, 25

   d. number of birds using a feeder each day for a 5-day period:
      8, 15, 12, 17, 23

7. Calvin was the high scorer in 6 basketball games this season. He
scored 22, 28, 18, 30, 22, and 24 points in the games. What are the
mean, the median, and the mode of Calvin's scores?

For use with Exploration 3

8. Emily recorded the amount of snowfall in her backyard for a week
for a winter science project. The snowfall amounts for the week, in
inches, were: 9, 3, 0, 4, 18, 1, and 0. Should Emily use the mean, the
mode, or the median as the average to report the average amount of
snowfall for the week in her report? Why?

9. Use a calculator to write each fraction as a decimal rounded to the
nearest hundredth.

   a. $\frac{3}{8}$ **b.** $\frac{3}{5}$ **c.** $\frac{7}{9}$

   d. $\frac{5}{3}$ **e.** $\frac{7}{6}$ **f.** $\frac{2}{7}$

   g. $\frac{5}{12}$ **h.** $\frac{9}{5}$ **i.** $\frac{8}{13}$

10. Round each decimal to the given place.

   a. 0.4829 (tenths)   **b.** 0.1564 (thousandths)

   c. 2.798 (hundredths)   **d.** 3.819 (tenths)

   e. 11.901 (ones)   **f.** 2.7005 (thousandths)

   g. 24.455 (tenths)   **h.** 59.45 (ones)

Name _____   Date _____

 **Study Guide**
For use with Section 2

Animal Averages   Line Plots and Averages

GOAL **LEARN HOW TO:** • draw and interpret line plots
              • use averages to describe data
              • write a fraction as a decimal using a calculator
              • choose appropriate averages
              • round decimal quotients

   AS YOU: • find averages for different data sets

Exploration 1: Line Plots

A **line plot** or **dot plot** displays data using a line marked with a scale. The scale must include the greatest and least values of the data. The line plot shown below models some data about ages of selected animals.

Maximum Recorded Ages of Selected Animals

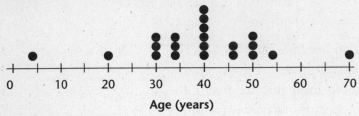

Age (years)

Range

The **range** of a set of numerical data is the difference between the greatest and least values. In a line plot, it is easy to identify the greatest and least data values.

Example
For the set of numbers 54, 32, 198, 107, and 136,   Range = greatest value – least value = 198 – 32 = 166.

Clusters and Gaps

A **cluster** in data is a place where the data items are bunched closely together. A **gap** in data is a large space where there are no data items. In the line plot above, there is a cluster from 30 to 54. There are gaps in the data between 4 and 20, between 20 and 30, and between 54 and 70.

Study Guide
For use with Section 2

Exploration 2: Finding Averages

Averages

One method of summarizing data is to calculate an **average** for the set of values. An average is a number used to describe a typical item in a data set. The *mean*, *median*, and *mode* are types of averages.

Mean: To find the mean, add all the values together and divide the sum by the number of values.

Data set: 30, 41, 32, 46, 37

$$\text{mean} = \frac{30 + 41 + 32 + 46 + 37}{5} = \frac{186}{5} = 37.2$$

Median: To find the median, arrange the values in order and find the middle value. If there are two middle values, the median is the mean of these two values.

Data set: 3, 4, 1, 1, 4, 6
In order, the data is 1, 1, 3, 4, 4, 6.
There are two middle numbers, 3 and 4.

$$\text{median} = \frac{3 + 4}{2} = \frac{7}{2} = 3.5$$

Mode: The mode is the value that occurs most often in a data set. There can be no mode or more than one mode for a data set.

Data set: 4, 3, 1, 1, 3, 1, 3, 4, 5, 6, 9
There are two modes, 1 and 3.

Depending on the situation and the data, one of these three averages may be more representative of the data than the others.

Exploration 3: Appropriate Averages

Writing a Fraction as a Decimal

You can use division to write a fraction as a decimal. For example, to write $\frac{3}{7}$ as a decimal, divide 3 by 7 by using a calculator. [3] [÷] [7] [=] [0.4285714]

Rounding Decimals

You round decimals in the same way that whole numbers are rounded. If the digit one place to the right of where you are rounding is 5 or greater, round up. Otherwise, leave the digit unchanged. For example, the result of rounding the decimal 2.483 to the nearest tenth is 2.5.

Name _____ Date _____

Study Guide: Practice & Application Exercises
For use with Section 2

Exploration 1

1. Terry recorded how long she spent exercising every day for two weeks. The times, in minutes, are: 40, 35, 40, 45, 45, 0, 60, 15, 40, 35, 40, 45, 50, 0.

   a. Make a line plot for the data. **b.** Find the range of the data.

   c. Identify any clusters or gaps in the data.

Exploration 2

Find the mean, the median, and the mode(s) of each data set.

2. masses of 5 marsupial mice (in grams): 8, 5, 7, 6, 4

3. litter sizes of 6 naked mole rats: 25, 12, 12, 12, 10, 13

4. lengths of 10 elephant tusks (in feet): 11, 10, 8, 10, 5, 8, 8, 10, 4, 9

For Exercises 5–7, tell whether the *mean*, *median*, or *mode* is being used.

5. Half of the houses sold were priced at $180,000 or less.

6. The average number of children in the households studied was 2.7.

7. The most popular women's shoe size is 7.

8. **Writing** Juan Ruiz owns a large citrus farm from which he has a monthly income of $8000. During the orange-picking season, Mr. Ruiz paid the four Mendez brothers $600, $700, $600, and $800 for part-time work during one month. Which type of average would you use as a fair representation of these 5 monthly incomes? Explain.

9. **Challenge** On her 5 math tests so far this grading period, Leah has earned grades of 94%, 86%, 92%, 80%, and 78%. The last math test for this grading period was this morning and Leah's mean grade on all 6 tests is 85%. What grade did Leah earn on the test this morning? What strategies did you use to obtain your answer?

Exploration 3

Calculator Write each fraction as a decimal rounded to the nearest hundredth.

10. $\frac{2}{9}$ 11. $\frac{9}{4}$ 12. $\frac{11}{8}$ 13. $\frac{8}{12}$

Round each decimal to the given place.

14. 9.3478 (tenths)   15. 0.3857 (hundredths)   16. 154.2395 (thousandths)

Name _____ Date _____

Mean Mass of Four Pikas (Use with Question 4 on page 232.)

Directions Follow the steps below to find $0.60 \div 4$.

a. The whole grid represents one unit. Each small square is what decimal part of the grid?

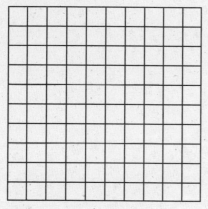

b. Shade 0.60 of the grid.

c. Divide the shaded portion into 4 equal-sized groups.

d. $0.60 \div 4 =$ _____

e. What is the mean mass of the four pikas? _____

....

Mean Body Length of Six Martens (Use with Question 5 on page 232.)

Directions Follow the steps below to find $2.40 \div 6$.

a. Shade 2.40 of the grids. (Shade 2 grids plus 0.40 of another grid.)

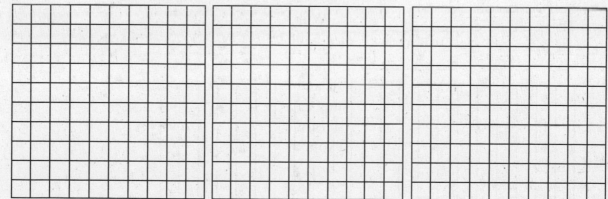

b. Divide the shaded area into 6 equal-sized groups.

c. Each group in part (b) is what part of a whole grid? _____
Write your answer as a decimal.

d. $2.40 \div 6 =$ _____

e. What is the mean body length of the six martens? _____

Math Thematics, Book 1

MODULE 4   LABSHEET **3B**

Decimal Division Grids (Use with Question 6 on page 232.)

Directions Use the grids below to find each quotient.

a. $0.06 \div 3 =$ _____

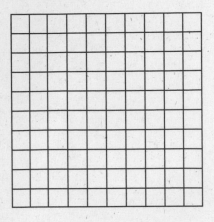

b. $0.36 \div 9 =$ _____

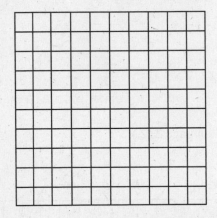

c. $2\overline{)1.30} =$ _____ $2\overline{)1.30}$ means $1.30 \div 2$.

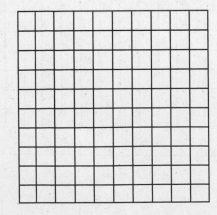 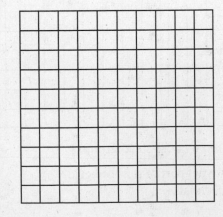

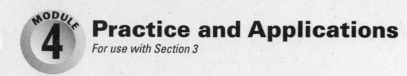

Practice and Applications

For use with Section 3

For use with Exploration 1

1. Use compatible numbers to check the position of the decimal point on each quotient. If a quotient is incorrect, give the correct quotient.

a. $8\overline{)32.48}$ (40.6)

b. $4\overline{)49.4}$ (1.235)

c. $20\overline{)84}$ (4.2)

2. Find each quotient. Use estimation to check that each quotient seems reasonable.

a. $11.32 \div 4$

b. $5\overline{)15.75}$

c. $6\overline{)31.35}$

d. $\dfrac{58}{8}$

e. $19.8 \div 8$

f. $12.6 \div 12$

g. $4\overline{)12.94}$

h. $6\overline{)30.15}$

i. $7\overline{)29.33}$

j. $17.1 \div 5$

k. $11.8 \div 4$

l. $18.63 \div 2$

3. Tell whether the quotient is correct in each division. If a quotient is not correct, give the correct quotient.

a. $4\overline{)145.8}$ (36.45)

b. $3\overline{)70.35}$ (20.345)

c. $3\overline{)15.9}$ (26.5)

4. Kristin needs a 13.68 m long piece of lace to use as trim around the edge of a square tablecloth. How long is each side of the tablecloth?

5. Andrew has 3 days to drive to 367.8 miles to Jackson. If he wants to drive the same distance each day, how many miles a day should he drive?

(continued)

Name _____ Date _____

Practice and Applications
For use with Section 3

For use with Exploration 2

a. Write an equation that the model represents.

b. Solve the equation that you wrote in part (a).

6. ⬚ + ⬚⬚⬚ = ⬚⬚⬚⬚⬚⬚
       ⬚⬚⬚   ⬚⬚⬚⬚⬚⬚⬚⬚

7. ⬚ + ⬚⬚⬚⬚ = ⬚⬚⬚⬚⬚⬚⬚⬚⬚⬚⬚

Write an addition equation to model each situation. Use one variable and tell what it represents.

8. Jane received 2 necklaces for her birthday. Now she has 5 necklaces.

9. Lance scored 3 points, giving his team a total score of 42 points.

Write a subtraction equation to model each situation. Use one variable and tell what it represents.

10. Kim gave away 6 books. She has 20 left.

11. Dan bought a shirt for $18.99 and received $1.01 in change.

For use with Exploration 3

Solve each equation. Check each solution.

12. $t - 3 = 18$ 13. $24 = k - 6$ 14. $n - 2.1 = 4.3$

15. $49 = 21 + b$ 16. $2.8 + m = 9.7$ 17. $6.5 + a = 12.3$

18. $0.75 + x = 3.6$ 19. $b - 35 = 15$ 20. $2.3 = n + 1$

21. $5 + w = 185$ 22. $y - 7.9 = 1.3$ 23. $10 = p + 6.4$

Tell whether you would use mental math or paper and pencil to solve each equation. Then solve.

24. $20.5 + a = 58.9$ 25. $t - 8.1 = 2$ 26. $25 = 9 + s$

27. $c + 71 = 560$ 28. $b - 10 = 3$ 29. $11.8 + z = 41.3$

30. $y - 315 = 10$ 31. $m - 6.4 = 5.7$ 32. $90 = 10 + n$

33. $d + 59 = 111$ 34. $q - 1 = 14$ 35. $r - 198 = 2$

Math Thematics, Book 1
Student Workbook

148

Name _____ Date _____

Study Guide
For use with Section 3

Little Critters   Dividing Decimals and Solving Equations

GOAL **LEARN HOW TO:** • divide a decimal by a whole number
• write addition and subtraction equations
• solve addition equations using models
• use inverse operations to solve addition and subtraction equations

AS YOU: • work with 10 × 10 grids
• examine the diets of zoo animals

Exploration 1: Dividing Decimals

Using a Grid to Divide

You can use a 10 × 10 grid to model division.

Example
Find 1.80 ÷ 3.

■ Sample Response ■

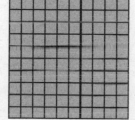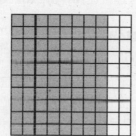

1. Shade 1.80 of the grids. Shade 1 grid plus 0.80 of another grid.

2. Divide the shaded area into 3 equal-sized groups.

3. So, 1.80 ÷ 3 = 0.60.

Divide a Decimal by a Whole Number

Divide as though both numbers, the dividend as well as the divisor, were whole numbers.

Write the decimal point in the quotient directly above the decimal point in the dividend.

$$
\begin{array}{r}
8.95 \\
4\overline{)35.80} \\
\underline{32} \\
3\,8 \\
\underline{3\,6} \\
20 \\
\underline{20} \\
0
\end{array}
$$

Write zeros to the right end of the dividend as needed to continue the division.

Study Guide
For use with Section 3

Estimating a Quotient

To check whether a quotient seems reasonable, use compatible numbers.

Example

The total mass of 10 apples is 19.3 kg. Could the mean of the masses of the apples be 0.25 kg? Why or why not?

Sample Response

Estimate $19.3 \div 10$ to check whether 0.25 is a reasonable answer.

$19.3 \div 10$ is slightly less than $20 \div 10$.

$20 \div 10 = 2$, so the answer of 0.25 is *not* reasonable.

Exploration 2: Writing and Modeling Equations

Modeling Equations

A value of a variable that makes an equation true is a **solution of the equation.** The process of finding solutions is called **solving an equation.**

Balance models can help you visualize an equation and remember that both sides represent the same amount. *Algebra tile models* can help you solve (find a solution of) an equation.

Example

Model this situation: Mrs. Cooper's art class has 12 students, including 7 female students. How many male students are in the class?

verbal statement:	male students	plus	female students	equals	total students
equation:	m	$+$	7	$=$	12

balance model:

m male students
+
7 female students   =   12 students

algebra tile model:

solution: There are 5 male students in Mrs. Cooper's art class.

Name _____ Date _____

Study Guide
For use with Section 3

Exploration 3: Using Inverse Operations

Using Inverse Operations to Solve

Addition and subtraction are **inverse operations.** They "undo" each other.

When you use symbols and variables to solve an equation, you are solving the equation *algebraically.* To solve an equation, remember these ideas:

- The goal is to get the variable alone on one side of the equation.
- Use inverse operations to "undo" one another.
- Any operation done on one side of an equation must also be done on the other side to keep the equation balanced.
- Check that your solution is correct by substituting the value for the variable into the equation.
- If necessary, use tiles to model the equation.

Subtraction "undoes" addition when you solve an equation.

Example

Solve $x + 7.2 = 9.3$.

Sample Response

$$x + 7.2 = 9.3$$
$$\underline{-7.2 = -7.2} \quad \leftarrow \text{Subtract 7.2 from both sides.}$$
$$x + 0 = 2.1$$
$$x = 2.1$$

Check:

$$x + 7.2 = 9.3 \quad \leftarrow \text{Substitute 2.1 for } x.$$
$$2.1 + 7.2 \stackrel{?}{=} 9.3$$
$$9.3 = 9.3 ✔$$

Addition "undoes" subtraction when you solve an equation.

Example

Solve $x - 7.2 = 9.3$.

Sample Response

$$x - 7.2 = 9.3$$
$$\underline{+ 7.2 = + 7.2} \quad \leftarrow \text{Add 7.2 to both sides.}$$
$$x + 0 = 16.5$$
$$x = 16.5$$

Check:

$$x - 7.2 = 9.3 \quad \leftarrow \text{Substitute 16.5 for } x.$$
$$16.5 - 7.2 \stackrel{?}{=} 9.3$$
$$9.3 = 9.3 ✔$$

Study Guide: Practice & Application Exercises

For use with Section 3

Exploration 1

For Exercises 1–3, find each quotient. Use estimation to check that each quotient seems reasonable.

1. $5\overline{)7.25}$

2. $24\overline{)21.48}$

3. $2.87 \div 14$

4. Eight cans of Pal Dog Food are stacked one upon the other. If the height of the stack is 99.2 cm, find the height of one can.

5. If 5 oranges cost \$2.25, what is the cost of 7 oranges? Explain.

Exploration 2

6. Write the equation represented by the model below.

$$\boxed{+} + \begin{array}{ccc} \boxed{+} & \boxed{+} & \boxed{+} \\ \boxed{+} & \boxed{+} & \boxed{+} & \boxed{+} \end{array} = \begin{array}{cccc} \boxed{+} & \boxed{+} & \boxed{+} & \boxed{+} \\ \boxed{+} & \boxed{+} & \boxed{+} & \boxed{+} & \boxed{+} \end{array}$$

7. Open-ended Describe a situation that can be modeled by the equation $y - 2 = 9$. Be sure to tell what the variable represents.

8. Make an algebra tile model that represents $x + 3 = 7$. Then use the model to help you find the solution.

9. Write an addition equation to model this situation: The book club gets 6 new members, raising the membership to 17. Use one variable and tell what it represents.

10. Write a subtraction equation to model this situation: Spending \$11, Phil had \$4 left. Use one variable and tell what it represents.

Exploration 3

For Exercises 11–19, solve each equation. Check each solution.

11. $b - 2.6 = 7.5$

12. $11 = 6 + y$

13. $0.56 + c = 3.1$

14. $42 = t - 8$

15. $a + 18 = 35$

16. $p + 0.03 = 7$

17. $z - 1.6 = 5.6$

18. $4.59 = w - 12.2$

19. $q - 14 = 16$

20. Is 9.25 a solution of the equation $1.75 + m = 10$? Explain.

Name _____ Date _____

Weights of Plant-Eating Dinosaurs
(Use with Questions 5 and 6 on page 250.)

Directions Complete parts (a)–(d) to make a
stem-and-leaf plot for the weights of the plant-eating
dinosaurs in the table.

a. Find the least and the greatest data items in the
table to help you choose the stem numbers. List
each stem in a column from least to greatest on
the blank stem-and-leaf plot below.

b. In the table, place a checkmark next to the data that
have a stem of 3. Use your list to write the leaves
for the stem 3 in order from least to greatest in
the stem-and-leaf plot below. Do this for each
stem using a different mark or color.

c. Fill in the key so that it tells the value represented
by a stem and leaf.

d. Write a title for the stem-and-leaf plot so that anyone
can tell what it is about.

Some Plant-Eating Dinosaurs	
Dinosaur	**Weight (tons)**
Anatosaurus	3.5
Ankylosaurus	5.0
Centrosaurus	2.6
Chasmosaurus	2.2
Corythosaurus	3.7
Edmontonia	3.9
Edmontosaurus	3.9
Euoplocephalus	3.0
Hadrosaurus	3.0
Pachyrhinosaurus	4.0
Panoplosaurus	4.0
Parasaurolophus	3.5
Parksosaurus	0.1
Sauropelta	2.7
Styracosaurus	2.7
Tenontosaurus	2.0
Torosaurus	5.0
Triceratops	5.3

List the stems here.

Title: _____

List the leaves to the
right of each stem.   Key: ☐|☐ means _____

MODULE 4   LABSHEET **4B**

Animal Division Grid (Use with Question 9 on page 251.)

Directions Complete parts (a)–(e) to divide 0.4 by 0.05.

A 6-kilogram *Microvenator* needed to eat about 0.4 kg of meat a day. Suppose the animals it hunted had a mass of about 0.05 kg each. To find how many animals a *Microvenator* needed to catch each day, you need to divide 0.4 by 0.05.

You can use a 10 × 10 grid to model the division. Let the grid represent one unit.

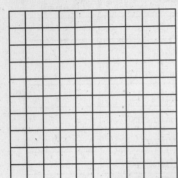

a. Shade 0.4 of the grid.

b. Divide the shaded area into equal-sized groups with 0.05 in each group.

c. How many equal-sized groups are there?

d. 0.4 ÷ 0.05 = _____

e. How many animals did a *Microvenator* need to catch each day?

· ·

Division Grids (Use with Question 10 on page 251.)

Directions Use each grid to find the quotient.

$$0.9 \div 0.45$$

a. 0.60 ÷ 0.15 = _____   b. 0.28 ÷ 0.04 = _____   c. 0.45$\overline{)0.9}$ = _____

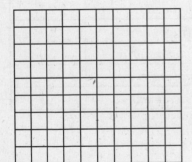   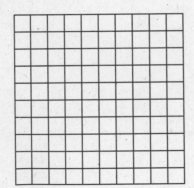   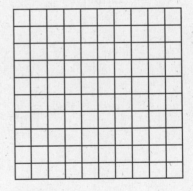

MODULE 4   LABSHEET **4C**

Guess My Rule (Use with Question 18 on page 254.)

Directions Cut out the rule cards, shuffle the cards, and place them in a pile face down. Follow the game rules in your book to play *Guess My Rule*.

Multiply the input by 7. $O = 7I$	Add 5 to the input. $O = I + 5$
Multiply the input by 3 and add 5. $O = 3I + 5$	Multiply the input by 8 and subtract 2. $O = 8I - 2$
Divide the input by 2. $O = I \div 2$	Multiply the input by 11. $O = 11I$
Multiply the input by 3 and divide by 2. $O = 3I \div 2$	Multiply the input by itself. $O = I \cdot I$ or $O = I^2$

This page has been
intentionally left blank
for ease of use of
surrounding labsheets.

MODULE 4   **LABSHEET** 4D

Rule Table (Use with Question 20 on page 255.)

Directions For each input value, apply the rule to find the output value. Then write each input and its output as an ordered pair.

Rule: Multiply the input by 2 and add 1.

Rule Table

Input	Applying the Rule	Output	Ordered Pair
3	$3 \cdot 2 + 1$	7	(3, 7)
4			
0			
2			
1			

Coordinate Grid
(Use with Question 22 on page 255.)

Directions Write the ordered pair for each point *A–D*.

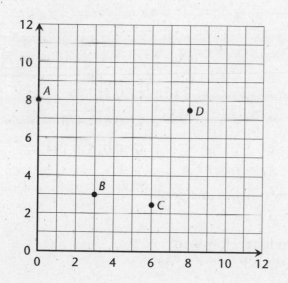

Empty Coordinate Grid
(Use with Questions 23–25 on page 255.)

Directions Follow the directions in your book to plot points.

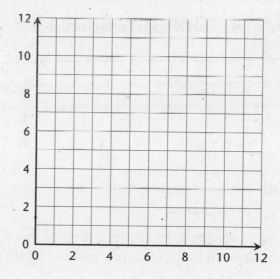

Name _____ Date _____

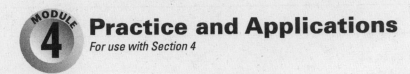

Practice and Applications
For use with Section 4

For use with Exploration 1

For Exercises 1–6, use the stem-and-leaf plot showing the spelling test scores for one class.

Spelling Test Scores

```
 6 | 8
 7 | 5 9
 8 | 0 0 2 6 7
 9 | 0 1 1 1 4 4 5 7
10 | 0
```

8 | 2 represents a score of 82

1. What was the low score in the class? the high score?

2. How many students scored in the 80s?

3. How many students took the spelling test?

4. How many students scored 94?

5. How many students scored 85?

6. Find the mean, the median, and the mode of the scores.

For use with Exploration 2

7. Find each quotient. Show your work.

   a. $0.08\overline{)5.6}$

   b. $3\overline{)0.09}$

   c. $0.4\overline{)0.96}$

   d. $0.3\overline{)0.2142}$

   e. $3.2\overline{)52}$

   f. $0.6\overline{)2.475}$

   g. $0.5\overline{)3.45}$

   h. $5.14\overline{)19.018}$

   i. $0.015\overline{)0.114}$

8. Melissa bought 4.25 lb of peanuts for $2.89. How much is one pound of the peanuts?

9. A carpenter has a piece of wood that is 210.7 cm long. How many 8.6 cm long pieces of wood can be cut from the wood?

(continued)

Name _____ Date _____

Practice and Applications

For use with Section 4

For use with Exploration 3

10. Apply the rule "multiply by 2 and then add 5" to each input. Write each input and output as an ordered pair.

a. 1 **b.** 3 **c.** 5

d. 9 **e.** 11 **f.** 20

11. Name the point that is the graph of each ordered pair.

a. $(3, 2)$ **b.** $\left(7, 4\frac{1}{2}\right)$ **c.** $(4, 6)$

d. $(0, 3)$ **e.** $\left(9, 1\frac{1}{2}\right)$ **f.** $(2, 5)$

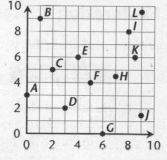

12. Write the coordinates of each point.

a. B **b.** I **c.** F

d. G **e.** K **f.** L

13. Copy the coordinate grid on graph paper. Graph each ordered pair on your coordinate grid. Label each point.

a. $(2, 5)$ **b.** $(0, 0)$ **c.** $(0, 2)$

d. $(4, 0)$ **e.** $\left(3\frac{1}{2}, 1\right)$ **f.** $(2, 1)$

g. $\left(2\frac{1}{2}, 4\right)$ **h.** $(3, 3)$ **i.** $(4, 3)$

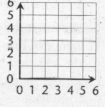

14. Draw a coordinate grid on graph paper.

a. Graph the ordered pairs in the table on your new coordinate grid.

b. Draw segments to connect the points you graphed in order from left to right.

c. Use your graph to predict the missing values.

input $2\frac{1}{2}$, output = ___?___   output 10, input = ___?___

Input	1	3	6	8
Output	4	6	9	11

Study Guide
For use with Section 4

Dinosaurs   Stem-and-Leaf Plots, Decimal Division, and Graphing

GOAL   **LEARN HOW TO:** • make and interpret a stem-and-leaf plot
• divide by a decimal
• graph pairs of values on a coordinate grid

AS YOU: • compare data

Exploration 1: Stem-and-Leaf Plots

A **stem-and-leaf plot** is used to compare data.

Example

The Baltimore Weather Bureau recorded these daily high temperatures, in °F, for the month of November. Make a stem-and-leaf plot of the data.

46	31	33	42	25	29	37	44	45	36
35	40	52	48	35	39	40	42	51	29
45	30	26	52	44	54	46	43	45	42

◀ Sample Response ▶

To make a stem-and-leaf plot for the data:

Note that the temperatures can be arranged into 4 groups: the 20's, the 30's, the 40's, and the 50's. Use the tens digits for the stems. List the stems in order from least to greatest.

```
stems
  2 |
  3 |
  4 |
  5 |
```

Now use the ones digits for the leaves. Read through the data, placing the leaves next to the corresponding stem in the order that the values appear in the data set.

```
leaves
  2 | 5 9 9 6
  3 | 1 3 7 6 5 5 9 0
  4 | 6 2 4 5 0 8 0 2 5 4 6 3 5 2
  5 | 2 1 2 4
```

Then rewrite the display with the leaves in order from least to greatest. Use a vertical line to separate the stems from the leaves.

```
  2 | 5 6 9 9
  3 | 0 1 3 5 5 6 7 9
  4 | 0 0 2 2 2 3 4 4 5 5 5 6 6 8
  5 | 1 2 2 4
```

Finally, write a title above the plot and a key below it.

November Daily High Temperatures in Baltimore

```
  2 | 5 6 9 9
  3 | 0 1 3 5 5 6 7 9
  4 | 0 0 2 2 2 3 4 4 5 5 5 6 6 8
  5 | 1 2 2 4
```

2 | 5 means 25° F

Math Thematics, Book 1
Student Workbook

 **Study Guide**
For use with Section 4

Exploration 2: Dividing by a Decimal

Example

Find the quotient 175.5 ÷ 0.25.

Sample Response

Multiply both numbers by 100 in order to change the divisor, 0.25, to a whole number. One zero must be inserted to the right of the dividend, 175.5, to accomplish this.

$$0.25\overset{\frown}{)}175.\overset{\frown}{5}0$$
$$\times 100 \times 100 \rightarrow 25\overline{)17550.}$$

Now divide as you would for whole numbers. Place the decimal point in the quotient directly above the decimal point in the dividend.

$$
\begin{array}{r}
702. \\
25\overline{)17550.} \\
-175\downarrow\downarrow \\
\hline
050 \\
-50 \\
\hline
0
\end{array}
$$

Exploration 3: Guess My Rule

An **ordered pair** consists of two pieces of data that go together. The order tells which comes first. An ordered pair of numbers, called *coordinates*, is used to indicate the location of a point on a **coordinate grid**. A coordinate grid is formed by a pair of number lines called **axes**.

Example

To graph the ordered pair (6, 3), begin at the **origin**, the point at which the axes meet.

The first number in the ordered pair tells how many units to move across the horizontal axis. In this ordered pair, the first number, 6, indicates a movement 6 units to the right.

The second number in the ordered pair tells how many units to move up the vertical axis. In this ordered pair, the second number, 3, indicates a movement 3 units up.

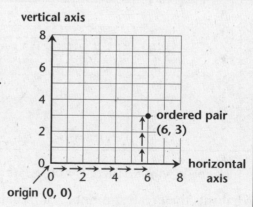

Name _____ Date _____

Study Guide: Practice & Application Exercises

MODULE 4

For use with Section 4

Exploration 1

For Exercises 1–7, use the stem-and-leaf plot.

Age Survey at a Movie Screening

```
2 | 1 3 3 6 8 8 9 9
3 | 2 3 5 7 9
4 | 0 1 4 6 8 9
5 | 1 3 4 7 8 9
```

2 | 1 means 21 years

1. How many people were surveyed?

2. How many people were younger than 25?

3. How many people were older than 45?

Find the following statistical values for the data.

4. the range   5. the mean   6. the median   7. the mode

Botany A researcher recorded the heights (in cm) of one specimen of each of 16 varieties of tulips. The data set is shown at the right.

```
31  42  28  27
35  38  49  19
25  37  43  36
40  41  39  24
```

8. Make a stem-and-leaf plot for the data.

9. Use your stem-and-leaf plot to find how many of the tulips

   a. were shorter than 36 cm.   b. were taller than 31 cm.

10. What percent of the tulips were between 20 cm and 29 cm tall?

Use the stem-and-leaf plot or the bar graph to answer Exercises 11–14. For each question, tell which display you used and why.

Medal Standings: 25th Summer Olympics

```
2  | 0 2 2 7 9 9
3  | 0 1
4  |
5  | 4
6  |
7  |
8  | 2
9  |
10 | 8
11 | 2
```

11 | 2 means 112 medals

11. Which team won 82 medals in the 25th Summer Olympics?

12. What was the greatest number of medals won by any team?

13. Which teams earned the same number of medals?

14. What was the total number of medals won by the 12 teams shown?

(continued)

Study Guide: Practice & Application Exercises
For use with Section 4

Exploration 2

For Exercises 15–18, find each quotient. Show your work.

15. $0.12\overline{)4.824}$ **16.** $1.7\overline{)159.12}$ **17.** $0.08\overline{)24.4}$ **18.** $0.009\overline{)8.127}$

19. The length of the living room in the McArdle house is to be 6.096 m. In the blueprint of the house, the architect has drawn that length as 4.8 cm. How many times the length of the blueprint measure will the actual length of the living room be?

Exploration 3

Apply the rule "divide by 5 and then add 5" to each input. Write each input and output as an ordered pair.

20. 10   **21.** 25   **22.** 5   **23.** 0

Use the diagram shown at the right. Write the coordinates of each point as an ordered pair.

24. M **25.** N

26. O **27.** P

28. Q **29.** R

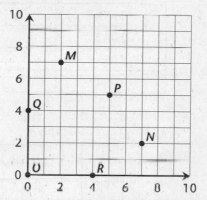

Graph each ordered pair on a coordinate grid. Label each point.

30. $A(7, 4)$ **31.** $B(1, 9)$ **32.** $C(0, 5)$ **33.** $D(6, 0)$

34. Writing Explain how the graph of $(7, 4)$ differs from that of $(4, 7)$.

35. Geometry Connection Draw a coordinate grid.

    a. Graph the ordered pairs $A(0, 5)$, $B(12, 5)$, $C(9, 8)$, and $D(3, 8)$.

    b. Draw segments to form polygon $ABCD$.

    c. Name polygon $ABCD$. Be as specific as possible.

    d. Transform polygon $ABCD$ by sliding it 4 units right and 4 units down. Label the vertices of the new polygon with their coordinates.

MODULE 4   **LABSHEET** **5A**

California Condor Population
(Use with Question 5 on page 265.)

Directions Follow the steps below to make two different line graphs of the condor population during the period 1953–1984.

  a. Plot a point on Graph A for each year and population listed in the table.

  b. Draw segments to connect the points in order.

  c. Plot a point on Graph B for each year and population listed in the table. Then draw segments to connect the points in order.

California Condor Population 1953–1984	
Year	Number of Condors
1953	60
1965	60
1967	60
1979	30
1982	27
1983	25
1984	27

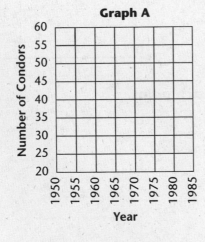

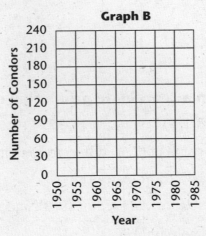

MODULE 4   **LABSHEET** **5B**

California Condor Population
(Use with Question 8(b) on page 266.)

Directions Follow the steps to make a line graph of the condor population during the period 1997–2003.

- Decide what intervals to use and mark the scales.

- Plot a point on the graph for each year and population.

- Draw segments to connect the points in order.

California Condor Population 1997–2003	
Year	Number of Condors
1997	132
1998	147
1999	158
2000	162
2001	182
2002	198
2003	223

California Condor Population 1997–2003

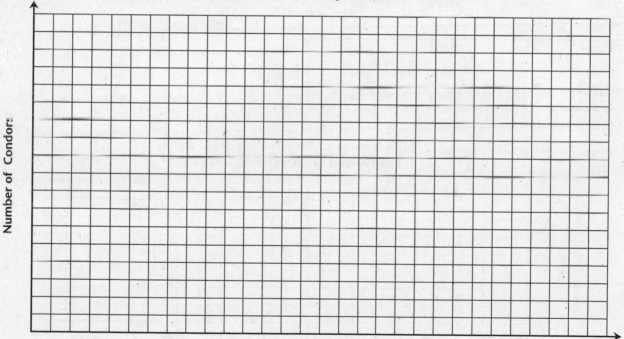

Number of Condors

Year

MODULE 4   **LABSHEET** **5C**

Endangered or Threatened Mammal Species Graphs
(Use with Question 10 on page 268.)

The table, stem-and-leaf plot, and line graph below show the number
of mammal species listed as endangered or threatened during the
period 1980–2001.

Total Number of Mammal Species Listed as Endangered or Threatened			
Year	Mammals	Year	Mammals
1980	36	1991	64
1981	36	1992	65
1982	36	1993	65
1983	39	1994	66
1984	42	1995	66
1985	48	1996	66
1986	49	1997	66
1987	52	1998	69
1988	56	1999	69
1989	58	2000	72
1990	61	2001	73

**Total Number of Mammal
Species Listed as
Endangered or Threatened
1980–2001**

```
3 | 6  6  6  9
4 | 2  8  9
5 | 2  6  8
6 | 1  4  5  5  6  6  6  6  9  9
7 | 2  3
```

4 | 8 means 48 species

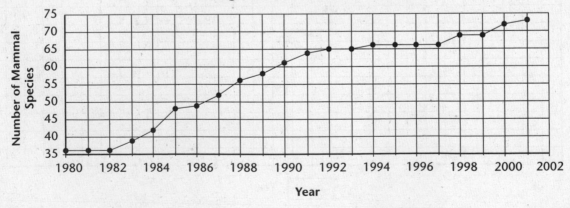

**Total Number of Mammal Species Listed as
Endangered or Threatened 1980–2001**

Name _____ Date _____

Commuter Data and Blank Grid
(Use with Exercises 3–5 on pages 271–272.)

Part I: Use with Exercise 3 on p. 271.

Directions The commuter data in the table were used to create Graph 1.
Study the graph to answer Exercise 3 on p. 271.

Graph 1

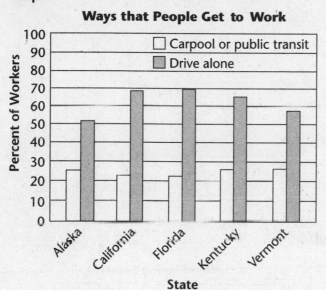

Ways that People Get to Work		
State	Percent of workers who carpool or use public transit	Percent of workers who drive alone
Alaska	25.2	52
California	22.8	68
Florida	22.7	69
Kentucky	25.5	65
Vermont	26.4	56

Part II: Use with Exercises 4–5 on pp. 271–272.

Directions Use the data in the table to create a second double bar graph on
the grid for Graph 2.

Graph 2

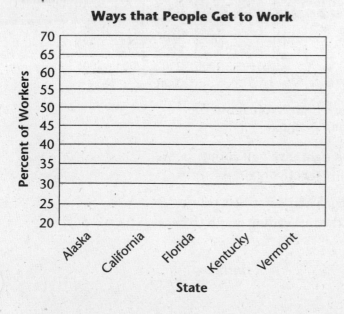

 Practice and Applications

For use with Section 5

For use with Exploration 1

Use the line graph to answer Exercises 1 and 2.

1. What does the line graph tell you about the number of large screen televisions from 1990 to 2006?

2. About how many more large screen televisions were there in 2006 than in 1990?

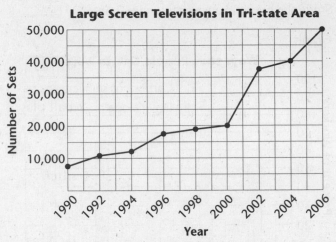

The bar graphs show the number of girls and boys who played soccer from 1998 to 2006 in Midvalley.

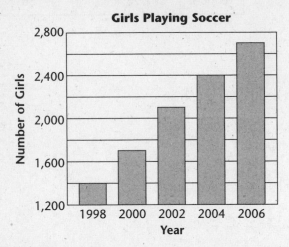

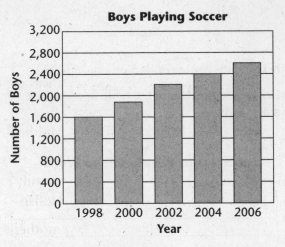

3. What impression does the bar graph on the left give you about the number of girls who played soccer from 1998 to 2006?

4. What impression does the bar graph on the right give you about the number of boys who played soccer from 1998 to 2006?

5. Explain how one of the graphs is misleading. Then describe a way that you could change the vertical scale of the misleading graph to create a different impression of the data.

(continued)

Name _____ Date _____

Practice and Applications

For use with Section 5

For use with Exploration 2

6. Tell whether the *mean*, the *median*, or the *mode* best describes each set of data. Explain your choice.

   a. Scores in eight geography quizzes:

89	95	91	61	98	89	94	93

   b. Heights (in inches) of five basketball players:

65	69	80	63	67

   c. Incomes (in dollars) of six baby sitters:

25	32	28	19	23	17

   d. Weights (in grams) of ten hummingbirds:

8	7	9	8	12	8	13	8	9	10

   e. Number of puppies in six litters:

6	7	8	8	5	9

7. Tell which type of average you think was used to make each statement. Explain your reasoning.

   a. Most of the students at Hillside Middle School said their favorite food is pizza.

   b. The average weight of the Jensen family pets is 28 oz. They have a dog, two hamsters, and eight goldfish.

   c. The average age of Jenny's grandmother, aunt, sister, and niece is 42.5 years.

   d. The number of students in five classes is 24.9.

Name _____ Date _____

Study Guide
For use with Section 5

Population Growth — Line Graphs and Choosing an Average

GOAL **LEARN HOW TO:** • make a line graph
• choose an appropriate average

AS YOU: • investigate changes in populations
• work wih statistics about population

Exploration 1: Representing Population Data

Line Graphs

A **line graph** is often used to show changes that take place over a period of time.

This line graph shows the population of the United States from 1970 through 2020. From 1970 through 2000, the data are actual census figures. The value for 2020 is a projection.

Misleading Graphs

Changing the scale on a bar graph or a line graph can give a very different impression of the data.

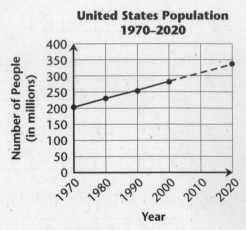

United States Population 1970–2020

Source: *U.S. Census Bureau*

Example

Both graphs below display the same data comparing the capacities of three nuclear power plants in the U.S., one in Texas, one in Arizona, and one in Ohio.

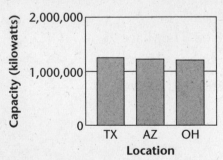

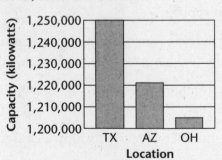

In the first graph, the capacities of the three plants appear to be about equal. In the second graph, the bar for the plant in Texas is 10 times the height of the bar for the plant in Ohio. The table at the right gives the actual data.

Location	Capacity (kilowatts)
Texas	1,250,000
Arizona	1,221,000
Ohio	1,205,000

Math Thematics, Book 1
Student Workbook

170

Copyright © McDougal Littell/Houghton Mifflin Company.
All rights reserved.

Name _____ Date _____

 **Study Guide**
For use with Section 5

Exploration 2: Choosing an Average

Statistical averages are often used to represent groups of data, giving "typical" data values. Recall that three of the types of averages are the *mean*, the *median*, and the *mode*. For a given data set, one type of average may be more appropriate than another.

Average	Condition for use or not	Example
Mean	If the data set contains one very high or one very low value, the mean will not be representative.	Data set: the heights of people in a kindergarten room. The teacher's height will inflate the mean height.
Median	If the data are clustered around two numbers with a large gap between them, the median will not be representative.	Data set: the heights of the people in a photo of two parents and their two small children. The heights of the small children are significantly different from the heights of their parents.
Mode	The mode is best used with categorical data, such as shoe size.	Data set: stock for a shoe store When ordering new stock for a store, more of the most common sizes are ordered.

Study Guide: Practice & Application Exercises

For use with Section 5

Exploration 1

1. Drawing two line graphs on one grid for the number of computers in use in Japan and in Germany can help you compare the data.

a. Find the range of the data to help you decide on the intervals for the vertical scale. Then draw the double line graph.

b. What is the general trend for the number of computers in use in Japan? in Germany?

c. How does the number of computers in Japan compare to the number of computers in Germany in the interval 1999 through 2005?

Computers in Use (in millions)

Year	Japan	Germany
1999	36.3	24.4
2000	40.0	27.6
2001	45.6	31.3
2002	48.7	35.6
2003	52.0	40.0
2004	69.2	45.0
2005	86.4	50.0

For Exercises 2–4, use the line graph.

2. What information does this graph display?

3. Explain how you could find the number of computers per 100 people in 2005.

4. Explain what you think a line graph of the number of computers per 100 people in the U.S. from 1999–2005 would look like.

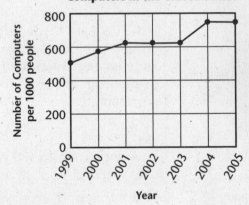

Use the two graphs shown below for Exercises 5–8 at the top of the next page.

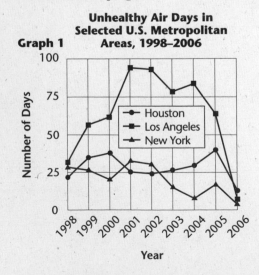

(continued)

Math Thematics, Book 1
Student Workbook

Study Guide: Practice & Application Exercises

MODULE 4

For use with Section 5

Displaying Data **Choose the graph from the previous page that best supports each statement. Explain your choice.**

5. The number of unhealthy air days in each of the three metropolitan areas did not change much in the years 1998–2006.

6. Between 2001 and 2005, the Los Angeles area almost cut the number of unhealthy air days in half.

7. Between 1998 and 2006, the number of unhealthy days in both the New York and Houston areas were about the same.

8. Of the three areas, Los Angeles made the most significant progress in eliminating unhealthy air days.

Use the table showing the carbon dioxide emissions of selected nations for Exercises 9–12.

9. Draw a bar graph to display the data.

10. What impression does your graph give about the emissions from the United States?

11. How could you change the emissions scale so that the bars look more even?

12. How could you change the emissions scale to make it seem that the emissions from Canada and Germany are insignificant?

Carbon Dioxide Emissions of Selected Nations

Nation	Emissions per year (millions of metric tons)
Canada	154
Germany	220
India	348
United States	1580

Source: *U.S. Department of Energy*

Writing **For Exercises 13–18, tell whether you would use a *line graph*, a *bar graph*, or a *stem-and-leaf plot* for each situation. Explain your choice.**

13. You want to see how your weight has changed over your lifetime.

14. Your teacher wants to show the scores on last week's quiz.

15. You took a survey of students' favorite books and want to make a graph to help you determine the top five books picked.

16. The track team coach wants to display the finish times of every runner in a race.

17. You're growing a sunflower and want to see how tall it grows during the spring and summer months.

18. Three movies were playing at the local theater. You find out the number of people who saw each movie and make a graph to illustrate your data.

(continued)

Study Guide: Practice & Application Exercises

For use with Section 5

Exploration 2

19. Astronomy The table lists the distances from Earth to each of the planets in our solar system when the planet is closest to Earth.

   a. Find the mean, the median, and the mode of the data.

   b. Which average do you think is most appropriate to describe the average closest approach to Earth by the planets in the solar system? Why?

Planet	Closest approach to Earth (mi)
Jupiter	390,000,000
Mars	35,000,000
Mercury	53,000,000
Neptune	2,678,000,000
Saturn	793,000,000
Uranus	1,700,000,000
Venus	25,000,000

20. The table lists the types of clouds that Mr. Slater's class saw in the sky last week.

   a. How would you describe the average cloud that Mr. Slater's class saw last week?

   b. Which average, the mean, the median, or the mode, did you use to answer part (a)? Explain.

   c. When is the mode the most appropriate average to use?

Day	Cloud Type
Sunday	cumulus
Monday	cumulus
Tuesday	cirrus
Wednesday	cirrostratus
Thursday	cumulus
Friday	cumulonimbus
Saturday	cumulus

Tell whether the *mean*, the *median*, or the *mode* best describes each set of data. Explain your choice.

21. Number of lions in 6 prides:
4, 12, 10, 8, 10, 10

22. Number of kindergartens in 8 schools:
2, 2, 1, 3, 2, 1, 3, 1

23. Heights (in.) of 7 people in a photo:
34, 64, 65, 65, 35, 36, 34

24. Weights (grams) of 5 gold bracelets:
6.8, 8.2, 8.1, 7.7, 9.1

Tell which average you think was used to make each statement. Explain your reasoning.

25. The average number of children in the families of Chet's classmates is 2.3.

26. The average dress size of the girls in Mrs. Appleby's class is 8.

27. The average math grade on the last test in Mr. Thor's class was B.

Name _____   Date _____

Practice and Applications

For use after Sections 1–5

For use with Section 1

1. Use the sorting grid to answer.

   a. Which months of the year begin with a vowel?

   b. Which month of the year begins with a vowel and ends with "r"?

   c. How many months end with "r"?

   d. Why are some of the months of the year outside of the sets?

	Months that begin with a vowel	Months that begin with a consonant
Months that end with an R	October	September, November, December
Months that end with another letter	April, August	January, February, March, May, June, July

2. Replace each ___?___ with the number that makes the statement true.

   a. 6 km = ___?___ m   **b.** 5.8 m = ___?___ cm   **c.** 418 m = ___?___ km

   d. 5270 mm = ___?___ m   **e.** 0.3 m = ___?___ mm   **f.** 75 cm = ___?___ mm

For use with Section 2

3. Students at Audy School collected aluminum cans for recycling. The number of pounds collected by each class were 7, 9, 12, 8, 9, 10, 9, 7, 6, 9, 10, and 8.

   a. Find the range of the pounds.

   b. Make a line plot for the data.

4. Tina runs after school. She keeps track of the number of miles she runs each week for 2 months: 12, 10, 8, 9, 10, 12, 15, and 10 miles. What are the mean, the median, and the mode of the data?

5. Use a calculator to write each fraction as a decimal rounded to the nearest hundredth.

   a. $\frac{4}{9}$ **b.** $\frac{7}{8}$ **c.** $\frac{1}{6}$

   d. $\frac{5}{4}$ **e.** $\frac{2}{3}$ **f.** $\frac{8}{7}$

(continued)

Name _____ Date _____

Practice and Applications
For use after Sections 1–5

For use with Section 3

6. Find each quotient.

   a. $15.92 \div 4$ **b.** $5\overline{)21.8}$ **c.** $18.6 \div 8$

7. Solve each equation. Check each solution.

   a. $t - 2.3 = 5.7$ **b.** $18 = 5 + d$

   c. $m + 9.1 = 12$ **d.** $24 = a + 7$

For use with Section 4

8. Use the stem-and-leaf plot showing the geography quiz scores for one class.

Geography Quiz Scores

```
 7 | 6 9
 8 | 3 3 5 6 8 8 9 9 9
 9 | 0 1 2 2 4 6 9
10 | 0 0
```

8 | 5 represents a score of 85

   a. What was the low score in the class? the high score?

   b. Find the mean, the mode, and the median of the scores.

9. Find each quotient.

   a. $2.4\overline{)8.64}$ **b.** $0.006\overline{)0.108}$ **c.** $8.4\overline{)55.02}$

10. The table shows the total cost for buying different numbers of magazines.

Number of Magazines (Input)	1	2	3	4	5	6	7
Total Cost in Dollars (Output)	2	4	6	?	10	?	?

   a. Write a rule for the output based on the input. Let c = cost and m = number of magazines.

   b. Use your rule to find the missing values in the table.

(continued)

Practice and Applications

For use after Sections 1–5

For use with Section 5

Use the line graph to answer Exercises 11–13.

11. What does the line graph tell you about the number of people who listened to radio shows from 1950–2000?

12. How could you alter the scale on the vertical axis to make it look like the number of people who listened to radio shows decreased slowly from 1950–2000?

13. How could you alter the scale on the horizontal axis to make it look like the number of people who listened to radio shows decreased rapidly from 1950–2000?

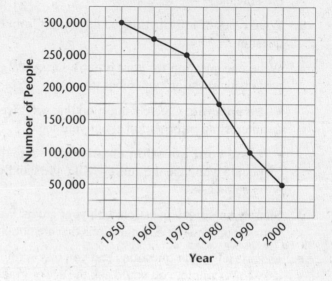

People Who Listened to Radio Shows in Twin Lake Area

14. Tell whether the *mean*, the *median*, or the *mode* best describes each set of data. Explain your choice.

a. Scores on six social studies tests:

85	91	62	89	88	86

b. Number of eggs in ten nests:

4	5	3	4	2	4	3	4	4	1

c. Number of students in five classes:

25	23	26	28	24

Name _____ Date _____

Survey Worksheet (Use with Project Question 3 on page 276.)

Directions Complete parts (a)–(c) on your own. Work with your group on parts (d)–(f).

a. How might someone answer each of the questions on the notepad?

b. What types of information would you get from each question?

c. Write one question for your group's survey. As you write your question remember to:

  • **Be specific.** Create a question that will give you interesting information about your topic.

  • **State your question clearly.** Make sure that people who take the survey will understand what is being asked.

d. Share your survey question with your group. With your group, rewrite any questions that are not clear.

e. Discuss any other questions that you may want to ask. For example, you could ask the age or grade level of the person you are surveying.

f. Combine your survey questions onto one sheet of paper. Make sure your group has at least five different questions.

Survey on Pets

1. How many pets do you own?

2. Name each kind of pet you own and how many of each kind you own.

3. What is your favorite pet?

Math Thematics, Book 1
Student Workbook

178

Name _____ Problem _____

☆ *The star indicates that you excelled in some way.*

 Problem Solving

❶   ❷   ❸   ❹   ❺

You did not understand the problem well enough to get started or you did not show any work.

You understood the problem well enough to make a plan and to work toward a solution.

You made a plan, you used it to solve the problem, and you verified your solution.

 Mathematical Language

❶   ❷   ❸   ❹   ❺

You did not use any mathematical vocabulary or symbols, or you did not use them correctly, or your use was not appropriate.

You used appropriate mathematical language, but the way it was used was not always correct or other terms and symbols were needed.

You used mathematical language that was correct and appropriate to make your meaning clear.

 Representations

❶   ❷   ❸   ❹   ❺

You did not use any representations such as equations, tables, graphs, or diagrams to help solve the problem or explain your solution.

You made appropriate representations to help solve the problem or help you explain your solution, but they were not always correct or other representations were needed.

You used appropriate and correct representations to solve the problem or explain your solution.

 Connections

❶   ❷   ❸   ❹   ❺

You attempted or solved the problem and then stopped.

You found patterns and used them to extend the solution to other cases, or you recognized that this problem relates to other problems, mathematical ideas, or applications.

You extended the ideas in the solution to the general case, or you showed how this problem relates to other problems, mathematical ideas, or applications.

 Presentation

❶   ❷   ❸   ❹   ❺

The presentation of your solution and reasoning is unclear to others.

The presentation of your solution and reasoning is clear in most places, but others may have trouble understanding parts of it.

The presentation of your solution and reasoning is clear and can be understood by others.

Content Used: _____ **Computational Errors:**   Yes ☐   No ☐

es on Errors: _____

Name _____ Problem _____

Student Self-Assessment Scales
For use with Module 5

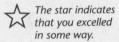 If your score is in the shaded area, explain why on the back of this sheet and stop.

☆ The star indicates that you excelled in some way.

 ## Problem Solving

①   ②   ③   ④   ⑤ ☆→

I did not understand the problem well enough to get started or I did not show any work.

I understood the problem well enough to make a plan and to work toward a solution.

I made a plan, I used it to solve the problem, and I verified my solution.

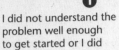 ## Mathematical Language

①   ②   ③   ④   ⑤ ☆→

I did not use any mathematical vocabulary or symbols, or I did not use them correctly, or my use was not appropriate.

I used appropriate mathematical language, but the way it was used was not always correct or other terms and symbols were needed.

I used mathematical language that was correct and appropriate to make my meaning clear.

 ## Representations

①   ②   ③   ④   ⑤ ☆→

I did not use any representations such as equations, tables, graphs, or diagrams to help solve the problem or explain my solution.

I made appropriate representations to help solve the problem or help me explain my solution, but they were not always correct or other representations were needed.

I used appropriate and correct representations to solve the problem or explain my solution.

 ## Connections

①   ②   ③   ④   ⑤ ☆→

I attempted or solved the problem and then stopped.

I found patterns and used them to extend the solution to other cases, or I recognized that this problem relates to other problems, mathematical ideas, or applications.

I extended the ideas in the solution to the general case, or I showed how this problem relates to other problems, mathematical ideas, or applications.

 ## Presentation

①   ②   ③   ④   ⑤ ☆→

The presentation of my solution and reasoning is unclear to others.

The presentation of my solution and reasoning is clear in most places, but others may have trouble understanding parts of it.

The presentation of my solution and reasoning is clear and can be understood by others.

Math Thematics, Book 1
Student Workbook

180

MODULE 5   **LABSHEET** **1A**

Paper Folding a Trihexaflexagon (Use with Question 2 on page 283.)

Directions

Step 1 Cut out the trapezoid.

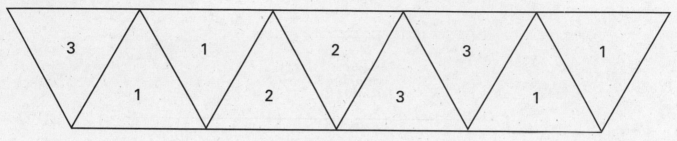

Step 2 Turn the strip over and number the triangles as shown in Figure 1.

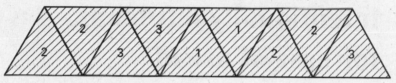

Figure 1

Step 3 Fold along the line segments separating the triangles several
times so the trihexaflexagon will be more flexible.

Step 4 Fold $\frac{2}{3}$ of the strip behind the front $\frac{1}{3}$, as shown in Figure 2.

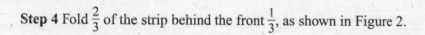

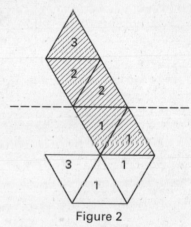

Figure 2

Step 5 Fold the triangles above the dashed segment in Figure 2
back to form a hexagon, as shown in Figure 3.

Figure 3

Step 6 Bring Triangle 1 in front of Triangle 3, as
shown in Figure 4.

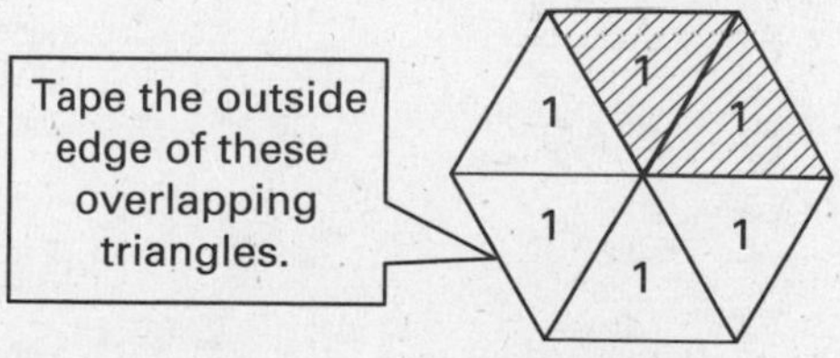

Tape the outside
edge of these
overlapping
triangles.

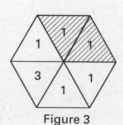

Figure 4

Math Thematics, Book 1
Student Workbook   **181**

This page has been
intentionally left blank
for ease of use of
surrounding labsheets.

MODULE 5   **LABSHEET** **1B**

Fraction Strips (Use with Questions 3 and 4 on page 284.)

Do NOT cut on dashed segments.

$\frac{1}{3}$

$\frac{1}{3}$

$\frac{1}{3}$

This page has been intentionally left blank for ease of use of surrounding labsheets.

Practice and Applications

For use with Section 1

For use with Exploration 1

1. Write an inequality that compares each fraction with $\frac{1}{2}$.

    a. $\frac{3}{8}$ **b.** $\frac{11}{12}$ **c.** $\frac{5}{8}$

    d. $\frac{3}{4}$ **e.** $\frac{5}{6}$ **f.** $\frac{1}{5}$

    g. $\frac{2}{9}$ **h.** $\frac{41}{50}$ **i.** $\frac{19}{90}$

2. Write the fractions in order from least to greatest.

    a. $\frac{3}{4}, \frac{3}{25}, \frac{3}{10}, \frac{3}{8}, \frac{3}{11}$ **b.** $\frac{1}{50}, \frac{1}{10}, \frac{1}{3}, \frac{1}{100}$

    c. $\frac{7}{12}, \frac{7}{8}, \frac{7}{10}, \frac{7}{100}, \frac{7}{9}$ **d.** $\frac{8}{9}, \frac{24}{25}, \frac{9}{10}, \frac{3}{4}, \frac{99}{100}$

    e. $\frac{2}{5}, \frac{1}{10}, \frac{7}{9}, \frac{5}{8}$ **f.** $\frac{29}{60}, \frac{12}{99}, \frac{19}{20}, \frac{15}{19}$

3. Replace each ____?____ with >, <, or =.

    a. $\frac{5}{9}$ __?__ $\frac{5}{11}$ **b.** $\frac{47}{48}$ __?__ $\frac{48}{49}$ **c.** $\frac{12}{25}$ __?__ $\frac{10}{12}$

    d. $\frac{24}{25}$ __?__ $\frac{8}{9}$ **e.** $\frac{14}{25}$ __?__ $\frac{14}{27}$ **f.** $\frac{9}{16}$ __?__ $\frac{13}{18}$

    g. $\frac{2}{3}$ __?__ $\frac{1}{5}$ **h.** $\frac{1}{2}$ __?__ $\frac{15}{30}$ **i.** $\frac{2}{9}$ __?__ $\frac{3}{4}$

    j. $\frac{3}{11}$ __?__ $\frac{5}{9}$ **k.** $\frac{7}{15}$ __?__ $\frac{7}{8}$ **l.** $\frac{1}{6}$ __?__ $\frac{1}{10}$

4. a. The inequality $x > \frac{1}{3}$ is true for every number greater than $\frac{1}{3}$. Give two values for x that are fractions and that make the inequality a true statement.

    b. The inequality $x < \frac{5}{8}$ is true for every number less than $\frac{5}{8}$. Give two values for x that are fractions and that make the inequality a true statement.

5. Sonya and Ivan each eat a piece of pie that is $\frac{1}{8}$ of the pie. How is it possible for Ivan to eat more pie than Sonya?

(continued)

Name _____ Date _____

Practice and Applications

For use with Section 1

For use with Exploration 2

6. Use a common denominator to compare the fractions.
Replace each ___?___ with >, <, or =.

a. $\frac{2}{3}$ __?__ $\frac{5}{8}$

b. $\frac{3}{8}$ __?__ $\frac{2}{5}$

c. $\frac{5}{12}$ __?__ $\frac{3}{4}$

d. $\frac{7}{12}$ __?__ $\frac{2}{3}$

e. $\frac{4}{12}$ __?__ $\frac{8}{24}$

f. $\frac{11}{30}$ __?__ $\frac{7}{15}$

g. $\frac{5}{8}$ __?__ $\frac{11}{24}$

h. $\frac{3}{14}$ __?__ $\frac{9}{28}$

i. $\frac{5}{6}$ __?__ $\frac{11}{24}$

7. Use decimals to compare. Replace each ___?___ with >, <, or =.

a. $\frac{75}{90}$ __?__ $\frac{128}{185}$

b. $\frac{78}{165}$ __?__ $\frac{13}{35}$

c. $\frac{86}{255}$ __?__ $\frac{48}{125}$

d. $\frac{134}{305}$ __?__ $\frac{79}{200}$

e. $\frac{23}{25}$ __?__ $\frac{218}{225}$

f. $\frac{315}{408}$ __?__ $\frac{94}{115}$

g. $\frac{23}{65}$ __?__ $\frac{138}{390}$

h. $\frac{72}{95}$ __?__ $\frac{150}{187}$

i. $\frac{18}{35}$ __?__ $\frac{23}{48}$

8. Use mental math, paper and pencil, or a calculator to compare the
fractions. Replace each ___?___ with >, <, or =.

a. $\frac{23}{25}$ __?__ $\frac{3}{5}$

b. $\frac{48}{205}$ __?__ $\frac{185}{315}$

c. $\frac{32}{125}$ __?__ $\frac{102}{212}$

d. $\frac{19}{50}$ __?__ $\frac{7}{20}$

e. $\frac{15}{51}$ __?__ $\frac{150}{521}$

f. $\frac{65}{97}$ __?__ $\frac{520}{776}$

g. $\frac{13}{26}$ __?__ $\frac{39}{52}$

h. $\frac{5}{9}$ __?__ $\frac{55}{99}$

i. $\frac{20}{81}$ __?__ $\frac{1}{4}$

j. $\frac{55}{102}$ __?__ $\frac{99}{200}$

k. $\frac{26}{75}$ __?__ $\frac{1}{3}$

l. $\frac{304}{512}$ __?__ $\frac{120}{200}$

9. Sarah needs $\frac{11}{18}$ yd of fabric to be able to sew a vest. She needs
$\frac{13}{18}$ yd of fabric to sew a skirt. Her mother gives her $\frac{2}{3}$ yd of fabric.
Which can Sarah sew, the vest or the skirt? Explain.

10. To pass inspection in the machine shop, the width of a widget must
be between $\frac{1}{8}$ cm and $\frac{3}{16}$ cm. Will a widget that is $\frac{7}{64}$ cm wide pass the
inspection? Explain.

Study Guide
For use with Section 1

Paper Folding   Comparing Fractions

GOAL   **LEARN HOW TO:** • use number sense to compare fractions
• use common denominators to write equivalent fractions
• use decimals to compare fractions

AS YOU: • fold fraction strips
• choose a method to compare fractions

Exploration 1: Fraction Number Sense

Inequalities

An **inequality** is a statement that uses the symbol > (*is greater than*) or
< (*is less than*) to compare two numbers. You will be writing inequalities
as you compare fractions.

Using Number Sense to Compare Fractions

There are three basic techniques that use number sense to compare
fractions.

1. See if the numerators or the $\frac{2}{5} > \frac{2}{9}$, since the numerators are the same and
   denominators are the same.   fifths are greater than ninths.

   $\frac{5}{7} < \frac{6}{7}$, since the denominators are the same
   and 5 < 6.

2. See if one fraction is greater than $\frac{7}{8} > \frac{2}{5}$, since $\frac{7}{8} > \frac{1}{2}$ and $\frac{2}{5} < \frac{1}{2}$.
   $\frac{1}{2}$ and the other is less than $\frac{1}{2}$.

3. See if both fractions are $\frac{10}{11} > \frac{4}{5}$, since $\frac{10}{11}$ is just $\frac{1}{10}$ less than a whole
   one part less than a whole.

   while $\frac{4}{5}$ is $\frac{1}{5}$ less than a whole, and $\frac{1}{11} < \frac{1}{5}$.

Exploration 2: Common Denominators

Using a Common Denominator to Compare Fractions

When two fractions have different denominators, you can compare them
more easily by rewriting them as equivalent fractions with a **common
denominator**, which is a common multiple of the two denominators.

Name _____   Date _____

 **Study Guide**
For use with Section 1

Example

Compare the fractions $\frac{5}{6}$ and $\frac{3}{4}$.

Sample Response

Examine the two denominators looking for their least common multiple, also called the **least common denominator (LCD)**.

    multiples of 6: 6, 12, 18, …   multiples of 4: 4, 8, 12, …

    12 is the least common denominator of 6 and 4.

Rewrite the fractions as equivalent fractions using the least common denominator.

$$\frac{5}{6} = \frac{5 \cdot 2}{6 \cdot 2} = \frac{10}{12} \qquad\qquad \frac{3}{4} = \frac{3 \cdot 3}{4 \cdot 3} = \frac{9}{12}$$

Since the fractions have the same denominator, look at the numerators to compare them.

Since $\frac{10}{12} > \frac{9}{12}$, therefore $\frac{5}{6} > \frac{3}{4}$.

Using Decimals to Compare Fractions

When the least common denominator of two fractions is too difficult to find, you can rewrite the fractions as decimals in order to compare them. You may want to use a calculator.

Example

Compare $\frac{7}{9}$ and $\frac{8}{13}$.

Sample Response

Step 1 Use division to rewrite each fraction as a decimal.

    [7] [÷] [9] [=] [0.77777777]

    [8] [÷] [1] [3] [=] [0.61538462]

Step 2 Compare the decimals.

    Since $0.77777777 > 0.61538462$, therefore $\frac{7}{9} > \frac{8}{13}$.

Math Thematics, Book 1
Student Workbook

188

Name _____   Date _____

 Study Guide: Practice & Application Exercises
MODULE 5
For use with Section 1

Exploration 1

Write an inequality that compares each fraction with $\frac{1}{2}$.

1. $\frac{5}{7}$ **2.** $\frac{6}{13}$ **3.** $\frac{358}{1000}$ **4.** $\frac{13}{9}$

Write the fractions in order from least to greatest.

5. $\frac{4}{7}, \frac{4}{13}, \frac{4}{100}, \frac{4}{3}, \frac{4}{5}$ **6.** $\frac{12}{13}, \frac{11}{12}, \frac{4}{5}, \frac{2}{3}, \frac{8}{9}$

Mental Math **For Exercises 7–10, use number sense to compare the fractions. Replace each __?__ with >, <, or =.**

7. $\frac{8}{11}$ __?__ $\frac{8}{9}$ **8.** $\frac{38}{39}$ __?__ $\frac{37}{38}$ **9.** $\frac{58}{120}$ __?__ $\frac{80}{110}$ **10.** $\frac{21}{43}$ __?__ $\frac{19}{43}$

11. **Writing** Jill filled a bag with $\frac{1}{2}$ kg of rocks and Jack filled a bag with $\frac{1}{2}$ kg of feathers. Jill said her bag of rocks was heavier than Jack's bag of feathers. Do you agree? Explain.

Exploration 2

Use a common denominator to compare the fractions. Replace each __?__ with >, <, or =.

12. $\frac{5}{6}$ __?__ $\frac{7}{12}$ **13.** $\frac{11}{16}$ __?__ $\frac{17}{32}$ **14.** $\frac{4}{7}$ __?__ $\frac{3}{5}$ **15.** $\frac{13}{20}$ __?__ $\frac{41}{50}$

For Exercises 16–19, use decimals to compare. Replace each __?__ with >, <, or =.

16. $\frac{9}{10}$ __?__ $\frac{17}{20}$ **17.** $\frac{71}{100}$ __?__ $\frac{333}{400}$ **18.** $\frac{103}{153}$ __?__ $\frac{178}{200}$ **19.** $\frac{387}{492}$ __?__ $\frac{58}{73}$

20. **Algebra Connection** The compound inequality $\frac{1}{2} < x < \frac{7}{8}$ means that x represents any number greater than $\frac{1}{2}$ and less than $\frac{7}{8}$. Give two values for x that are fractions and that make the inequality true.

21. Dustin needs to replace a button on a shirt. A $\frac{1}{2}$-inch button is too small. A $\frac{3}{4}$-inch button is too large. He has other buttons that are $\frac{5}{8}$-inch, $\frac{13}{16}$-inch, and 1-inch in diameter. Which one should he use? Explain.

Name _____   Date _____

Part I Conversion Facts (Use with Question 12 on page 299.)

To convert customary measurements, you must know the
facts for how different measurement units are related.
Complete the following.

1 ft = 12 in.	and	1 in. = _____ ft
1 yd = _____ ft	and	1 ft = $\frac{1}{3}$ yd
_____ yd = 36 in.	and	1 in. = $\frac{1}{36}$ yd
1 mi = 1760 yd	and	1 yd = _____ mi
1 mi = _____ ft	and	_____ ft = $\frac{1}{5280}$ mi

Part II Converting Yards to Feet (Use with Question 13(b) on page 299.)

Step 1: Write the conversion fact for changing 1 yd to feet.

$$1 \text{ yd} = \_\_\_\_\_ \text{ ft}$$

Step 2: Multiply by 8, since you are converting 8 yd to feet.

$$8 \cdot 1 \text{ yd} = \_\_\_\_\_ \cdot \_\_\_\_\_ \text{ ft}$$

Step 3: Complete the multiplication from Step 2.

$$8 \text{ yd} = \_\_\_\_\_ \text{ ft}$$

Part III Converting Inches to Feet (Use with Question 14(b) on page 299.)

Step 1: Write the conversion fact for changing 1 in. to feet.

$$1 \text{ in.} = \_\_\_\_\_ \text{ ft}$$

Step 2: Multiply by 1044, since you are converting 1044 in. to feet.

$$1044 \cdot 1 \text{ in.} = \_\_\_\_\_ \cdot \_\_\_\_\_ \text{ ft}$$

Step 3: Complete the multiplication from Step 2.

$$1044 \text{ in.} = \_\_\_\_\_ \text{ ft}$$

Name _____   Date _____

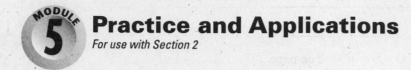

Practice and Applications

For use with Section 2

For use with Exploration 1

1. For each situation, name an appropriate customary unit or
    combination of units for measuring.

    a. checking that the perimeter of the goalie box meets regulations
    in soccer

    b. finding the distance across town

    c. measuring the length of your arm

2. Use a customary ruler to measure the length of the crayon to the
    nearest $\frac{1}{2}$ in., the nearest $\frac{1}{4}$ in. and the nearest $\frac{1}{8}$ in.

For use with Exploration 2

3. Replace each ___?___ with the number that makes the statement true.

    a. 6 yd = ___?___ ft

    b. 26,400 yd = ___?___ mi

    c. $6\frac{1}{3}$ yd = ___?___ in.

    d. 39 in. = ___?___ ft

    e. $5\frac{3}{4}$ ft = ___?___ in.

    f. 14 ft = ___?___ yd

4. Write each measurement as a fraction of a yard.

    a. 24 in.

    b. 8 ft

    c. 10 ft

5. Add or subtract. Simplify answers when possible.

    a.
    2 yd 1 ft
    + 5 yd 2 ft

    b.
    6 yd 1 ft
    − 4 yd 2 ft

    c.
    3536 ft
    + 1744 ft

    d.
    7 ft 8 in.
    − 2 ft 10 in.

    e.
    4 ft 7 in.
    + 6 ft 8 in.

    f.
    6 yd
    − 2 yd 1 ft

6. A carpenter has a 12 ft long piece of lumber. He cuts a section off
    that is $6\frac{3}{4}$ ft long. How long (in yd, ft, and in.) is the remaining piece
    of lumber?

Study Guide
For use with Section 2

Building the Great Wall Customary Units of Length

GOAL **LEARN HOW TO:** • develop benchmarks for an inch, a foot, and a yard
• find fractional measures on a ruler
• convert between customary units of length
• add and subtract lengths

AS YOU: • find the lengths of everyday objects
• explore the dimensions of various landmarks

Exploration 1: Investigating Benchmarks

Measuring Length in Customary Units

Parts of your body or common objects make good benchmarks for
estimating lengths in **inches (in.)**, **feet (ft)**, **yards (yd)**, or **miles (mi)**.
For instance, on the hand of an average-sized adult, the distance from
the knuckle of the thumb to the end of the thumb is about 1 inch.

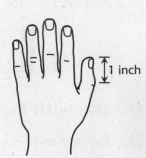

Reading a Ruler

You can use a ruler to find more accurate measurements. The markings
on a ruler indicate lengths such as inches, half-inches, quarter-inches,
and eighth-inches.

Example

Measure the length of the line segment to the nearest inch, $\frac{1}{2}$ in., and $\frac{1}{4}$ in.

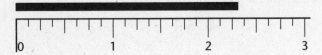

To the nearest inch: 2 in. To the nearest $\frac{1}{2}$ in.: $2\frac{1}{2}$ in. To the nearest $\frac{1}{4}$ in.: $2\frac{1}{4}$ in.

Some measurements are given using a combination of units. For
example, on a high school football field, the distance between the
uprights on the goal posts is 23 ft 4 in.

Study Guide
For use with Section 2

Exploration 2: Converting Customary Units of Length

The customary units of length are related in the following ways.

$1 \text{ in.} = \frac{1}{12} \text{ ft} = \frac{1}{36} \text{ yd}$ $1 \text{ ft} = 12 \text{ in.} = \frac{1}{3} \text{ yd} = \frac{1}{5280} \text{ mi}$

$1 \text{ yd} = 3 \text{ ft} = 36 \text{ in.} = \frac{1}{1760} \text{ mi}$ $1 \text{ mi} = 1760 \text{ yd} = 5280 \text{ ft}$

To convert from a larger unit to a smaller unit, you multiply. To convert from a smaller unit to a larger unit, you divide. You can multiply by the conversion fact to convert one customary unit to another.

Example

Convert 4 mi to feet.

$1 \text{ mi} = 5280 \text{ ft}$

$4 \cdot 1 \text{ mi} = 4 \cdot 5280 \text{ ft}$

$4 \text{ mi} = 21,120 \text{ ft}$

Convert 72 in. to yards.

$1 \text{ in.} = \frac{1}{36} \text{ yd}$

$72 \cdot 1 \text{ in.} = 72 \cdot \frac{1}{36} \text{ yd}$

$72 \text{ in.} = 2 \text{ yd}$

Adding and Subtracting Lengths in Customary Units

When adding and subtracting customary measurements, you may need to regroup units.

Example

Find each sum or difference. Simplify answers when possible.

8 ft 9 in.		8 ft 9 in.		8 ft 9 in.
+ 5 ft 6 in.	→	+ 5 ft 6 in.	→	+ 5 ft 6 in.
		13 ft 15 in.		14 ft 3 in.

Regroup 12 in. as 1 ft.

Regroup 1 yd as 3 ft.

7 yd 1 ft		⁶ ⁴ 7 yd 1 ft		⁶ ⁴ 7 yd 1 ft
− 4 yd 2 ft	→	− 4 yd 2 ft	→	− 4 yd 2 ft
				2 yd 2 ft

Name _____   Date _____

Study Guide: Practice & Application Exercises
For use with Section 2

Exploration 1

Use a benchmark to estimate the measurement.

1. the height of your classroom, to the nearest yard

2. the distance from your knee to your ankle, to the nearest foot

For each situation in Exercises 3 and 4, name an appropriate customary unit or combination of units for measuring.

3. measuring the length of the route you travel from home to school

4. finding the altitude (height above sea level) of the city in which you live

5. What is the length of the segment to the nearest

    a. inch?   **b.** $\frac{1}{2}$ inch?

    c. $\frac{1}{4}$ inch?   **d.** $\frac{1}{8}$ inch?

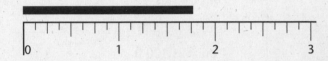

Exploration 2

For Exercises 6–8, replace each __?__ with the number that makes the statement true.

6. 18 yd = __?__ ft   **7.** 34,320 ft = __?__ mi   **8.** 114 in. = __?__ ft

9. Social Studies Some units of measurement can be traced to the Middle Ages.

    a. The *furlong* was originally a "furrow long," the length of a plowed strip of land in the division of medieval manors. If 8 furlongs = 1 mi, how many feet are in 1 furlong?

    b. The *rod* originated from the length of the pole used by a plowman to measure a furrow. If 40 rods = 1 furlong, how many feet are in 1 rod?

Find each sum or difference. Simplify answers when possible.

10.   6 mi 5176 ft   **11.**   14 ft 8 in.   **12.**   10 yd 1 ft
       + 10 mi 943 ft   − 8 ft 10 in.   + 4 yd 2 ft

13.   1 ft 5 in.   **14.**   3 yd 1 ft   **15.**   3 mi 1260 yd
     −   9 in.   + 9 yd 2 ft   − 2 mi 890 yd

MODULE 5   **LABSHEET** **3A**

Creating a Tetra-tetraflexagon (Use with the Setting the Stage on page 307.)

Follow the directions below to build your tetra-tetraflexagon.

1. Cut along *solid* lines both inside and around the edge of the flexagon. Then fold and crease all *dotted* lines. Notice the shapes that appear on the back side of the page.

2. Fold section F behind section E, wrapping section G around and on top of E.

3. Fold section D back behind C, then sections C and D behind section B.

4. Tape section G to section D at the X's. Each section facing you should have a circle in it.

5. Now you are ready to fold your flexagon. Using the photos in the *Setting the Stage* as a guide, close both sides of the flexagon together like a book and then open it from the spine in the back. Continue closing and opening. When the flexagon cannot be opened any further, reverse the direction by closing the flexagon back away from you and pulling it open from the spine in the front.

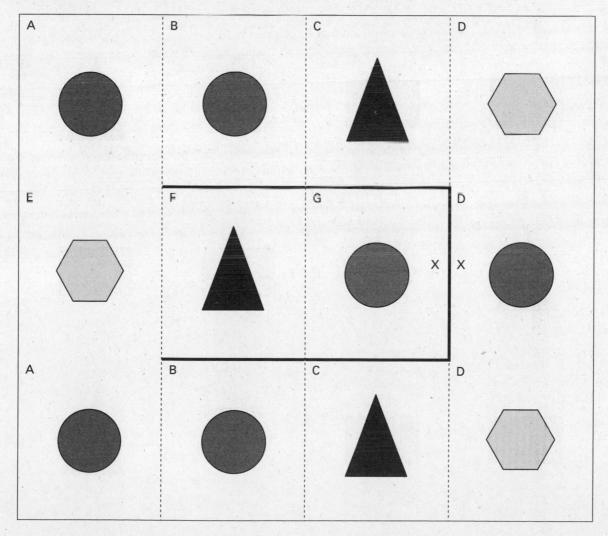

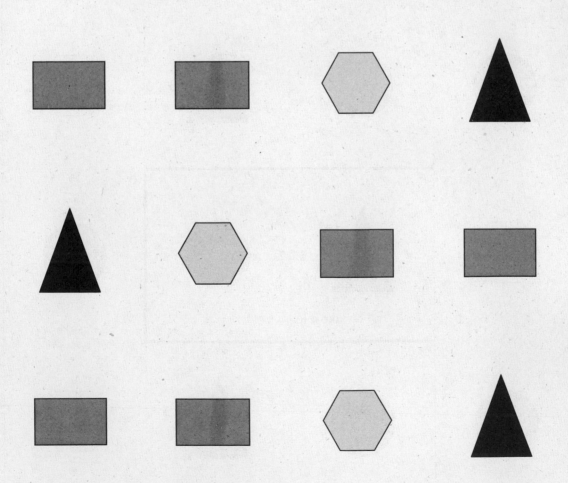

Name _____   Date _____

Practice and Applications
For use with Section 3

For use with Exploration 1

1. Find each sum. Write each answer in lowest terms.

   a. $\dfrac{1}{4} + \dfrac{3}{5}$ **b.** $\dfrac{5}{8} + \dfrac{1}{4}$ **c.** $\dfrac{5}{12} + \dfrac{3}{8}$

   d. $\dfrac{3}{8} + \dfrac{5}{6}$ **e.** $\dfrac{5}{6} + \dfrac{3}{5}$ **f.** $\dfrac{5}{12} + \dfrac{8}{9}$

2. Find each difference. Write each answer in lowest terms.

   a. $\dfrac{7}{10} - \dfrac{3}{5}$ **b.** $\dfrac{8}{9} - \dfrac{5}{12}$ **c.** $\dfrac{7}{8} - \dfrac{1}{2}$

   d. $\dfrac{15}{16} - \dfrac{3}{8}$ **e.** $\dfrac{5}{6} - \dfrac{5}{12}$ **f.** $\dfrac{5}{8} - \dfrac{2}{5}$

3. Find each sum or difference. Write each answer in lowest terms.

   a. $\dfrac{1}{2} + \dfrac{4}{5}$ **b.** $\dfrac{11}{12} \quad \dfrac{5}{8}$ **c.** $\dfrac{4}{15} + \dfrac{2}{3}$

   d. $\dfrac{3}{4} - \dfrac{2}{7}$ **e.** $\dfrac{7}{16} + \dfrac{3}{4}$ **f.** $\dfrac{2}{3} - \dfrac{4}{9}$

4. Find the value of each expression. Write each answer in lowest terms.

   a. $\dfrac{7}{9} - \dfrac{3}{18}$ **b.** $\dfrac{3}{7} + \dfrac{4}{5}$ **c.** $\dfrac{8}{9} - \dfrac{3}{4}$

   d. $\dfrac{3}{4} - \dfrac{1}{2} + \dfrac{5}{8}$ **e.** $\dfrac{2}{3} + \dfrac{1}{6} + \dfrac{2}{5}$ **f.** $\dfrac{9}{16} + \dfrac{1}{4} \quad \dfrac{3}{8}$

   g. $\dfrac{5}{9} - \dfrac{1}{3} + \dfrac{5}{6}$ **h.** $\dfrac{7}{10} - \dfrac{1}{4} + \dfrac{1}{8}$ **i.** $\dfrac{3}{8} + \dfrac{5}{16} + \dfrac{1}{4}$

5. Lana has 48 rocks in her rock collection. Of the rocks, $\dfrac{3}{8}$ are quartz and $\dfrac{1}{3}$ are granite. How many of Lana's rocks are quartz or granite?

6. Ryan has $\dfrac{7}{8}$ c oil. He uses $\dfrac{3}{4}$ c oil to make a loaf of bread. He needs $\dfrac{1}{3}$ c oil to make some vegetables. How much more oil does Ryan need to make the vegetables?

7. Evaluate each expression when $n = \dfrac{2}{3}$. Write each answer in lowest terms.

   a. $n + \dfrac{3}{4}$ **b.** $\dfrac{8}{9} - n$ **c.** $\dfrac{1}{3} + n$

   d. $n - \dfrac{2}{5}$ **e.** $\dfrac{7}{8} - n$ **f.** $n + \dfrac{1}{2}$

Name _____   Date _____

Study Guide
For use with Section 3

Flex This!   Addition and Subtraction of Fractions

GOAL   **LEARN HOW TO:** • add and subtract fractions
AS YOU: • explore the measurements of several flexagons

Exploration 1: Adding and Subtracting Fractions

Adding Fractions

To add fractions, follow these steps:

Step 1   Rewrite the fractions using a common denominator.

Step 2   Add the numerators and write the sum over the common denominator.

Add: $\frac{3}{5} + \frac{2}{7}$

The least common denominator is 35.

$$\frac{3 \cdot 7}{5 \cdot 7} + \frac{2 \cdot 5}{7 \cdot 5} = \frac{21}{35} + \frac{10}{35}$$

$$= \frac{21 + 10}{35}$$

$$= \frac{31}{35}$$

Subtracting Fractions

To subtract fractions, follow these steps:

Step 1   Rewrite the fractions using a common denominator.

Step 2   Subtract the numerators and write the difference over the common denominator.

Step 3   Write the answer in lowest terms.

Subtract: $\frac{11}{6} - \frac{1}{3}$

The least common denominator is 6.

$$\frac{11}{6} - \frac{1 \cdot 2}{3 \cdot 2} = \frac{11}{6} - \frac{2}{6}$$

$$= \frac{11 - 2}{6}$$

$$= \frac{9}{6}$$

$$= \frac{3}{2} \text{ or } 1\frac{1}{2}$$

Name _____   Date _____

Study Guide: Practice & Application Exercises
For use with Section 3

Exploration 1

Find each sum. Write each answer in lowest terms.

1. $\frac{1}{2} + \frac{2}{5}$

2. $\frac{3}{5} + \frac{3}{10}$

3. $\frac{5}{6} + \frac{3}{11}$

4. $\frac{4}{27} + \frac{1}{3} + \frac{5}{9}$

For Exercises 5–8, find each difference. Write each answer in lowest terms.

5. $\frac{7}{9} - \frac{3}{5}$

6. $\frac{3}{4} - \frac{5}{16}$

7. $\frac{4}{5} - \frac{1}{3}$

8. $\frac{12}{7} - \frac{2}{3}$

Find the value of each expression. Write each answer in lowest terms.

9. $\frac{1}{3} + \frac{7}{15} + \frac{3}{5}$

10. $\frac{1}{2} - \frac{7}{18} + \frac{8}{9}$

11. $\frac{35}{39} + \frac{7}{13} - \frac{1}{3}$

Evaluate each expression when $n = \frac{1}{4}$. Write each answer in lowest terms.

12. $n + \frac{9}{16}$

13. $\frac{5}{8} - n$

14. $\frac{3}{7} + n$

15. The first step in refining coal tar is a distillation process used to obtain three different liquid parts called *fractions* of the coal tar and an undistillable residue called *pitch*. The table gives data about the fractions of the coal tar that are distillable. What part of the unrefined coal tar is pitch?

Name of fraction	Size of fraction
light oil	$\frac{1}{20}$
middle oil	$\frac{17}{100}$
heavy oil	$\frac{4}{25}$

16. Displaying Data The circle graph shows educational achievement levels in the U.S. in 2005.

a. About what fraction have a college degree? have a high school diploma?

b. Compare those with a college degree to those with only some college.

c. Write a fraction for those who did not graduate high school.

U.S. Educational Achievement in 2005

Source: *U.S. Census Bureau*

This page has been
intentionally left blank
for ease of use of
surrounding labsheets.

Name _____   Date _____

1 in. by 1 in. Squares (Use with the Extended Exploration on page 317.)

Directions Cut out the squares.

This page has been intentionally left blank for ease of use of surrounding labsheets.

MODULE 5   **LABSHEET** **4A**

Mask (Use with Questions 2 and 3 on pages 318–319 and Question 11 on page 321.)

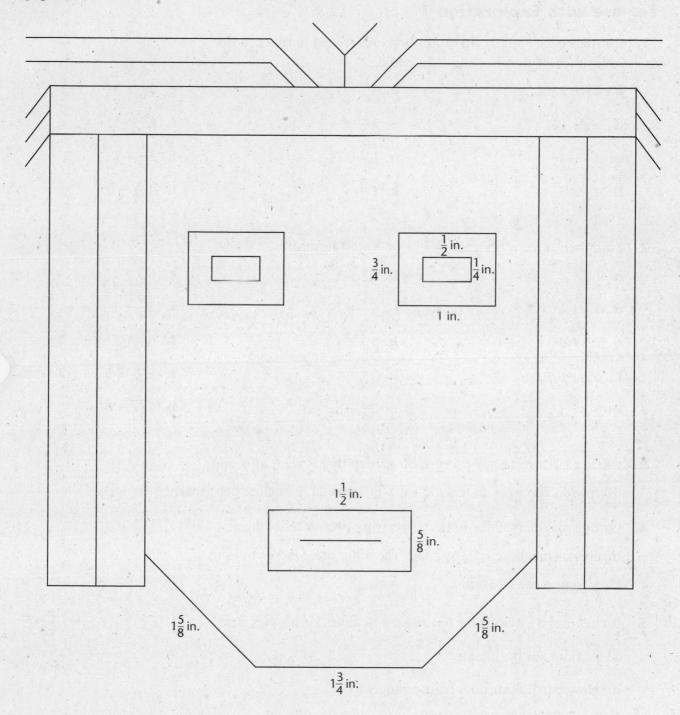

Name _____   Date _____

 Practice and Applications
For use with Section 4

For use with Exploration 1

1. Estimate each sum by first rounding each mixed number to the nearest whole number and then adding.

a. $4\frac{7}{8} + 2\frac{1}{4}$ **b.** $5\frac{1}{6} + 3\frac{1}{5}$ **c.** $2\frac{1}{9} + 3\frac{5}{6}$

d. $5\frac{7}{9} + 1\frac{2}{7}$ **e.** $2\frac{11}{12} + 4\frac{8}{9}$ **f.** $6\frac{3}{10} + 2\frac{6}{7}$

g. $2\frac{1}{5} + 4\frac{1}{8}$ **h.** $1\frac{7}{8} + 2\frac{1}{3}$ **i.** $2\frac{2}{7} + 1\frac{1}{10}$

j. $4\frac{4}{5} + 3\frac{1}{7}$ **k.** $2\frac{3}{10} + 1\frac{2}{3}$ **l.** $4\frac{1}{12} + 1\frac{9}{10}$

2. Find each sum. Write each answer in lowest terms.

a. $1\frac{2}{3} + 2\frac{1}{4}$ **b.** $3\frac{1}{5} + 4\frac{2}{3}$ **c.** $6\frac{1}{4} + 2\frac{5}{8}$

d. $3\frac{4}{5} + 1\frac{1}{4}$ **e.** $6\frac{1}{2} + 2\frac{2}{3}$ **f.** $2\frac{5}{9} + 1\frac{1}{6}$

g. $2\frac{1}{6} + 3\frac{2}{3}$ **h.** $3\frac{3}{8} + 4\frac{3}{4}$ **i.** $5\frac{1}{6} + 7\frac{1}{2}$

j. $4\frac{2}{9} + 6\frac{1}{2}$ **k.** $7\frac{2}{3} + 4\frac{5}{9}$ **l.** $8\frac{3}{10} + 5\frac{4}{5}$

m. $6\frac{3}{8} + 1\frac{5}{6}$ **n.** $2\frac{5}{6} + 5\frac{3}{5}$ **o.** $7\frac{5}{12} + 3\frac{8}{9}$

3. Christy has a rectangular vegetable garden that is $8\frac{1}{2}$ ft long and $6\frac{3}{4}$ ft wide. How much fencing will Christy need to enclose her garden?

4. George makes a tail for his kite by sewing two pieces of fabric together. One piece is $2\frac{3}{5}$ m long. The other piece is $3\frac{7}{10}$ m long. How long is the kite tail?

5. A chef uses $8\frac{1}{2}$ c flour for his cakes, $9\frac{3}{4}$ c flour for his pies, and $25\frac{2}{3}$ c flour for his breads.

   a. How much flour does he use altogether?

   b. Will he have any flour left from a 50 lb bag of flour?

(continued)

Name _____   Date _____

Practice and Applications

For use with Section 4

For use with Exploration 2

6. Use mental math to find each difference.

a. $7\frac{1}{4} - 2$ **b.** $9 - \frac{2}{3}$ **c.** $8\frac{7}{8} - 3$

d. $9\frac{1}{3} - 5\frac{2}{3}$ **e.** $6\frac{3}{4} - 2\frac{1}{2}$ **f.** $15 - 4\frac{7}{12}$

g. $6\frac{1}{2} - 5\frac{1}{4}$ **h.** $10 - 7\frac{1}{3}$ **i.** $3\frac{1}{2} - 2\frac{2}{5}$

7. Find each difference. Write each answer in lowest terms.

a. $4\frac{1}{2} - 2\frac{1}{6}$ **b.** $6\frac{4}{5} - 2\frac{3}{10}$ **c.** $9\frac{5}{8} - 6\frac{1}{4}$

d. $8\frac{2}{3} - \frac{3}{12}$ **e.** $10\frac{5}{9} - 4\frac{1}{6}$ **f.** $15\frac{1}{2} - 8\frac{3}{4}$

g. $9\frac{3}{4} - 5\frac{1}{5}$ **h.** $19\frac{1}{3} - 6\frac{1}{2}$ **i.** $8\frac{3}{5} - 4\frac{3}{4}$

j. $15\frac{1}{2} - 12\frac{7}{8}$ **k.** $18\frac{5}{8} - 12\frac{1}{2}$ **l.** $23\frac{1}{8} - 10\frac{2}{3}$

8. Find each sum or difference. Write each answer in lowest terms.

a. $3\frac{2}{3} + 1\frac{5}{9}$ **b.** $6\frac{2}{3} - 4\frac{2}{5}$ **c.** $48\frac{1}{3} - 26\frac{1}{2}$

d. $6\frac{3}{4} + 9\frac{5}{6}$ **e.** $6\frac{3}{4} - 2\frac{1}{2}$ **f.** $15 - 4\frac{7}{12}$

g. $78\frac{1}{2} - 24\frac{3}{4}$ **h.** $12\frac{1}{2} + 8\frac{7}{10}$ **i.** $18\frac{5}{6} - 4\frac{3}{5}$

j. $16\frac{2}{3} - 5\frac{3}{4}$ **k.** $10\frac{1}{3} + 45\frac{7}{8}$ **l.** $98\frac{1}{2} - 32\frac{2}{3}$

9. To make costumes for a school play, the costume designer needs $25\frac{5}{8}$ yd of fabric.

a. She has $18\frac{2}{3}$ yd of fabric. How many more yards of fabric does she need?

b. A parent donates $5\frac{1}{2}$ yd of fabric to use for the costumes. How many more yards of fabric will the costume designer need now?

c. How much fabric will the costume designer have left if she buys 2 yd of fabric to complete the costumes? Is it more or less than $\frac{1}{2}$ yd of fabric?

Name _____ Date _____

Study Guide
For use with Section 4

Masks Addition and Subtraction of Mixed Numbers

GOAL **LEARN HOW TO:** • add mixed numbers
• subtract mixed numbers

AS YOU: • determine the amount of string needed for a mask
• design a pin

Exploration 1: Adding Mixed Numbers

Using Estimation

One way to estimate the sum of two mixed numbers is to round each number to the nearest whole number. For example, the sum $6\frac{1}{3} + 3\frac{3}{4}$ is about $6 + 4$, or 10.

Using Paper and Pencil

To add mixed numbers, add the whole numbers and the fractions separately.

> **Example**
>
> To add: Use a common denominator.
>
> $$6\frac{1}{3} \rightarrow 6\frac{1 \cdot 4}{3 \cdot 4} \rightarrow 6\frac{4}{12}$$
>
> $$+ 3\frac{3}{4} \rightarrow 3\frac{3 \cdot 3}{3 \cdot 4} \rightarrow + 3\frac{9}{12}$$
>
> $$9\frac{13}{12} \rightarrow 9 + 1\frac{1}{12} = 10\frac{1}{12}$$

Exploration 2: Subtracting Mixed Numbers

Using Paper and Pencil

To subtract mixed numbers, subtract the fractions first and then the whole numbers, regrouping if necessary.

> **Example**
>
> To subtract: Use a common denominator.   Regroup.
>
> $$6\frac{1}{3} \rightarrow 6\frac{4}{12} \rightarrow 5 + \frac{12}{12} + \frac{4}{12} \rightarrow 5\frac{16}{12}$$
>
> $$- 3\frac{3}{4} \rightarrow - 3\frac{9}{12} \rightarrow - 3\frac{9}{12} \rightarrow - 3\frac{9}{12}$$
>
> $$2\frac{7}{12}$$

Math Thematics, Book 1
Student Workbook

206

Name _____ Date _____

Exploration 1

Estimate each sum by first rounding each mixed number to the nearest whole number and then adding.

1. $7\frac{2}{9} + 11\frac{5}{6}$
2. $10\frac{1}{3} + 18\frac{7}{17}$
3. $14\frac{7}{11} + 3\frac{16}{19}$
4. $20\frac{60}{128} + 16\frac{200}{412}$

Find each sum. Write each answer in lowest terms.

5. $6\frac{2}{5} + 13\frac{3}{10}$
6. $3\frac{1}{2} + 7\frac{2}{5}$
7. $6\frac{1}{3} + 5\frac{3}{4}$
8. $7\frac{2}{3} + 6\frac{5}{8}$

For Exercises 9–11, use compatible numbers to find each sum. Look for fraction parts with a sum of 1.

9. $5\frac{5}{6} + 9\frac{1}{8} + 3\frac{1}{6}$
10. $12\frac{2}{3} + 4\frac{7}{9} + 14\frac{1}{3}$
11. $6\frac{1}{5} + 7\frac{3}{7} + 4\frac{4}{5} + 2\frac{4}{7}$

Estimate each sum by first rounding each mixed number to the nearest half.

12. $7\frac{3}{5} + 8\frac{9}{11}$
13. $23\frac{5}{8} + 7\frac{7}{12}$
14. $16\frac{5}{9} + 30\frac{5}{13}$
15. $100\frac{17}{20} + 200\frac{27}{40}$

Exploration 2

Find each difference. Write each answer in lowest terms.

16. $8\frac{2}{3} - 4\frac{1}{5}$
17. $4\frac{7}{12} - 1\frac{3}{8}$
18. $3\frac{1}{6} - 1\frac{3}{4}$
19. $12\frac{2}{5} - 3\frac{3}{4}$

Use mental math to find each difference. Explain your steps.

20. $10 - 4\frac{2}{5}$
21. $16 - 9\frac{7}{9}$
22. $13\frac{3}{7} - 8$
23. $29 - 11\frac{5}{12}$

Use the table to answer Exercises 24 and 25.

24. Which of the horses covered the greatest distance in one race?

25. What was the difference in distances covered by Street Sense and Curlin in the two races they won?

2007 Winners in Races for 3-Year Old Horses

Race	Distance (mi)	Winner
Kentucky Derby	$1\frac{1}{4}$	Street Sense
Preakness Stakes	$1\frac{3}{16}$	Curlin
Belmont Stakes	$1\frac{1}{2}$	Rags to Riches

MODULE 5   **LABSHEET** **5A**

Parallelograms A–D (Use with Question 19 on page 335.)

Directions For each parallelogram, label a pair of bases and draw and label the height. Next measure the length of a base and the height to the nearest tenth of a centimeter. Then find the area.

A.

B.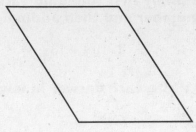

C.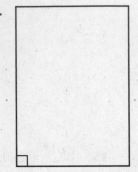

D.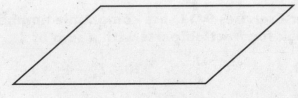

Parallelograms E–H (Use with Exercise 13 on page 341.)

Directions For each parallelogram, label a pair of bases and draw and label the height. Next measure the length of a base and the height to the nearest tenth of a centimeter. Then find the area.

E.

F.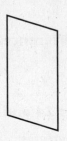

G.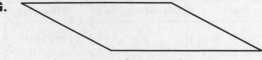

H.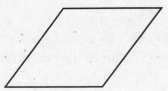

Math Thematics, Book 1
Student Workbook

MODULE 5   LABSHEET **5B**

Triangles A–D (Use with Question 26 on page 336.)

Directions For each triangle, label a base and draw and label the height. Next measure the length of the base and the height to the nearest tenth of a centimeter. Then find the area.

A.

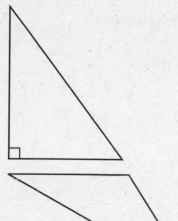

B.

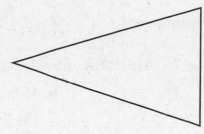

C.

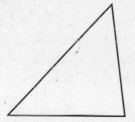

D.

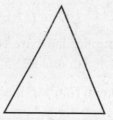

Triangles E–H (Use with Exercise 16 on page 341.)

Directions For each triangle, label a base and draw and label the height. Next measure the length of the base and the height to the nearest tenth of a centimeter. Then find the area.

E.

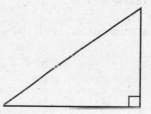

F.

G.

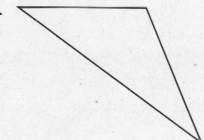

H.

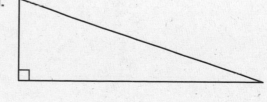

Math Thematics, Book 1

Practice and Applications

For use with Section 5

For use with Exploration 1

1. Estimate the area of each object in customary units.

    a. a door in your home

                                 b. a table in your home

2. Replace each __?__ with the number that makes the statement true.

    a. $126 \text{ yd}^2 = \underline{\ ?\ } \text{ ft}^2$ **b.** $36 \text{ ft}^2 = \underline{\ ?\ } \text{ yd}^2$ **c.** $108 \text{ in.}^2 = \underline{\ ?\ } \text{ ft}^2$

    d. $16 \text{ ft}^2 = \underline{\ ?\ } \text{ in.}^2$ **e.** $135 \text{ ft}^2 = \underline{\ ?\ } \text{ yd}^2$ **f.** $288 \text{ in.}^2 = \underline{\ ?\ } \text{ ft}^2$

For use with Exploration 2

3. Find the area of a parallelogram with the given dimensions.

    a. $b = 4.6$ cm   **b.** $b = 7$ mm   **c.** $b = 6\frac{3}{4}$ ft

       $h = 3.8$ cm $h = 12$ mm $h = 8$ ft

    d. $b = 20$ cm   **e.** $b = 11.5$ cm   **f.** $b = 24$ in.

       $h = 15$ cm $h = 8$ cm $h = 18$ in.

    g. 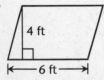   **h.** 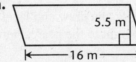   **i.**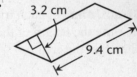

4. The dimensions of a rectangular lawn are 18 ft by 30 ft. Mr. Blane wants to put sod in the lawn. It costs $8.95 a square yard.

    a. Find the area of the lawn that Mr. Blane wants to sod.

    b. How much will the sod for the lawn cost?

(continued)

Name _____   Date _____

For use with Exploration 3

5. Find the area of each figure.

a.
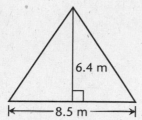
6.4 m
8.5 m

b.
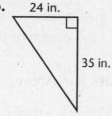
24 in.
35 in.

c.
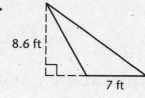
8.6 ft
7 ft

d.
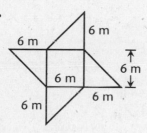
6 m
6 m
6 m
6 m
6 m
6 m
6 m

e.
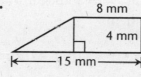
8 mm
4 mm
15 mm

f.
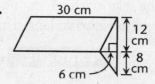
30 cm
12 cm
8 cm
6 cm

6. Write and solve an equation to find the missing dimension for each figure.

a.
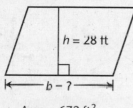
$h = 28$ ft
$b = ?$
Area = 672 ft^2

b.
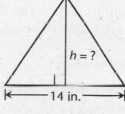
$h = ?$
14 in.
Area = 126 in.^{2}

c.
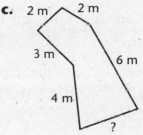
2 m   2 m
3 m   6 m
4 m
?
Perimeter = 22 m

7. The area of the rectangular family room in the Robin's home is 1440 ft^2. The width of the family room is 32 ft. What is the length of the room?

8. Find the unknown value in each equation.

    a. $28 + n = 57$ **b.** $6 \cdot x = 192$

Study Guide
For use with Section 5

The Taj Mahal   Area

GOAL   **LEARN HOW TO:** • measure area and convert between its customary units
• find the area of a parallelogram and a triangle
• find a missing dimension

AS YOU: • explore the size and design of the Taj Mahal

Exploration 1: Customary Units for Area

Area is the number of **square units** that cover a surface. To find
the relationships among square units, you can begin with the unit
relationships of length and square them.

Example

1 ft = 12 in.	1 yd = 3 ft	1 yd = 36 in.
$(1 \text{ ft})^2 = (12 \text{ in.})^2$	$(1 \text{ yd})^2 = (3 \text{ ft})^2$	$(1 \text{ yd})^2 = (36 \text{ in.})^2$
So, $1 \text{ ft}^2 = 144 \text{ in.}^2$	So, $1 \text{ yd}^2 = 9 \text{ ft}^2$	So, $1 \text{ yd}^2 = 1296 \text{ in.}^2$

Exploration 2: Area of a Parallelogram

Area can also be measured in metric units. 1 m = 100 cm,
so $(1 \text{ m})^2 = (100 \text{ cm})^2$ or $1 \text{ m}^2 = 10{,}000 \text{ cm}^2$.

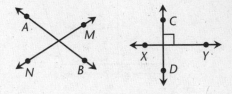

Lines or segments that meet at a point **intersect**. $\overleftrightarrow{AB}$
intersects $\overleftrightarrow{MN}$. Recall that lines that intersect at right angles
are perpendicular. $\overleftrightarrow{CD}$ is perpendicular to $\overleftrightarrow{XY}$.

The measures that determine the area of a parallelogram are
called the *base* and the *height*. When a segment is drawn from
one side perpendicular to the opposite parallel side, the length
of the segment is the **height** of the parallelogram and those
two parallel sides are the **bases** of the parallelogram.

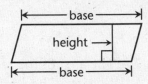

Example

Find the area of a parallelogram with height 4 cm and base 9 cm.

▩ Sample Response ▩

Area = length of base • height
    = 9 • 4
    = 36   So the area of the parallelogram is 36 cm².

Name _____ Date _____

Study Guide
For use with Section 5

Exploration 3: Area of a Triangle

Any side of a triangle can be its **base** (of length *b*). The **height** (*h*) of the triangle is the length of the segment from the vertex opposite the base drawn perpendicular to the base. You may have to extend the base to intersect with the height.

  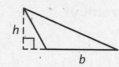   Area $= \frac{1}{2} \cdot b \cdot h$

Example

Find the area of a triangle with base 6.5 in. and height 4 in.

▪ Sample Response ▪

$A = \frac{1}{2} \cdot b \cdot h$

$= \frac{1}{2} \cdot 6.5 \cdot 4$

$= 3.25 \cdot 4$

$= 13$ So, the area of the triangle is 13 in.^{2}

Finding Unknown Values

Using an area formula, you can write and solve an equation to find a missing dimension.

Example

The area of a triangle is 56 ft^2. If the length of its base is 14 ft, find the height of the triangle.

▪ Sample Response ▪

$A = \frac{1}{2} \cdot b \cdot h$

$56 = \frac{1}{2} \cdot 14 \cdot h$ ← Substitute the known values into the formula.

$56 = 7 \cdot h$

$8 = h$ ← Divide both sides by 7.

So, the height of the triangle is 8 ft.

Study Guide: Practice & Application Exercises

For use with Section 5

Exploration 1

Estimate the area of each object in customary units and explain your method. Then measure the length and width and use the area formula to check your estimates.

1. the cover of your math textbook
2. the surface of your classroom desk

Replace each __?__ with the missing measurement.

3. 288 ft² = __?__ in.²
4. 48 in.² = __?__ ft²
5. 102 yd² = __?__ ft²

6. The wool rug in Nick's bedroom has an area of 11,520 in.² What is the rug's area in square feet?

Exploration 2

For Exercises 7–12, find the area of a parallelogram with the given dimensions.

7. $b = 14$ in., $h = 25$ in.
8. $b = 5\frac{1}{3}$ yd, $h = 18$ yd
9. $b = 4.6$ ft, $h = 3.2$ ft

10. $b = 7.1$ cm, $h = 3.2$ cm
11. $b = 6$ mm, $h = 9$ mm
12. $b = 8$ m, $h = 10.5$ m

13. Mr. Adams is building a rectangular dog enclosure. He plans to use the back wall of his house as one side of the enclosure and a total of 60 ft of fencing for the other three sides. What are the dimensions of the rectangular enclosure with the greatest area that he can build?

Exploration 3

Find the area of a triangle with the given dimensions.

14. $b = 23$ ft, $h = 16$ ft
15. $b = 8\frac{1}{4}$ in., $h = 24$ in.
16. $b = 16.3$ cm, $h = 4.8$ cm

For Exercises 17–19, write and solve an equation to find the missing dimension for each figure.

17.
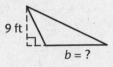
9 ft
$b = ?$
Area = 54 ft²

18.
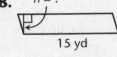
$h = ?$
15 yd
Area = 48 yd²

19.
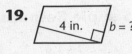
4 in.
$b = ?$
Area = 9.4 in.²

20. Plot the points $A(1, 2)$, $B(9, 2)$, and $C(1, 6)$ on a coordinate grid. Draw line segments connecting the points. Find the area of $\triangle ABC$.

Math Thematics, Book 1
Student Workbook

214

Name _____   Date _____

Ruler Models (Use with Questions 10 and 11 on page 348.)

Directions Complete each problem using the ruler given.

Problem 1 How many times does $\frac{1}{4}$ in. fit into 3 in.?

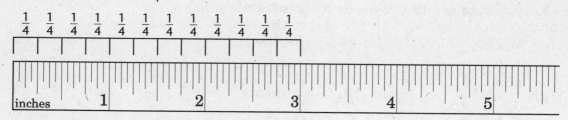

Use your answer to complete the division: $3 \div \frac{1}{4} =$ _____.

You can also find the answer by multiplying. Since there are _____ fourths in 1,

there are _____ • _____ = _____ fourths in 3.

Problem 2 How many times does $\frac{1}{8}$ in. fit into $1\frac{1}{4}$ in.?

Use your answer to complete the division: $1\frac{1}{4} \div$ _____ = _____.

You can also find out by multiplying. Since there are _____ eighths in 1,

there are _____ • _____ = _____ eighths in $1\frac{1}{4}$.

Problem 3 How many times does $\frac{3}{4}$ in. fit into $2\frac{1}{4}$ in.?

Use your answer to write and complete the division:

_____ ÷ _____ = _____ • _____ = _____

Name _____   Date _____

Practice and Applications
For use with Section 6

For use with Exploration 1

1. Find each quotient. Write each answer in lowest terms.

a. $1 \div \frac{1}{3}$ **b.** $8 \div \frac{1}{4}$ **c.** $4 \div \frac{2}{3}$

d. $4 \div \frac{1}{5}$ **e.** $14 \div \frac{7}{12}$ **f.** $6 \div \frac{3}{5}$

g. $9 \div \frac{3}{5}$ **h.** $12 \div \frac{3}{4}$ **i.** $10 \div \frac{5}{6}$

j. $8 \div \frac{4}{7}$ **k.** $4 \div \frac{2}{5}$ **l.** $20 \div \frac{10}{11}$

m. $15 \div \frac{1}{2}$ **n.** $16 \div \frac{4}{5}$ **o.** $20 \div \frac{5}{9}$

2. Find each quotient. Write each answer in lowest terms.

a. $2\frac{1}{5} \div \frac{1}{5}$ **b.** $8\frac{1}{2} \div \frac{5}{8}$ **c.** $2\frac{3}{4} \div \frac{1}{3}$

d. $5\frac{3}{5} \div \frac{9}{10}$ **e.** $3\frac{5}{8} \div \frac{1}{2}$ **f.** $3\frac{3}{4} \div \frac{1}{3}$

g. $1\frac{3}{5} \div \frac{1}{8}$ **h.** $6\frac{1}{2} \div \frac{3}{4}$ **i.** $3\frac{1}{4} \div \frac{1}{2}$

j. $7\frac{5}{6} \div \frac{1}{6}$ **k.** $4\frac{1}{5} \div \frac{2}{3}$ **l.** $6\frac{4}{7} \div \frac{1}{2}$

m. $8\frac{1}{6} \div \frac{4}{9}$ **n.** $7\frac{1}{2} \div \frac{2}{5}$ **o.** $10\frac{1}{9} \div \frac{1}{3}$

3. The art teacher has 50 oz of clay. He divides the clay into $\frac{3}{4}$ oz pieces for his classes.

  a. How many pieces of clay does he have for his classes?

  b. Is there any clay left over? If so, how much?

4. Carter wants to paint a banner of colored stripes. He cuts a piece of paper that is $3\frac{3}{5}$ m long.

  a. If he makes each stripe $\frac{3}{8}$ m long, how many different stripes can Carter make?

  b. Carter wants to have some room left to fold over the edges of the banner after each stripe is painted. Will he have some room to do this? If so, how much?

(continued)

Name _____ Date _____

Practice and Applications
For use with Section 6

For use with Exploration 2

5. Find each quotient. Write each answer in lowest terms.

a. $\dfrac{3}{4} \div \dfrac{3}{8}$ **b.** $\dfrac{18}{5} \div \dfrac{3}{8}$ **c.** $\dfrac{5}{12} \div \dfrac{3}{4}$

d. $7 \div 3\dfrac{1}{2}$ **e.** $\dfrac{9}{11} \div \dfrac{2}{3}$ **f.** $5\dfrac{2}{3} \div 1\dfrac{3}{5}$

g. $4\dfrac{2}{7} \div 2$ **h.** $3\dfrac{1}{4} \div 1\dfrac{1}{2}$ **i.** $\dfrac{13}{14} \div \dfrac{1}{7}$

j. $6\dfrac{1}{2} \div 1\dfrac{3}{4}$ **k.** $2\dfrac{8}{9} \div 1\dfrac{1}{3}$ **l.** $4\dfrac{2}{3} \div 2\dfrac{1}{3}$

m. $3\dfrac{1}{6} \div 1\dfrac{2}{3}$ **n.** $5\dfrac{1}{2} \div 3\dfrac{3}{4}$ **o.** $6\dfrac{1}{4} \div 2\dfrac{2}{5}$

p. $1\dfrac{3}{4} \div 1\dfrac{5}{7}$ **q.** $6 \div 3\dfrac{3}{4}$ **r.** $2\dfrac{1}{3} \div 1\dfrac{1}{2}$

s. $3\dfrac{1}{5} \div 2\dfrac{1}{4}$ **t.** $7\dfrac{1}{8} \div 1\dfrac{1}{2}$ **u.** $2\dfrac{1}{5} \div 3$

v. $4\dfrac{3}{8} \div 2$ **w.** $4\dfrac{4}{5} \div 2\dfrac{3}{4}$ **x.** $9\dfrac{1}{3} \div 1\dfrac{1}{6}$

6. Find each quotient where $n = \dfrac{2}{5}$.

a. $11 \div n$ **b.** $n \div \dfrac{3}{4}$ **c.** $n \div n$

d. $n \div 1\dfrac{1}{2}$ **e.** $6 \div n$ **f.** $2\dfrac{1}{5} \div n$

g. $4\dfrac{1}{3} \div n$ **h.** $9\dfrac{1}{2} \div n$ **i.** $n \div \dfrac{7}{9}$

j. $5 \div n$ **k.** $n \div 3\dfrac{1}{4}$ **l.** $3\dfrac{2}{3} \div n$

7. A pizza maker at a pizza parlor uses $1\dfrac{3}{4}$ c flour for each small pizza he makes. He uses $2\dfrac{1}{3}$ c flour for every large pizza he makes. He always makes the same number of small and large pizzas.

a. How much flour does he use for one small and one large pizza?

b. How many pizzas can he make from 26 c of flour? How many large? How many small?

c. Is there any flour left over?

Name _____ Date _____

 **Study Guide**
For use with Section 6

Designing a Border Division with Fractions

GOAL **LEARN HOW TO:** • divide whole numbers and mixed numbers by fractions
• divide by fractions and mixed numbers

AS YOU: • design a border for the cover of your math book

Exploration 1: Dividing by a Fraction

To divide by a fraction, you can multiply by its **reciprocal**.

> **Example**
>
> $12 \div \frac{1}{2} = 12 \cdot \frac{2}{1} = \frac{24}{1}$, or 24 $2\frac{3}{5} \div \frac{7}{10} = 2\frac{3}{5} \cdot \frac{10}{7} = \frac{13}{5} \cdot \frac{10}{7} = \frac{130}{35} = 3\frac{5}{7}$

Exploration 2: Dividing Fractions and Mixed Numbers

Using Number Sense in Division

When you divide a number by a smaller number, the quotient is greater than 1.

Divide $\frac{5}{6} \div \frac{1}{3}$.

Multiply by the reciprocal of the divisor.

$$\frac{5}{6} \div \frac{1}{3} = \frac{5}{6} \cdot \frac{3}{1}$$

$$= \frac{15}{6} \text{ or } 2\frac{1}{2}$$

The quotient is greater than 1. _____↑

When you divide a number by a larger number, the quotient is less than 1.

Divide $\frac{1}{3} \div \frac{5}{6}$.

Multiply by the reciprocal of the divisor.

$$\frac{1}{3} \div \frac{5}{6} = \frac{1}{3} \cdot \frac{6}{5}$$

$$= \frac{6}{15} \text{ or } \frac{2}{5}$$

The quotient is less than 1. _____↑

Dividing by a Mixed Number

When dividing a mixed number by a mixed number, first write each mixed number as a fraction. Then multiply by the reciprocal of the divisor.

> **Example**
>
> To divide $2\frac{5}{6} \div 5\frac{1}{2}$, follow these steps:
>
> **Step 1** Write each mixed number as a fraction. $2\frac{5}{6} \div 5\frac{1}{2} = \frac{17}{6} \div \frac{11}{2}$
>
> **Step 2** Multiply by the reciprocal of the divisor. $= \frac{17}{6} \cdot \frac{2}{11}$
>
> **Step 3** Reduce to lowest terms, if possible. $= \frac{34}{66}$, or $\frac{17}{33}$

Math Thematics, Book 1
218 Student Workbook

Name _____   Date _____

Study Guide: Practice & Application Exercises
For use with Section 6

Exploration 1

Write the reciprocal of each number.

1. 15

2. $6\frac{1}{3}$

3. $\frac{3}{5}$

4. $\frac{9}{2}$

For Exercises 5–12, find each quotient. Write each answer in lowest terms.

5. $6 \div \frac{2}{3}$

6. $16 \div \frac{3}{4}$

7. $20 \div \frac{4}{5}$

8. $18 \div \frac{3}{2}$

9. $2\frac{1}{3} \div \frac{7}{8}$

10. $5\frac{1}{2} \div \frac{3}{4}$

11. $3\frac{4}{7} \div \frac{1}{4}$

12. $1\frac{5}{6} \div \frac{5}{12}$

13. Mr. Tomkins wants to put a "No Trespassing" sign in the middle of every $\frac{1}{4}$ mi section of a $3\frac{1}{2}$ mi long fence on his farm. How many signs will he need?

14. A jogging trail is $\frac{5}{8}$ mi long. How many times must Rachel run the trail in order to run a total of 20 mi?

Exploration 2

For Exercises 15–18, find each quotient. Write each answer in lowest terms.

15. $\frac{3}{4} \div \frac{1}{8}$

16. $\frac{14}{35} \div \frac{2}{7}$

17. $3\frac{1}{3} \div 5\frac{1}{2}$

18. $6\frac{7}{8} \div 1\frac{2}{3}$

Find each quotient where $n = \frac{2}{3}$.

19. $n \div \frac{1}{2}$

20. $5 \div n$

21. $3\frac{7}{8} \div n$

22. $n \div n$

23. **Aerodynamics** The largest helicopter ever built has a rotor diameter of $219\frac{5}{6}$ ft, while the smallest helicopter ever built has a rotor diameter of just $14\frac{3}{4}$ ft. About how many times as great is the larger rotor diameter than the smaller one?

24. Paco has a board $4\frac{1}{2}$ ft long. He wants to cut it into pieces that are each $1\frac{1}{2}$ ft long.

   a. Draw a diagram showing where he should cut the board.

   b. How many pieces will he have?

   c. What quotient does your diagram model?

Name _____ Date _____

Practice and Applications

For use after Sections 1–6

For use with Section 1

1. Write the fractions in order from least to greatest.

   a. $\dfrac{74}{75}, \dfrac{12}{25}, \dfrac{1}{50}, \dfrac{99}{100}, \dfrac{1}{3}$

   b. $\dfrac{5}{6}, \dfrac{3}{5}, \dfrac{1}{8}, \dfrac{3}{4}, \dfrac{1}{9}$

2. Replace each ___?___ with >, <, or =.

   a. $\dfrac{4}{5}$ ___?___ $\dfrac{4}{15}$

   b. $\dfrac{7}{8}$ ___?___ $\dfrac{8}{9}$

   c. $\dfrac{2}{5}$ ___?___ $\dfrac{2}{3}$

   d. $\dfrac{8}{15}$ ___?___ $\dfrac{64}{120}$

   e. $\dfrac{11}{12}$ ___?___ $\dfrac{23}{27}$

   f. $\dfrac{19}{37}$ ___?___ $\dfrac{41}{95}$

For use with Section 2

3. Replace each ___?___ with the number that makes the statement true.

   a. 7 yd = ___?___ ft

   b. 15,840 yd = ___?___ ft

   c. $3\dfrac{2}{3}$ yd = ___?___ in.

   d. 57 in. = ___?___ ft

   e. $8\dfrac{1}{2}$ ft = ___?___ in.

   f. 10 ft = ___?___ yd

4. Add or subtract. Simplify when possible.

   a. 3 yd 2 ft
      + 1 yd 2 ft

   b. 3 ft 8 in.
      − 1 ft 10 in.

   c. 6 ft
      − 3 ft 3 in.

For use with Section 3

5. Find each sum or difference. Write each answer in lowest terms.

   a. $\dfrac{3}{8} + \dfrac{2}{5}$

   b. $\dfrac{7}{12} - \dfrac{3}{8}$

   c. $\dfrac{3}{5} + \dfrac{1}{2}$

   d. $\dfrac{7}{9} - \dfrac{2}{3}$

   e. $\dfrac{5}{6} + \dfrac{3}{4}$

   f. $\dfrac{8}{9} - \dfrac{1}{8}$

6. Find the value of each expression. Write each answer in lowest terms.

   a. $\dfrac{7}{8} - \dfrac{3}{4} + \dfrac{1}{2}$

   b. $\dfrac{2}{3} - \dfrac{1}{6} + \dfrac{1}{4}$

   c. $\dfrac{3}{5} + \dfrac{2}{3} + \dfrac{7}{10}$

7. Max ate $\dfrac{1}{3}$ of a tomato pie. Mitch ate $\dfrac{2}{9}$ of the pie. Mason ate $\dfrac{1}{6}$ of the pie. Did the three boys eat the whole pie? Explain.

(continued)

Name _____   Date _____

Practice and Applications
For use after Sections 1–6

For use with Section 4

8. Estimate each sum by first rounding each mixed number to the nearest whole number and then adding.

   a. $3\frac{7}{9} + 2\frac{1}{8}$ **b.** $4\frac{1}{6} + 1\frac{1}{4}$ **c.** $2\frac{5}{6} + 2\frac{11}{12}$

9. Find each sum. Write each answer in lowest terms.

   a. $5\frac{1}{6} + 2\frac{3}{8}$ **b.** $1\frac{4}{7} + 2\frac{2}{3}$ **c.** $3\frac{7}{12} + 1\frac{7}{8}$

10. Use mental math to find each difference.

   a. $8\frac{6}{7} - 3$ **b.** $4 - 1\frac{3}{8}$ **c.** $12\frac{3}{8} - 5\frac{1}{4}$

11. Find each sum or difference. Write each answer in lowest terms.

   a. $4\frac{1}{2} + 3\frac{5}{9}$ **b.** $8\frac{2}{3} - 1\frac{5}{9}$ **c.** $4\frac{2}{5} - 1\frac{3}{4}$

   d. $3\frac{1}{6} + 2\frac{7}{9}$ **e.** $4\frac{7}{8} - 2\frac{1}{2}$ **f.** $20 - 12\frac{3}{5}$

For use with Section 5

12. Find the area of each figure.

   a. 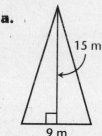   **b.** 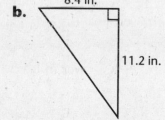   **c.**

13. Find the unknown value in each equation.

   a. $12 + y = 90$ **b.** $9 \cdot x = 234$

For use with Section 6

14. Find each quotient. Write each answer in lowest terms.

   a. $8 \div \frac{5}{6}$ **b.** $3\frac{1}{4} \div 1\frac{3}{4}$ **c.** $6 \div 1\frac{5}{9}$

   d. $9 \div \frac{3}{8}$ **e.** $2\frac{5}{6} \div \frac{1}{3}$ **f.** $2\frac{4}{9} \div \frac{2}{3}$

MODULE 5   **REVIEW AND ASSESSMENT LABSHEET**

Polygons (Use with Exercises 36 and 37 on page 361.)

Name _____   Problem _____

Teacher Assessment Scales

For use with Module 6

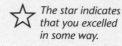
The star indicates
that you excelled
in some way.

 Problem Solving

❶ ❷ ❸ ❹ ❺

You did not understand the problem well enough to get started or you did not show any work.

You understood the problem well enough to make a plan and to work toward a solution.

You made a plan, you used it to solve the problem, and you verified your solution.

 Mathematical Language

❶ ❷ ❸ ❹ ❺

You did not use any mathematical vocabulary or symbols, or you did not use them correctly, or your use was not appropriate.

You used appropriate mathematical language, but the way it was used was not always correct or other terms and symbols were needed.

You used mathematical language that was correct and appropriate to make your meaning clear.

 Representations

❶ ❷ ❸ ❹ ❺

You did not use any representations such as equations, tables, graphs, or diagrams to help solve the problem or explain your solution.

You made appropriate representations to help solve the problem or help you explain your solution, but they were not always correct or other representations were needed.

You used appropriate and correct representations to solve the problem or explain your solution.

 Connections

❶ ❷ ❸ ❹ ❺

You attempted or solved the problem and then stopped.

You found patterns and used them to extend the solution to other cases, or you recognized that this problem relates to other problems, mathematical ideas, or applications.

You extended the ideas in the solution to the general case, or you showed how this problem relates to other problems, mathematical ideas, or applications.

Presentation

❶ ❷ ❸ ❹ ❺

The presentation of your solution and reasoning is unclear to others.

The presentation of your solution and reasoning is clear in most places, but others may have trouble understanding parts of it.

The presentation of your solution and reasoning is clear and can be understood by others.

Content Used: _____   **Computational Errors:**   Yes ☐ No ☐

Notes on Errors: _____

Name _____   Problem _____

Student Self-Assessment Scales

For use with Module 6

▬▬ *If your score is in the shaded area, explain why on the back of this sheet and stop.*

☆ *The star indicates that you excelled in some way.*

 Problem Solving

① ② ③ ④ ⑤ ☆

① I did not understand the problem well enough to get started or I did not show any work.

③ I understood the problem well enough to make a plan and to work toward a solution.

⑤ I made a plan, I used it to solve the problem, and I verified my solution.

 Mathematical Language

① ② ③ ④ ⑤ ☆

① I did not use any mathematical vocabulary or symbols, or I did not use them correctly, or my use was not appropriate.

③ I used appropriate mathematical language, but the way it was used was not always correct or other terms and symbols were needed.

⑤ I used mathematical language that was correct and appropriate to make my meaning clear.

 Representations

① ② ③ ④ ⑤ ☆

① I did not use any representations such as equations, tables, graphs, or diagrams to help solve the problem or explain my solution.

③ I made appropriate representations to help solve the problem or help me explain my solution, but they were not always correct or other representations were needed.

⑤ I used appropriate and correct representations to solve the problem or explain my solution.

 Connections

① ② ③ ④ ⑤ ☆

① I attempted or solved the problem and then stopped.

③ I found patterns and used them to extend the solution to other cases, or I recognized that this problem relates to other problems, mathematical ideas, or applications.

⑤ I extended the ideas in the solution to the general case, or I showed how this problem relates to other problems, mathematical ideas, or applications.

 Presentation

① ② ③ ④ ⑤ ☆

① The presentation of my solution and reasoning is unclear to others.

③ The presentation of my solution and reasoning is clear in most places, but others may have trouble understanding parts of it.

⑤ The presentation of my solution and reasoning is clear and can be understood by others.

MODULE 6   **LABSHEET** **1A**

Measuring a Mug (Use with Question 3 on page 366.)

Directions You will need pennies. Work with a partner to measure as directed below.

a. Measure and record the height of the mug (the distance between the two parallel segments) in pennies. _____ pennies

b. Using the squares next to the mug, measure and record the height of the mug in squares. _____ squares

Practice and Applications
For use with Section 1

For use with Exploration 1

1. Write each ratio in three ways.

    a. cases of apples to cases of oranges

    b. cases of pears to cases of grapes

    c. cases of bananas to cases of apples

    d. cases of grapes to cases of oranges

    e. cases of apples to cases of pears

    f. cases of oranges to cases of bananas

Fruit Supply Warehouse	
Fruit	Number of Cases
apples	248
oranges	160
pears	38
bananas	90
grapes	52

2. Draw a picture to show each ratio.

    a. Number of circles to number of squares is four to seven.

    b. Number of stars to number of diamonds is 3 : 8.

    c. Number of mugs to number of glasses is $\frac{5}{2}$.

    d. Number of bananas to number of apples is two to three.

    e. Number of triangles to number of rectangles is 6 : 1.

3. Tell whether the ratios are equivalent.

    a. 8 : 3 and 24 : 9   **b.** 5 : 8 and 30 : 40   **c.** 15 : 9 and 9 : 15

    d. $\frac{12}{15}$ and $\frac{4}{5}$ **e.** $\frac{45}{6}$ and $\frac{90}{12}$ **f.** $\frac{6}{9}$ and $\frac{10}{15}$

    g. 7 to 9 and 35 to 45   **h.** 3 to 8 and 13 to 8   **i.** 5 to 12 and 120 to 50

4. There are 8 pencils for every 5 students.

    a. Write the ratio of pencils to students in three ways.

    b. Write the ratio of students to pencils in three ways.

5. For each of the following, find the number *n* that makes the ratios equivalent.

    a. $\frac{2}{5} = \frac{n}{75}$ **b.** 13 : 39 and 26 : *n*   **c.** 21 to 14 and *n* to 2

    d. $\frac{8}{32} = \frac{9}{n}$ **e.** 20 : *n* and 5 : 20   **f.** $\frac{n}{18} = \frac{8}{24}$

Name _____ Date _____

Study Guide
For use with Section 1

Take a Closer Look   Exploring Ratios

GOAL **LEARN HOW TO:** • make comparisons using ratios
• recognize and write equivalent ratios

AS YOU: • explore how characters in movies can appear to be
shorter or taller than their actual heights

Exploration 1: Comparing Measures

Ratios

A **ratio** is a special type of comparison of two numbers or measures. A
ratio can be written in three ways: (1) using the word *to*, (2) with a colon,
and (3) as a fraction.

> **Example**
>
> The ratio comparing 6 to 12 can be written in these three ways:
>
> | using the word *to* | with a colon | as a fraction |
> |:---:|:---:|:---:|
> | 6 to 12 | 6 : 12 | $\frac{6}{12}$ |
>
> The order of the numbers in a ratio is important. 6 : 12 is not the same as 12 : 6.

Equivalent Ratios

Sometimes a ratio of two measures can be shown another way by
separating the two measures into the same number of groups.

> **Example**
>
> In 3rd period study hall, there are 20 boys and 12 girls. You can compare the
> number of boys to the number of girls by using the ratio 20 to 12,
>
> or by using 2 groups of each kind   or by using 4 groups of each kind.
>
> | BBBBB | ↔ | GGG |
> | BBBBB | ↔ | GGG |
>
> | BBBBBBBBBB | ↔ | GGGGGG | | BBBBB | ↔ | GGG |
> | BBBBBBBBBB | ↔ | GGGGGG | | BBBBB | ↔ | GGG |
>
>   10 boys   to   6 girls   5 boys   to   3 girls
>
> So, to compare the number of boys to the number of girls in the study hall, you can
> use the ratio 20 : 12, or the ratio 10 : 6, or the ratio 5 : 3.

Name _____   Date _____

Study Guide

For use with Section 1

Ratios that can be written as equivalent fractions are called **equivalent ratios**.

Example

The table shows that the ratio 20 : 12 is equivalent to the ratio 10 : 6.

Ratio	Fraction	Equivalent Fraction
20 : 12	$\frac{20}{12}$	$\frac{5}{3}$
10 : 6	$\frac{10}{6}$	$\frac{5}{3}$

You can use equivalent ratios to solve problems.

Example

Julia built a scale model of her house using a ratio of 1 in. to 8 in. That means that every 1 in. on the scale model represented 8 in. in real life.

A doorway in Julia's house is 96 in. tall in real life. Find n in the ratio $n : 96$ to make it equivalent to the ratio 1 : 8. How tall is the doorway in the scale model?

Sample Response

$\frac{1}{8} = \frac{n}{96}$ ← Set up ratios to represent the situation.

$\frac{1 \cdot 12}{8 \cdot 12} = \frac{n}{96}$ ← Multiply the numerator and the denominator by 12.

$\frac{12}{96} = \frac{n}{96}$ ← Simplify.

The doorway in the scale model is 12 in. tall.

Study Guide: Practice & Application Exercises

For use with Section 1

Exploration 1

1. a. In one study hall, there are 16 boys and 12 girls. In another study hall, there are 20 boys and 15 girls. What is the ratio of boys to girls in each study hall?

   b. Are the ratios you found in part (a) equivalent? Explain.

2. Physics An *inclined plane*, such as a *ramp*, is a simple machine that is designed to move an object. When a man rolls a heavy barrel up a ramp of length *l* to a height of *h*, the man exerts less force than he would if he were to lift the barrel straight up from the ground to the same height *h*. An inclined plane provides a mechanical advantage equal to the *ratio of the length of the plane to its height.*

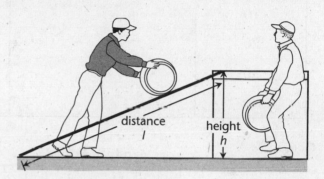

distance *l*

height *h*

   a. Suppose a man is rolling a barrel a distance of 5 ft along a ramp in order to raise the barrel to a height of 3 ft. Write the mechanical advantage of this inclined plane as a ratio in three different ways.

   b. Suppose the barrel was rolled 10 ft along a ramp to raise it to a height of 6 ft. Write this mechanical advantage as a ratio in three different ways.

   c. Are the ratios you wrote in parts (a) and (b) equivalent? Explain.

For Exercises 3–6, tell whether the ratios are equivalent.

3. $\frac{2}{3}$ and $\frac{4}{9}$ **4.** $\frac{4}{7}$ and $\frac{16}{28}$ **5.** $1:5$ and $15:3$ **6.** $2:9$ and and $8:36$

7. Probability When a coin is tossed, there are two possible outcomes, *heads* or *tails*. These outcomes are equally likely. Write the ratio that expresses the theoretical probability of getting *heads* in one toss of the coin.

8. Writing The triangles represent the inclines for two hills. Which hill do you think is harder to climb? Explain.

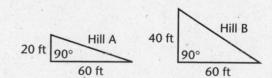

20 ft | 90° | Hill A | 60 ft

40 ft | 90° | Hill B | 60 ft

MODULE 6   **LABSHEET** 2A

Sandbag Brigade Data (Use with Exercise 18 on page 378.)

Directions Use your class's data to complete the table. Then plot the distance and time data on the grid below. Draw segments to connect the points in order from left to right.

Number of students	Length of the brigade (feet)	Time to pass the sandbag from end to end (seconds)
10		
20		
30		
40		

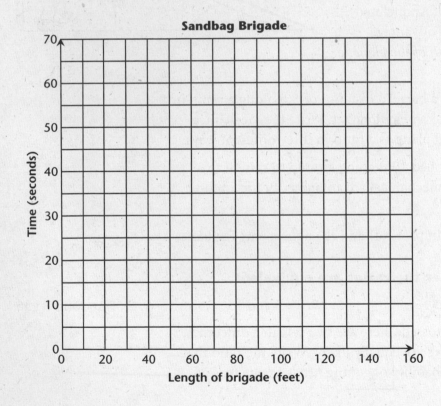

Sandbag Brigade

Name _____   Date _____

Practice and Applications

For use with Section 2

For use with Exploration 1

1. Tell whether each ratio is a rate.

    a. 60 words in 2 min

    c. 5 min for every 30 min

    e. 95 m in 4 sec

    g. 7 km for every 15 km

    i. 3 baskets in 5 free throws

    b. 6 ft in 1 sec

    d. 8 ft to 80 ft

    f. 12 pages in 3 min

    h. 8 gal per minute

2. Tell whether the rates are equivalent.

    a. $\dfrac{9 \text{ pages}}{5 \text{ min}}, \dfrac{90 \text{ pages}}{45 \text{ min}}$

    c. $6 for 8 lb, $36 for 48 lb

    b. $\dfrac{120 \text{ words}}{4 \text{ min}}, \dfrac{480 \text{ words}}{16 \text{ min}}$

    d. 65 mi on 12 gal, 6.5 mi on 6 gal

3. Find a unit rate for each rate.

    a. 15 pages in 5 min

    b. 3000 km in 4 days

    c. 92 mi on 4 gal

    d. 300 ft in 125 steps

    e. $50 for 8 books

    f. 20 ft in 3 min

4. Tell which is a better buy.

    a. $1.62 for 9 lb of onions or
       $2.25 for 15 lb of onions

    c. $2.88 for 24 oz of grape juice or
       $11.52 for 64 oz of grape juice

    b. $12.70 for 9 lb of peanuts or
       $10.90 for 8 lb of peanuts

    d. $2.10 for 6 apples or
       $5.25 for 15 apples

5. Copy and complete the table.

Number of miles	5	10	15	20	?
Time (minutes)	6	?	?	?	30

6. Kevin runs about 300 ft in 15 seconds.

    a. At this rate, how far does he run in 1 minute? in 10 minutes?

    b. Does it take Kevin more or less than 10 minutes to run 1 mile?
       Explain.

Study Guide
For use with Section 2

The Sandbag Brigade   Rates

GOAL   **LEARN HOW TO:** • use rates to make predictions
                              • find unit rates

AS YOU: • analyze data from your class's sandbag brigade

Exploration 1: Using Rates and Unit Rates

Rates

A **rate** is a ratio that compares two quantities measured in different units.
For instance, taking 20 min to read 2 pages is a rate. Rates may also be
expressed as equivalent ratios.

<table>
<tr><td colspan="3">Example</td></tr>
<tr>
<td>

The pairs of numbers in this table
form equivalent ratios.

$\dfrac{20 \text{ min}}{2 \text{ pages}} = \dfrac{30 \text{ min}}{3 \text{ pages}} = \cdots$

</td>
<td colspan="2">

Time (min)	Pages read
20	2
30	3
40	4
50	5

</td>
</tr>
</table>

Unit Rates

A rate that gives an amount per one unit is called a **unit rate.**

Example

To find a unit rate for the situation discussed in the previous example, you need to
find an equivalent ratio with a denominator of 1 page.

First write the given rate as a ratio. $\dfrac{20 \text{ min}}{2 \text{ pages}}$

Then set up a rate for the number of
minutes per one page. Use the variable $\dfrac{20 \text{ min}}{2 \text{ pages}} = \dfrac{x \text{ min}}{1 \text{ page}}$
x to represent the number of minutes.

To find the value of x, compare the   Since you must divide 2 pages by 2 to
denominators.   obtain 1 page, divide the numerator,
                                            20 min, by 2 also: $20 \div 2 = 10$.

                                            So, $x = 10$.

The unit rate for the situation is $\dfrac{10 \text{ min}}{1 \text{ page}}$, or 10 min/page (read "10 minutes per page").

Name _____ Date _____

Study Guide
For use with Section 2

Using Unit Rates to Make Predictions

When you know a unit rate, you can use that value to make predictions.

Example

Use the unit rate $\frac{10 \text{ min}}{1 \text{ page}}$ to predict how long it will take a person reading at this rate to read 15 pages.

■ Sample Response ■

Set up equivalent ratios. Use the variable y to represent the number of minutes.

$$\frac{10 \text{ min}}{1 \text{ page}} = \frac{y \text{ min}}{15 \text{ pages}}$$

To find the value of y, compare the denominators.

Since you must multiply 1 page by 15 to obtain 15 pages, multiply the numerator, 10 min, by 15: $10 \cdot 15 = 150$.

So, $y = 150$.

So, at a rate of 10 min/page, it would take 150 min (or 2 hr 30 min) to read 15 pages.

Study Guide: Practice & Application Exercises

For use with Section 2

Exploration 1

Tell whether the rates are equivalent ratios.

1. $\dfrac{2 \text{ nurses}}{5 \text{ patients}}, \dfrac{6 \text{ nurses}}{15 \text{ patients}}$

2. $\dfrac{275 \text{ students}}{11 \text{ teachers}}, \dfrac{50 \text{ students}}{2 \text{ teachers}}$

3. $\dfrac{86 \text{ baskets}}{100 \text{ attempts}}, \dfrac{40 \text{ baskets}}{50 \text{ attempts}}$

4. $2.80 for 14 pens, $5.60 for 30 pens

5. 450 words in 10 min, 135 words in 3 min

For Exercises 6–8, find a unit rate for each rate.

6. 234 km in 6 hr   **7.** $48.60 for 12 hr   **8.** 208 mi on 16 gal

9. Mr. Foy, a certified public accountant, can complete 54 basic tax forms in 18 hr.

   a. Find a unit rate in forms per hour.

   b. Working at this rate, how long would it take Mr. Foy to complete 144 such forms?

10. The length of runway recommended for a commercial passenger plane to land safely is related to its airspeed (in knots) when it touches down. A 727 jet touching down at 168 knots requires a 6000 ft runway.

   a. Find a unit rate.

   b. If an air traffic controller must direct a 727 jet to a 5000 ft runway, what is the maximum permissible touchdown speed its pilot can use?

11. As a salesperson Nat earns a *commission*. A commission is an amount of money based on the dollar amount of sales. The table shows Nat's commissions for the last 4 weeks.

Commission ($)	Sales ($)
100	1000
125	1250
75	750
150	1500

   a. Graph the data in the table. Draw segments connecting the points you graphed in order from left to right.

   b. Use your graph to predict the amount of commission Nat would earn if his sales were $900.

   c. Use a ruler to extend the line of your graph to predict Nat's commission for sales of $2000.

   d. Find a unit rate for the data. Use the unit rate to make the predictions asked for in parts (b) and (c). Compare the predictions you made using a unit rate with those you made using the graph.

Name _____ Date _____

Body Measurements Table

(Use with Questions 11–12 on page 385, Questions 21–22 on page 388,
Exercise 12 on page 391, and Exercise 18 on page 392.)

	Person number	Height (cm)	Tibia (cm)	Radius (cm)	Reach (cm)
Your group	1				
	2				
	3				
	4				
Two other groups	5				
	6				
	7				
	8				
	9				
	10				
	11				
	12				

Body Ratios Table

(Use with Question 12 on page 385, Questions 14–16 on page 386,
and Question 22 on page 388.)

Group member	$\dfrac{\text{Tibia}}{\text{Height}}$	$\dfrac{\text{Radius}}{\text{Height}}$	$\dfrac{\text{Reach}}{\text{Height}}$
1			
2			
3			
4			
Mean			
"Nice" fraction			

Math Thematics, Book 1

Reach Compared to Height Graph
(Use with Questions 18–20 and 22 on pages 387–388.)

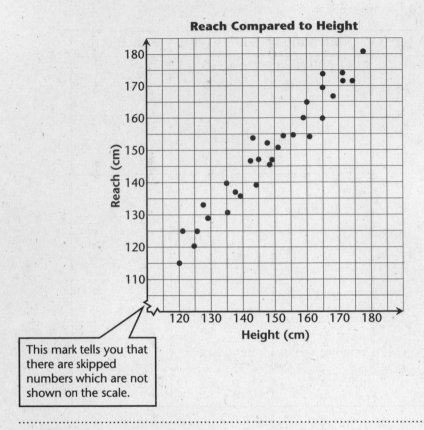

This mark tells you that there are skipped numbers which are not shown on the scale.

Points on the Line Table
(Use with Question 22 on page 388.)

Directions Use the fitted line on your scatter plot to complete the table.

Tibia (cm)				40	45
Height (cm)	130	140	150		
Tibia / Height					

Name _____   Date _____

Practice and Applications
For use with Section 3

For use with Exploration 1

1. Use the ratio 1 : 3 as an estimate for the body ratios *thumb length to hand length*, *hand length to shoulder width*, and *shoulder width to body length*. Suppose the length of Mark's hand is 12 cm.

   a. Estimate his thumb length.

   b. Estimate his shoulder width.

   c. Estimate his body length.

2. Write each ratio as a decimal rounded to the nearest hundredth.

   a. 5 : 7   **b.** 4 : 9   **c.** 2 : 11

   d. 8 : 15   **e.** 7 : 12   **f.** 3 : 16

For use with Exploration 2

3. Write a "nice" fraction for each ratio.

   a. 4 : 23   **b.** 0.69   **c.** $\dfrac{11}{45}$

   d. 0.8 to 1   **e.** 6 : 50   **f.** $\dfrac{9}{44}$

For Exercise 4, use the data in the table.

Child	A	B	C	D	E
Seated height (cm)	62	72	69	74	81
Standing height (cm)	98	115	112	114	128

4. a. Write each *seated height* to *standing height* ratio as a decimal rounded to the nearest thousandth.

   b. Find the mean of the ratios you found in part (a).

   c. Write a "nice" fraction that is close to the mean.

   d. Use your "nice" fraction to estimate the missing entries in the table.

Seated height (cm)	68	?	?	75
Standing height (cm)	?	120	124	?

(continued)

Practice and Applications
For use with Section 3

For use with Exploration 3

For Exercise 5, use the data in the table, which shows the seated height and standing height of five children.

Seated height (cm)	65	74	68	77	83
Standing height (cm)	102	120	108	122	132

5. a. Make a scatter plot that shows the relationship between the seated height and the standing height of each child in the table.

b. Draw a fitted line on your scatter plot.

c. Use your scatter plot to estimate the missing entries in the table.

Seated height (cm)	67	?	?	79
Standing height (cm)	?	112	126	?

6. a. Which fitted line would you use to make predictions about the shoulder width of a child or predictions about a child's height? Why?

Height Compared to Shoulder Width

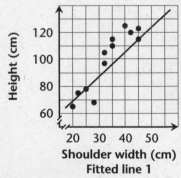

Fitted line 1

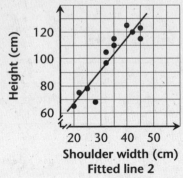

Fitted line 2

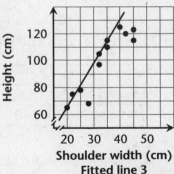

Fitted line 3

b. Use your choice from part (a) to predict the height of a child with a shoulder width of 35 cm.

Study Guide
For use with Section 3

Body Ratios   Using Ratios

GOAL   **LEARN HOW TO:** • use measurements to decide whether a ratio is reasonable
            • write a ratio as a decimal and find a ratio to describe data
            • use ratios and scatter plots to make predictions

   AS YOU: • analyze body ratio data

Exploration 1: Comparing Ratios

The decimal form of a ratio can help you to compare ratios. To find its
decimal form, first write the ratio as a fraction.

Example

Hildie, who is 5 ft 4 in. tall, found that the distance from the middle of her abdomen
to the floor is 39 in. Write the ratio *total height* : *distance from mid-abdomen to floor* as
a decimal, rounded to the nearest hundredth.

Sample Response

First, write the ratio as a fraction.
Convert 5 ft 4 in. to 64 in.

$$\frac{\text{total height}}{\text{distance from mid-abdomen to floor}} = \frac{64 \text{ in.}}{39 \text{ in.}}$$

Then divide the numerator by
the denominator.

$$\begin{array}{r} 1.641 \\ 39\overline{)64.000} \end{array}$$ ← Carry to 3 decimal places in order
                        to round to the nearest hundredth.

So, for Hildie, the ratio to the nearest hundredth is 1.64

Exploration 2: Estimating Ratios

"Nice" fractions such as $\frac{1}{2}, \frac{2}{3}$, and $\frac{3}{4}$ are often used to describe ratios in a

simple way, making further computation easier.

Example

Use Hildie's ratio to predict Rick's total height if the distance from his mid-abdomen
to the floor is 35 in.

Sample Response

Hildie's ratio of 1.64 is close to 1.6, which
equals a mixed number with a "nice" fraction.

$1.64 \approx 1\frac{6}{10} = \frac{3}{5}$, or $\frac{8}{5}$

Predict Rick's total height.

$\frac{8}{5} = \frac{?}{35}$ Observe: $\frac{8 \times 7}{5 \times 7} = \frac{56}{35}$

So, Rick's total height is about 56 in. or 4 ft 8 in.

Name _____   Date _____

Study Guide

For use with Section 3

Exploration 3: Predicting with a Graph

To display a relationship between two sets of data, you can use a graph called a **scatter plot**.

Example

The data for Hildie and nine other people are shown in this table. Construct a scatter plot of the data.

Mid-abdomen to floor (in.)	39	35	40	38	36	37	38	39	37	35
Total height (in.)	64	56	63	62	57	60	60	60	57	55

■ Sample Response ■

Prepare a coordinate grid with appropriate axes and scales.

If necessary, show a "break" in the axes to indicate that part of the graph is not shown. (This may only be done if the omitted part of the graph does not distort the appearance of the graphed data.) Different scales may be used on the two axes. Each scale must include the entire range of values for the portion of the data represented along its axis.

Draw a line segment on the graph that lies close to most of the points. Try to have about the same number of points on each side of the segment. The segment may pass through some of the points. This segment, drawn to fit the data, is called a **fitted line**.

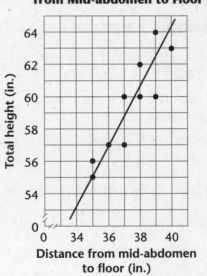

Total Height Compared to Distance from Mid-abdomen to Floor

You can use the fitted line on a scatter plot to make predictions. The fitted line on the graph above shows that:

• for a mid-abdomen-to-floor distance of 38.5 in., the corresponding total height is about 61.5 in.

• for a total height of 58 in., the corresponding mid-abdomen-to-floor distance is about 36.5 in.

You can extend a fitted line to make predictions for values that are outside the range of the graphed data. When extended, the fitted line above would show that for a mid-abdomen-to-floor distance of 41 in., the corresponding total height is about 66 in.

Math Thematics, Book 1
240 Student Workbook

Name _____ Date _____

Study Guide: Practice & Application Exercises

MODULE 6

For use with Section 3

Exploration 1

For Exercises 1–4, write each ratio as a decimal to the nearest hundredth.

1. 5 : 9   **2.** 7 : 11   **3.** 3 : 7   **4.** 6 : 13

5. Each of these rectangles has a height of 9 m.

a. For each rectangle, write the ratio *width to height* as a fraction and as a decimal.

b. What do the ratios in part (a) tell you about the general shape of the rectangles?

12 m   18 m   9 m   4.5 m

Exploration 2

Write a "nice" fraction for each ratio.

6. 4 : 19   **7.** 15 : 42   **8.** 0.42   **9.** 0.7 to 1

Use the ratio 1.6 : 1, or more simply, 1.6 as an estimate for the body ratio *shoulder to fingertip* : *elbow to fingertip*.

10. If Al's shoulder-to-fingertip distance is 28 in., estimate his elbow-to-fingertip distance.

11. If Bo's elbow-to-fingertip distance is 14 in., estimate her shoulder-to-fingertip distance.

Exploration 3

For Exercises 12–14, use the data at the right, which compares tree seedling growth to weekly rainfall.

12. On graph paper, make a scatter plot with a fitted line that shows the relationship between rainfall and tree seedling growth.

13. Predict the growth of the seedling during a week when it received 3.5 cm of rain.

14. Predict the amount of rainfall during a week when the seedling grew 9 cm. Explain.

Rainfall (cm)	Growth (cm)
0	3
0	1
1	4
1	2
2	6
2	7
3	5
3	10
4	8
4	14

Practice and Applications
For use with Section 4

For use with Exploration 1

1. Use cross products to tell whether the ratios are equivalent.

    a. $\dfrac{36}{45}$ and $\dfrac{12}{15}$

    b. $\dfrac{17}{24}$ and $\dfrac{51}{72}$

    c. $\dfrac{8}{9}$ and $\dfrac{36}{40}$

    d. $\dfrac{3}{8}$ and $\dfrac{15}{24}$

    e. $\dfrac{16}{30}$ and $\dfrac{56}{105}$

    f. $\dfrac{26}{15}$ and $\dfrac{65}{38}$

2. Find all the equivalent ratios in each list.

    a. $\dfrac{12}{30}, \dfrac{27}{72}, \dfrac{4.5}{12}, \dfrac{60}{150}, \dfrac{18}{48}$

    b. $\dfrac{5}{9}, \dfrac{14}{8.5}, \dfrac{40}{72}, \dfrac{7}{12}, \dfrac{56}{34}$

3. Find the missing term in each proportion.

    a. $\dfrac{4}{18} = \dfrac{10}{x}$

    b. $\dfrac{8}{14} = \dfrac{12}{n}$

    c. $\dfrac{9}{15} = \dfrac{b}{75}$

    d. $\dfrac{m}{8} = \dfrac{4.2}{2.4}$

    e. $\dfrac{24}{18} = \dfrac{38.4}{s}$

    f. $\dfrac{6}{y} = \dfrac{21}{52.5}$

    g. $14 : 5 = 70 : c$

    h. $a : 20 = 24 : 96$

    i. $9 : p = 45 : 18$

For use with Exploration 2

4. If appropriate, use a proportion to solve each problem. If it is not appropriate to use a proportion, explain why not.

    a. Six pairs of shorts cost $96. How much will nine pairs of shorts cost?

    b. Carmen used 5 ft of string to make 4 mobiles. How much string will she need to make 18 mobiles?

    c. Five art magazines cost $14.25. How much will eight art magazines cost?

    d. Four baseball caps cost $25. How many baseball caps can you buy with $43.75?

    e. Two helicopters were used for rescue missions from 8 A.M. to 11 A.M. How many helicopters will be used for rescue missions in a twelve hour period?

Name _____   Date _____

Study Guide
For use with Section 4

Jumping Ability   Proportions

GOAL   **LEARN HOW TO:** • use cross products to find equivalent ratios
• find the missing term in a proportion
• write a proportion to solve a problem
• use a proportion to make a prediction

AS YOU: • analyze real-world situations and make predictions

Exploration 1: Exploring Proportions

Recognizing Proportions

A **proportion** is an equation stating that $\frac{5}{10} = \frac{1}{2}$ is a proportion.
two ratios are equivalent. The **cross**
products in a proportion are equal. $10 \times 1 = 5 \times 2$

One method for determining if two ratios are equivalent is to compare
cross products.

> ### Example
>
> To tell whether $\frac{10}{15}$ and $\frac{32}{48}$ are equivalent ratios, compare the cross products.
>
> $15 \times 32 = 480$ and $10 \times 48 = 480$
>
> Since the cross products are equal, the ratios are equivalent.

Finding a Missing Term in a Proportion

You can use cross products to find the missing term in a proportion.

> ### Example
>
> Find the missing term in the proportion $\frac{18}{72} = \frac{x}{144}$.
>
> ### Sample Response
>
> Use cross products to write an equation. $72 \cdot x = 18 \cdot 144$
> $72 \cdot x = 2592$
> Then use division to find the value of the variable. $x = 2592 \div 72$
> $x = 36$
>
> Check by substituting 36 for x to verify that the ratios are equivalent.
>
> $\frac{18}{72} \overset{?}{=} \frac{36}{144}$
>
> $\frac{1}{4} = \frac{1}{4}$ ✔   So, since the ratios are equivalent when $x = 36$, the missing term of
> the proportion is 36.

Study Guide
For use with Section 4

Exploration 2: Using Proportions

Writing a Proportion

When you write a proportion to solve a problem, it is important to use the correct order.

Example

The North American jumping mouse has very long hind legs and is able to leap 9–15 ft. Suppose that leaping distance is related to body length for these mice. If a 6 in. jumping mouse can leap 9 ft, predict how far an 8 in. jumping mouse can leap.

Sample Response

Determine what measurements are being compared and what units are being used.

$$\frac{\text{leap distance (ft)}}{\text{body length (in.)}}$$

Decide what ratios to show in the proportion. Let x represent the missing term, which in this problem is the leaping distance of the bigger mouse.

$$\frac{\text{Ratio for}}{\text{smaller mouse}} = \frac{\text{Ratio for}}{\text{bigger mouse}}$$

$$\frac{9 \text{ ft}}{6 \text{ in.}} = \frac{x \text{ ft}}{8 \text{ in.}}$$

Use the cross products.

$$6 \cdot x = 9 \cdot 8$$
$$6 \cdot x = 72$$

Divide.

$$x = 72 \div 6$$
$$x = 12$$

Check by substituting 12 for x to verify that the ratios are equivalent.

$$\frac{9}{6} \stackrel{?}{=} \frac{12}{8}$$
$$\frac{3}{2} = \frac{3}{2} ✔$$

So, an 8 in. jumping mouse should leap about 12 ft.

Name _____   Date _____

Study Guide: Practice & Application Exercises

MODULE 6

For use with Section 4

Exploration 1

Find all the equivalent ratios in each list.

1. $\dfrac{24}{36}, \dfrac{8}{24}, \dfrac{30}{45}, \dfrac{25}{15}, \dfrac{30}{90}$

2. $\dfrac{250}{1000}, \dfrac{8}{2}, \dfrac{67.6}{16.9}, \dfrac{7.2}{28.8}, \dfrac{3.5}{14}$

Use cross products to tell whether the ratios are equivalent.

3. $\dfrac{2}{3}$ and $\dfrac{12}{18}$

4. $\dfrac{5.2}{13}$ and $\dfrac{7.6}{19}$

5. $\dfrac{5}{11}$ and $\dfrac{11}{23}$

Find the missing term in each proportion.

6. $\dfrac{3}{5} = \dfrac{18}{n}$

7. $4 : 6 = z : 42$

8. $\dfrac{x}{9} = \dfrac{35}{63}$

9. $16 : y = 12 : 9$

Exploration 2

10. Choose the two proportions that have been set up correctly for solving the problem.

    At Old Faithful in Yellowstone National Park, the best-known geyser in the United States, an eruption that rises to a height of 115 ft discharges about 10,000 gal of water. About how many gallons of water are discharged by an eruption that rises to a height of 165 ft?

    A. $\dfrac{10,000}{115} = \dfrac{x}{165}$

    B. $\dfrac{115}{10,000} = \dfrac{165}{x}$

    C. $\dfrac{115}{10,000} = \dfrac{x}{165}$

11. Choose the proportion that is *not* correctly set up for solving the problem.

    If 48 oz of a certain juice cost $1.89, what will 72 oz of the juice cost?

    A. $\dfrac{48}{1.89} = \dfrac{72}{x}$

    B. $\dfrac{48}{72} = \dfrac{1.89}{x}$

    C. $\dfrac{1.89}{72} = \dfrac{x}{48}$

    D. $\dfrac{1.89}{48} = \dfrac{x}{72}$

12. Because of large-scale commercial seal hunting operations, certain species of fur seals were brought close to extinction. In 1972, the United States prohibited the hunting of seals in its waters. The National Marine Fisheries Service monitors the fur seal population. Suppose that to estimate the number of fur seal pups in a rookery during one summer breeding season, workers tagged 2734 of the pups. Several weeks later, 600 pups in the same rookery were inspected and 163 of these were found to have already been tagged. Use a proportion to estimate the number of fur seals in the rookery.

13. Damon can shovel the snow off of 15 ft of sidewalk in 10 min. Assuming he can maintain this speed, how many feet of sidewalk can he shovel in 75 min?

MODULE 6   **LABSHEET** **5A**

Polygon Pairs (Use with Question 9 on page 409.)

Directions For each pair of polygons:

- Measure and record all of the side lengths in centimeters.

- Check the measures of corresponding angles by using a protractor or a tracing of one of the polygons.

- Tell whether the polygons in each pair are similar. For the similar polygons, tell which are congruent. If they are not similar, explain how you know.

a.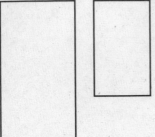

b.

c.

d.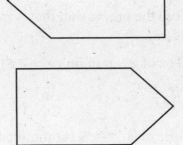

Name _____ Date _____

Practice and Applications
For use with Section 5

For use with Exploration 1

1. The figures in each pair are similar. List all the pairs of corresponding angles and corresponding sides.

   a.
   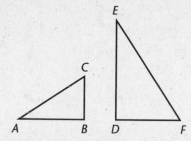

   b.
   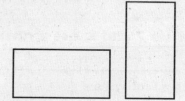

2. Tell whether the figures in each pair are similar or congruent. If they are not similar, explain how you know.

   a.
   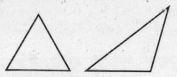

   b.

3. The figures in each pair are similar. Use proportions to find the missing lengths.

   a.
   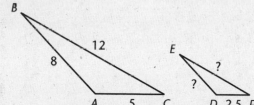

   b.
   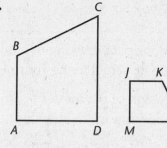

4. A rectangular tablecloth is similar to a rectangular table. The table is 8 ft long by 6 ft wide. How wide is the tablecloth if it is 10 ft long?

   (continued)

Name _____ Date _____

Practice and Applications
For use with Section 5

For use with Exploration 2

5. For each scale, find how long a measure of 4 in. on the drawing would be on the actual object.

    a. 1 in. : 8 ft   **b.** 2 in. : 5 ft   **c.** $\frac{1}{2}$ in. : $3\frac{1}{2}$ in.

6. a. In a floor plan drawing of a home, the living room is 3.4 in. wide. The actual living room is 51 ft wide. What is the scale?

    b. The length of the master bedroom is 37.5 ft. What is the length of the bedroom in the drawing?

    c. The width of the hallway in the drawing is 0.5 in. How wide is the actual hallway?

    d. In the drawing, the length of the house is 8 in. and the width is 5 in. What is the perimeter of the actual house?

For Exercises 7 and 8, use a ruler and the map below.

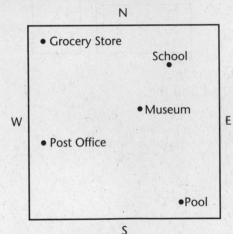

Scale: 1 in. = 9 mi

7. Use the scale on the map to estimate the actual distance between each pair of locations.

    a. the grocery store and the post office

    b. the post office and the school

    c. the school and the museum

8. Omar starts at the school and travels south, about 13 mi. Where does he end up?

Math Thematics, Book 1
Student Workbook

248

Name _____ Date _____

Study Guide
For use with Section 5

Very Similar   Geometry and Proportions

GOAL   **LEARN HOW TO:** • identify similar and congruent figures
• use proportions to find missing lengths
AS YOU: • compare pattern block shapes
• work with scale models and drawings

Exploration 1: Comparing Shapes

Similar and Congruent Figures

Similar figures have the same shape but not necessarily the same size.

The symbol ~ means "is similar to."

When two figures are similar, for each part of one figure there is a **corresponding part** on the other figure.

In similar figures, the corresponding angles have the same measure and the ratios of the lengths of the corresponding sides are equivalent. AB means the length of $\overline{AB}$.

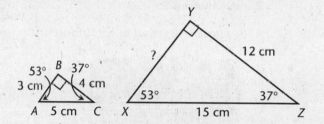

In the similar triangles above, $\angle A$ corresponds to $\angle X$ and $\overline{BC}$ corresponds to $\overline{YZ}$.

The measures of $\angle A$ and $\angle X$ are both 53°.

$$\frac{AB}{XY} = \frac{BC}{YZ} = \frac{AC}{XZ}$$

Congruent figures are a special type of similar figures that are the same shape and *the same size*.

Exploration 2: Models and Scale Drawings

You can use proportions to find missing lengths in similar figures.

> **Example**
>
> Find XY in the similar triangles above by writing a proportion.
>
> ▬ **Sample Response** ▬
>
> $\frac{AB}{XY} = \frac{AC}{XZ}$ → $\frac{3}{XY} = \frac{5}{15}$
>
> $5 \cdot XY = 3 \cdot 15$ ← The cross products are equal.
>
> $XY = 45 \div 5$ ← Divide both sides by 5.
>
> $XY = 9$ cm

Study Guide
For use with Section 5

Proportions and Scale

The ratio of a measurement on a drawing (or model) to the corresponding measurement on the actual object is called the **scale** of the drawing. You can use the scale of a drawing to write a proportion to find the measurements of an actual object.

Example

Suppose a drawing of a computer chip uses a scale of 1 in. : 0.5 mm.

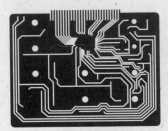

In the drawing, the width of the chip is 1.5 in. To find the width of the actual chip, use a proportion.

$$\frac{\text{drawing measure}}{\text{actual measure}} = \frac{\text{drawing measure}}{\text{actual measure}}$$

Let x represent the unknown dimension.

$$\frac{1 \text{ in.}}{0.5 \text{ mm}} = \frac{1.5 \text{ in.}}{x \text{ mm}}$$

$$1 \cdot x = 1.5 \cdot 0.5$$

$$x = 0.75$$

So, the width of the actual chip is 0.75 mm.

Study Guide: Practice & Application Exercises

For use with Section 5

Exploration 1

For Exercises 1 and 2, the figures in each pair are similar. Make a table showing all the pairs of corresponding angles and corresponding sides.

1.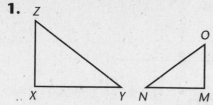

2.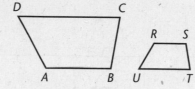

3. a. Of figures A, B, and C, which two triangles are similar?

   b. What is the ratio of the lengths of the corresponding sides?

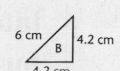

Exploration 2

4. The two quadrilaterals are similar. Find the missing lengths.

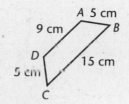

5. One of the four basic sizes of model railroads uses the HO scale, $\frac{1}{8}$ in. : 1 ft. Using this scale, what would be the actual length of a freight car if the length of its model is 5 in.?

6. Tyra's class is painting a mural. The finished mural will be 18 ft wide. They are making a scale model of the mural that is 3 ft wide.

   a. Find the scale used to create the model.

   b. The class wants to paint a tree in the center of the mural. They want the tree to be 5 ft tall and 2 ft wide in the actual mural. How many inches tall will the tree be in the model?

   c. If the class used 1.5 gal of paint for the model mural, about how many gallons will they need for the actual mural?

This page has been
intentionally left blank
for ease of use of
surrounding labsheets.

MODULE 6   LABSHEET **6A**

Olympic Sporting Events Survey (Use with the *Setting the Stage* and Question 1 on page 419, Question 22 on page 425, and Question 26 on page 427.)

Directions Tally the number of students who choose each Olympic sporting event as their first choice to attend. Then write the total in the *Total* column.

Sporting Event	Tally	Total
Aquatics		
Basketball		
Boxing		
Cycling		
Fencing		
Field hockey		
Gymnastics		
Kayak		
Rowing		
Soccer		
Softball		
Tae Kwon Do		
Track and Field		
Volleyball		
Weightlifting		

1. What sporting event was most popular?

2. Is there any event that more than half of the class chose to attend?

3. Use the survey results to find the ratio of each of the following to the number of students in the class.

   a. the number of students who chose track and field

   b. the number of students who chose gymnastics

   c. the number of students who chose soccer

   d. the number of students who chose a sporting event other than track and field, gymnastics, or soccer

This page has been intentionally left blank for ease of use of surrounding labsheets.

MODULE 6

Common Fraction, Decimal, and Percent Equivalents
(Use with Question 8 on page 421.)

Directions For each fraction in the tables, write an equivalent fraction in hundredths. Then write a percent and a decimal for each fraction.

Fraction	Equivalent Fraction in Hundredths	Percent	Decimal
$\frac{1}{2}$	$\frac{50}{100}$		
$\frac{2}{2}=1$			

Fraction	Equivalent Fraction in Hundredths	Percent	Decimal
$\frac{1}{4}$			
$\frac{2}{4}=\frac{1}{2}$			
$\frac{3}{4}$			
$\frac{4}{4}=1$			

Fraction	Equivalent Fraction in Hundredths	Percent	Decimal
$\frac{1}{10}$			
$\frac{2}{10}=\frac{1}{5}$			
$\frac{3}{10}$			
$\frac{4}{10}=\frac{2}{5}$			
$\frac{5}{10}=\frac{1}{2}$			
$\frac{6}{10}=\frac{3}{5}$			
$\frac{7}{10}$			
$\frac{8}{10}=\frac{4}{5}$			
$\frac{9}{10}$			
$\frac{10}{10}=1$			

Fraction	Equivalent Fraction in Hundredths	Percent	Decimal
$\frac{1}{5}$			
$\frac{2}{5}$			
$\frac{3}{5}$			
$\frac{4}{5}$			
$\frac{5}{5}=1$			

Name _____   Date _____

Grid for Thirds (Use with Question 15 on page 423.)

Directions Complete parts (a)–(i) to write $\frac{1}{3}$ and $\frac{2}{3}$ as percents.

  a. Divide the 100 squares into 3 groups with the same number of whole squares in each group.

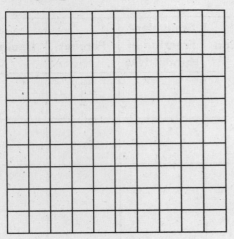

  b. How many squares are in each group? _____

  c. How many squares are left over? _____

  d. Shade one of the groups from part (a).

  e. Divide the left-over squares from part (a) into 3 equal-sized parts. Shade one of the parts.

  f. In all, how many squares and parts of squares did you shade on the grid? _____

  g. How many hundredths of the grid did you shade? _____

  h. Write a percent for $\frac{1}{3}$. _____

  i. Use your answer to part (h) to write a percent for $\frac{2}{3}$. _____ Explain how you found your answer.

Name _____   Date _____

Shading Percents (Use with Exercise 1 on page 429.)

Directions Shade the part of the grid represented by each percent.
Write a fraction and a decimal for the shaded part.

a. 1%

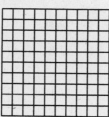

fraction _____

decimal _____

b. 10%

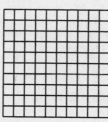

fraction _____

decimal _____

c. 25%

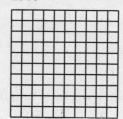

fraction _____

decimal _____

d. 46%

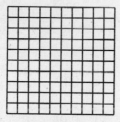

fraction _____

decimal _____

e. 67%

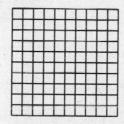

fraction _____

decimal _____

f. 100%

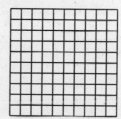

fraction _____

decimal _____

Math Thematics, Book 1
Student Workbook   **257**

Practice and Applications
For use with Section 6

For use with Exploration 1

1. Write each percent as a fraction and as a decimal.

    a. 40%   **b.** 98%   **c.** 65%

    d. 11%   **e.** 75%   **f.** 57%

2. Write each decimal as a fraction and as a percent.

    a. 0.35   **b.** 0.2   **c.** 0.17

    d. 0.08   **e.** 0.24   **f.** 0.75

3. Write each fraction as a decimal and as a percent.

    a. $\dfrac{7}{100}$ **b.** $\dfrac{4}{25}$ **c.** $\dfrac{3}{5}$

    d. $\dfrac{4}{10}$ **e.** $\dfrac{9}{20}$ **f.** $\dfrac{140}{200}$

4. Replace each ____?____ with >, <, or =.

    a. $\dfrac{2}{5}$ __?__ 0.25   **b.** 0.132 __?__ 13%   **c.** 0.04 __?__ 4%

    d. 48% __?__ $\dfrac{1}{2}$ **e.** 20% __?__ $\dfrac{2}{5}$ **f.** 0.04 __?__ 4%

5. At the University Bookstore, 2500 textbooks were sold last month. Math and science book sales totaled 1800 books. Write a fraction and a percent for the number of math and science books sold out of all the books sold.

For use with Exploration 2

6. Use a fraction in lowest terms to find each value.

    a. 20% of 65   **b.** 10% of 70   **c.** 25% of 56

    d. 30% of 400   **e.** 75% of 112   **f.** 5% of 500

    g. 70% of 30   **h.** 80% of 60   **i.** 90% of 40

(continued)

Practice and Applications

For use with Section 6

7. A jacket is discounted 25%. The original cost of the jacket is $50.

   a. Use mental math to find 10% of $50.

   b. Use mental math to find 20% of $50.

   c. Use mental math to find 5% of $50.

   d. Use parts (a)–(c) to find 25% of $50.

   e. Use mental math to find 50% of $50.

   f. Use mental math to find $\frac{1}{2}$ of 50% or 25% of $25. Which method do you think is easier for finding 25% of $50?

8. Estimate a percent for each fraction.

   a. $\frac{45}{85}$ **b.** $\frac{21}{80}$ **c.** $\frac{22}{52}$

   d. $\frac{11}{30}$ **e.** $\frac{63}{81}$ **f.** $\frac{48}{99}$

9. Lindsay scored in about 76% of the basketball games in which she played. She played in 21 games. Use a "nice" fraction to estimate the number of games in which she scored. Is your estimate higher or lower than the actual number of games? Why?

For use with Exploration 3

10. The table at the right shows the favorite pets of 35 students.

   a. Write a "nice" fraction for the number of students who chose each pet.

   b. Use the "nice" fractions from part (a) to estimate the percent of students who chose each pet.

   c. Use the percents from part (b) to estimate the angle measures for each pet in a circle graph.

   d. Use a compass or a round object to draw a circle and find its center. Use a protractor to mark off each angle you found in part (c). Label your graph with the name of each pet and write a title.

Pet	Number of Students
Dog	15
Cat	10
Bird	5
Fish	5

Name _____ Date _____

Playing the Percentages   Percents and Circle Graphs

GOAL   **LEARN HOW TO:** • write a percent
• relate fractions, decimals, and percents
• use a fraction to find a percent of a number
• use a fraction to estimate a percent of a number
• display data in a circle graph
• use percents and fractions to estimate angle measures

AS YOU: • compare samples that have different sizes
• examine data

Exploration 1: Writing Percents

Understanding Percent

Percent means *per hundred* or *out of 100*. In the 10×10
grid at the right, 40 of the 100 squares are shaded.
In percent form: 40% of the squares are shaded.
In decimal form: 0.40 (or 0.4) of the squares are shaded.

In fraction form $\frac{40}{100}$ $\left(\text{or } \frac{2}{5}\right)$ of the squares are shaded.

Using Percents or Decimals to Compare

To compare fractions using percents or decimals, first rewrite the fractions
so their denominators are 100.

Example

Which is greater, $\frac{7}{20}$ or $\frac{14}{200}$?

■ **Sample Response** ■

Find the equivalent fractions with denominators of 100 so that you can rewrite each
fraction as a percent. Then compare the percents.

$\frac{7}{20} = \frac{7 \cdot 5}{20 \cdot 5} = \frac{35}{100} = 0.35 = 35\%$ $\frac{14}{200} = \frac{14 \div 2}{200 \div 2} = \frac{7}{100} = 0.07 = 7\%$

Since 35% > 7%, therefore $\frac{7}{20} > \frac{14}{200}$.

Study Guide
For use with Section 6

Exploration 2: Using Fractions for Percents

When percents are equivalent to "nice" fractions, it is convenient to use the fractional form.

Find 40% of 175.

40% is equivalent to $\frac{40}{100}$ or $\frac{2}{5}$.

Then $\frac{2}{5} \cdot \overset{35}{\underset{1}{175}} = 70$

So, 40% of 175 is 70.

"Nice" fractions can also be used to estimate a percent of a number.

Use a "nice" fraction to estimate 73% of 120.

Note that 73% is close to 75%,

which is equivalent to $\frac{75}{100}$ or $\frac{3}{4}$.

Since $\frac{1}{4}$ of 120 is 30, $\frac{3}{4}$ of 120 is 90.

So, 73% of 120 is about 90.

Exploration 3: Circle Graphs

To show a part to whole relationship, data can be displayed in a **circle graph** or **pie chart**. The entire 360° circle represents the whole, or 100%. You can use percents to find angle measures for each section of the circle graph.

Example

Jenna, Leah, and Ryan worked together to rake their neighbor's yard. Jenna raked 36%, Leah raked 20%, and Ryan raked 44%. Create a circle graph to represent this data.

Sample Response

$\frac{36}{100}, \frac{20}{100}, \frac{44}{100}$ ← Write each percent as a fraction over 100.

$\frac{36}{100} = \frac{x}{360}$; $x = 129.6°$

$\frac{20}{100} = \frac{x}{360}$; $x = 72°$ ← Use a proportion to find each angle measure in a circle graph.

$\frac{44}{100} = \frac{x}{360}$; $x = 158.4°$

Leaves Raked

← Use a compass to draw a circle and find its center. Then use a protractor to mark off each angle measure you found. Label your graph and write a title.

Name _____ Date _____

Study Guide: Practice & Application Exercises

MODULE 6

For use with Section 6

Exploration 1

Write each percent as a fraction and as a decimal.

1. 70%   **2.** 38%   **3.** 8%   **4.** 15%

Write each fraction as a decimal and as a percent.

5. $\frac{7}{100}$ **6.** $\frac{11}{25}$ **7.** $\frac{100}{400}$ **8.** $\frac{12}{100}$

Exploration 2

For Exercises 9–12, use a fraction in lowest terms to find each value.

9. 50% of 359   **10.** 20% of 295   **11.** 60% of 1000   **12.** 5% of 460

13. The tuition for the first year at the college that Adelle Simpson is planning to attend is $12,000. The college is offering 25% of the tuition in financial aid. What is the remaining amount of the tuition that the Simpson family must pay?

14. Jorge had a total of 25 math tests for the year. He achieved an honors grade in 76% of them. Use a "nice" fraction to estimate the number of math tests in which Jorge achieved an honors grade. Is your estimate higher or lower than the actual number of tests? Explain.

Estimate a percent for each fraction.

15. $\frac{23}{49}$ **16.** $\frac{61}{80}$ **17.** $\frac{32}{91}$ **18.** $\frac{15}{74}$

Exploration 3

19. a. The table at right is based on a survey of Mr. Green's 6th grade class. Use the data to construct a circle graph.

b. What percent of the students in Mr. Green's class spent less than 6 hours on homework each week?

c. What is the angle measure of the section of the graph that represents the number of students who spent more than 8 hours a week on homework?

Hours Spent on Homework Each Week	Number of Students
0–2 hours	6
3–5 hours	10
6–8 hours	2
More than 8 hours	2
Total Students	**20**

Name _____ Date _____

Practice and Applications

For use after Sections 1–6

For use with Section 1

1. Write each ratio three ways.

   a. number of circles to number of squares

   b. number of diamonds to number of triangles

2. Tell whether the ratios are equivalent.

   a. 7 : 5 and 49 : 35
   b. $\frac{26}{32}$ and $\frac{65}{80}$
   c. 15 to 18 and 5 to 9

3. There are 3 soccer balls for every 4 players on the soccer team. What is the ratio of players to balls? Write the ratio three ways.

For use with Section 2

4. Find a unit rate for each rate.

   a. 1125 mi in 5 days
   b. $144 for 6 art books
   c. 128 km on 4 gal

5. Tell which is a better buy.

   a. $1.40 for 5 oranges or $1.84 for 8 oranges

   b. $2.40 for 16 oz of cherry juice or $3.84 for 24 oz of cherry juice

6. Cindy can read 48 pages in 24 minutes. At this rate, how many pages can Cindy read in one half hour? in two hours?

For use with Section 3

7. Write each ratio as a decimal rounded to the nearest hundredth.

   a. 3 : 7
   b. 2 : 9
   c. 7 : 11

   d. 16 : 19
   e. 4 : 15
   f. 5 : 12

8. Write a "nice" fraction for each ratio.

   a. 24 : 31
   b. 0.29
   c. $\frac{12}{52}$

(continued)

Practice and Applications

For use after Sections 1–6

For use with Section 4

9. Find the missing term in each proportion.

a. $\dfrac{8}{15} = \dfrac{28}{x}$

b. $\dfrac{7}{n} = \dfrac{112}{384}$

c. $\dfrac{12}{76} = \dfrac{b}{171}$

For use with Section 5

10. The figures in each pair are similar. Use proportions to find the missing lengths.

a.

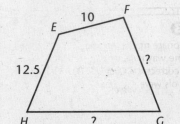

b.

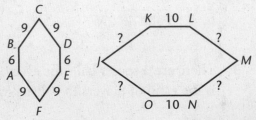

11. For each scale, find how long a measure of 3 in. on the drawing would be on the actual object.

a. 1 in. : 15 ft

b. 2 in. : 7 ft

c. $\dfrac{1}{2}$ in. : $5\dfrac{1}{2}$ yd

For use with Section 6

12. Write each fraction as a decimal and as a percent.

a. $\dfrac{7}{25}$

b. $\dfrac{2}{5}$

c. $\dfrac{11}{20}$

13. Use a fraction in lowest terms to find each value.

a. 75% of 80

b. 40% of 55

c. 60% of 90

14. Estimate a percent for each fraction.

a. $\dfrac{38}{79}$

b. $\dfrac{1}{9}$

c. $\dfrac{41}{52}$

15. Find the angle measure of the section of a circle graph to represent each percent.

a. 50%

b. 20%

c. 75%

Name _____ Problem _____

Teacher Assessment Scales

For use with Module 7

 ☆ *The star indicates that you excelled in some way.*

 ## Problem Solving

❶   ❷   ❸   ❹   ❺   ☆→

❶ You did not understand the problem well enough to get started or you did not show any work.

❸ You understood the problem well enough to make a plan and to work toward a solution.

❺ You made a plan, you used it to solve the problem, and you verified your solution.

 ## Mathematical Language

❶   ❷   ❸   ❹   ❺   ☆→

❶ You did not use any mathematical vocabulary or symbols, or you did not use them correctly, or your use was not appropriate.

❸ You used appropriate mathematical language, but the way it was used was not always correct or other terms and symbols were needed.

❺ You used mathematical language that was correct and appropriate to make your meaning clear.

 ## Representations

❶   ❷   ❸   ❹   ❺   ☆→

❶ You did not use any representations such as equations, tables, graphs, or diagrams to help solve the problem or explain your solution.

❸ You made appropriate representations to help solve the problem or help you explain your solution, but they were not always correct or other representations were needed.

❺ You used appropriate and correct representations to solve the problem or explain your solution.

 ## Connections

❶   ❷   ❸   ❹   ❺   ☆→

❶ You attempted or solved the problem and then stopped.

❸ You found patterns and used them to extend the solution to other cases, or you recognized that this problem relates to other problems, mathematical ideas, or applications.

❺ You extended the ideas in the solution to the general case, or you showed how this problem relates to other problems, mathematical ideas, or applications.

Presentation

❶   ❷   ❸   ❹   ❺   ☆→

❶ The presentation of your solution and reasoning is unclear to others.

❸ The presentation of your solution and reasoning is clear in most places, but others may have trouble understanding parts of it.

❺ The presentation of your solution and reasoning is clear and can be understood by others.

Content Used: _____

Computational Errors: Yes ☐   No ☐

Notes on Errors: _____

_____

Name _____   Problem _____

▬ *If your score is in the shaded area, explain why on the back of this sheet and stop.*

☆ *The star indicates that you excelled in some way.*

 Problem Solving

① ② ③ ④ ⑤

I did not understand the problem well enough to get started or I did not show any work.

I understood the problem well enough to make a plan and to work toward a solution.

I made a plan, I used it to solve the problem, and I verified my solution.

 Mathematical Language

① ② ③ ④ ⑤

I did not use any mathematical vocabulary or symbols, or I did not use them correctly, or my use was not appropriate.

I used appropriate mathematical language, but the way it was used was not always correct or other terms and symbols were needed.

I used mathematical language that was correct and appropriate to make my meaning clear.

 Representations

① ② ③ ④ ⑤

I did not use any representations such as equations, tables, graphs, or diagrams to help solve the problem or explain my solution.

I made appropriate representations to help solve the problem or help me explain my solution, but they were not always correct or other representations were needed.

I used appropriate and correct representations to solve the problem or explain my solution.

 Connections

① ② ③ ④ ⑤

I attempted or solved the problem and then stopped.

I found patterns and used them to extend the solution to other cases, or I recognized that this problem relates to other problems, mathematical ideas, or applications.

I extended the ideas in the solution to the general case, or I showed how this problem relates to other problems, mathematical ideas, or applications.

 Presentation

① ② ③ ④ ⑤

The presentation of my solution and reasoning is unclear to others.

The presentation of my solution and reasoning is clear in most places, but others may have trouble understanding parts of it.

The presentation of my solution and reasoning is clear and can be understood by others.

MODULE 7   **LABSHEET** **1A**

Net 1 (Use with Questions 4, 5, 7, and 8 on pages 441–442 and the *Setting the Stage* on page 452.)

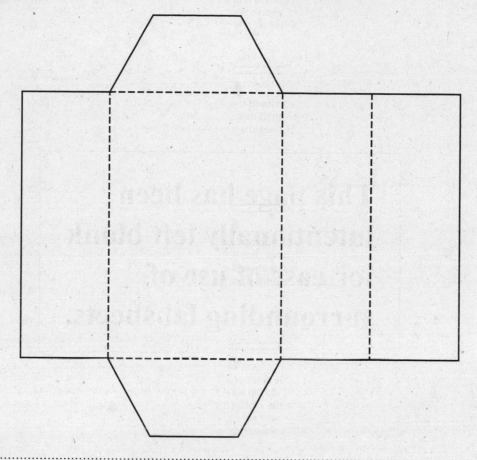

Net 2 (Use with Questions 4, 7, and 8 on pages 441–442.)

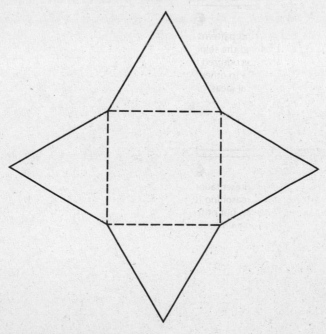

This page has been
intentionally left blank
for ease of use of
surrounding labsheets.

MODULE 7   **LABSHEET** **1B**

Net 3 (Use with Questions 15–17 on page 445.)

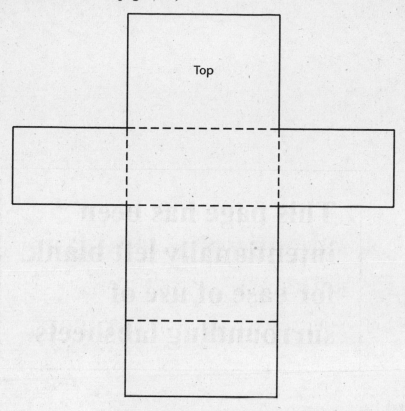

Net 4 (Use with Questions 19 and 20 on page 446.)

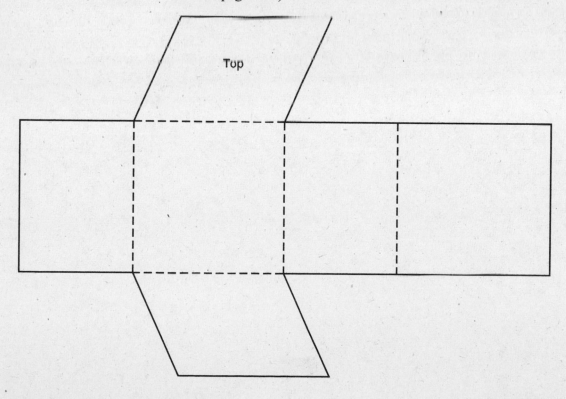

This page has been
intentionally left blank
for ease of use of
surrounding labsheets.

Name _____   Date _____

Practice and Applications
For use with Section 1

For use with Exploration 1

1. For each net, tell whether the polyhedron it will form is a prism. If it is, tell what shape the bases are and name the prism if you can.

a.
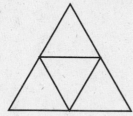

b.
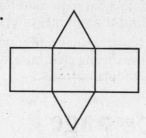

c.
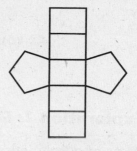

2. A hexahedron is a polyhedron that has 6 faces and 12 edges. How many vertices does a hexahedron have?

3. Use the methods you learned in this section to draw a hexagonal prism.

For use with Exploration 2

4. Find the volume of each prism.

a.
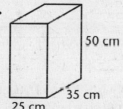
50 cm
35 cm
25 cm

b.
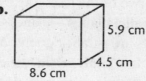
5.9 cm
4.5 cm
8.6 cm

c.
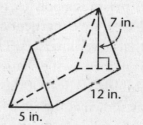
7 in.
12 in.
5 in.

5. Replace each ___?___ with the missing measurement for a prism with a base area B, height h, and volume V.

a. $B = 26$ ft^2
   $h = $ ___?___
   $V = 104$ ft^3

b. $B = $ ___?___
   $h = 19$ cm
   $V = 798$ cm^3

c. $B = 122$ mm^2
   $h = 15$ mm
   $V = $ ___?___

6. A box that is 9 in. long, 5 in. wide, and 3 in. high is shaped like a rectangular prism. Will it hold the liquid contents of a cube with side length of 5 in.? Explain.

Name _____ Date _____

Study Guide
For use with Section 1

Race to the Sky   Three-Dimensional Geometry

GOAL   **LEARN HOW TO:** • recognize prisms
• draw prisms
• fold a flat pattern to form a polyhedron
• find the volumes of prisms

AS YOU: • develop spatial visualization skills
• build prisms using centimeter cubes
• fold nets to form prisms

Exploration 1: Figures in Space

Parts of a Polyhedron

A **polyhedron** is a three-dimensional object made up of flat
surfaces, or **faces**, shaped like polygons. Pairs of faces meet
in segments called **edges**. Edges meet in points called **vertices**.
The plural of polyhedron is **polyhedra**.

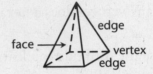

This polyhedron has 5 faces,
8 edges, and 5 vertices.

Prisms

A **prism** is a polyhedron in which two of the faces, the
bases, are congruent and lie in **parallel planes**—planes
that never intersect. The other faces are parallelograms. A prism
is named by the shape of its bases. In a **right prism**, the edges
joining vertices of the two bases are perpendicular to the bases,
as shown at the right. In **oblique prisms**, those edges are not
perpendicular to the bases and the prisms are slanted when
they sit on one of the bases.

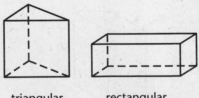

triangular   rectangular
prism   prism

Drawing and Constructing Polyhedra

One way to draw a prism is to draw the bases first and then connect the
corresponding vertices. Finally, decide which lines would be hidden from
view, and change them to dashed lines.

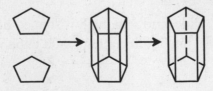

Math Thematics, Book 1
Student Workbook

272

Name _____ Date _____

Study Guide

For use with Section 1

Using Nets

A **net** is a flat pattern that can be cut out and folded to form a three-dimensional object. After copying the first figure at the right onto a sheet of paper, you would cut along each solid line, fold the paper along each dashed line, and then tape the edges together to form the triangular prism shown.

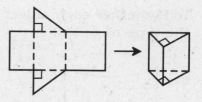

Exploration 2: Volumes of Prisms

Volume is the number of **cubic units** contained within a three-dimensional object. Examples of cubic units are **cubic centimeters** or cubic feet.

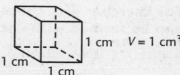

The height of a prism is the perpendicular distance between its bases. You can find the volume of a prism built with centimeter cubes using its height and base plan, which is found by tracing the base of the prism. To find the volume, multiply the height of the prism by the number of centimeter cubes shown in the base plan. For example, a prism with a height of 5 cm and a base plan made of 4 centimeter cubes has a volume of 20 cm^3.

To find the volume (V) of any prism, you can multiply the area of a base (B) of the prism by the height (h) of the prism, or $V = B \cdot h$.

Example

A triangular prism has a height of $13\frac{1}{2}$ ft. If the triangular bases have a base length of 18 ft and a height of 9 ft, what is the volume of the prism?

Sample Response

$V = B \cdot h$ ← The base of the prism is a triangle. Use $\frac{1}{2} \cdot b \cdot h$ to find its area.

$= \left(\frac{1}{2} \cdot 18 \cdot 9 \right) \cdot 13\frac{1}{2}$ ← For the triangular base, $b = 18$ and $h = 9$.

$= 1093\frac{1}{2}$

So, the volume of the prism is $1093\frac{1}{2}$ ft^3.

Study Guide: Practice & Application Exercises
For use with Section 1

Exploration 1

Tell whether each object is shaped like a prism. If it is, name the type of prism.

1.
2.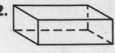
3.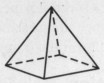

For Exercises 4–6, choose the letter of the polyhedron that can be formed with each net.

4.
5.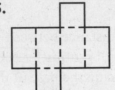
6.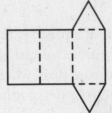

A.   B.   C.   D.

7. Which of polyhedra A, B, C, and D in Exercises 4–6 above are prisms? For those polyhedra that are not prisms, tell why they are not.

8. A cuboctahedron has 14 faces and 24 edges. How many vertices does a cuboctahedron have?

9. An icosahedron has 20 faces and 12 vertices. How many edges does an icosahedron have?

10. A dodecahedron has 30 edges and 20 vertices. How many faces does a dodecahedron have?

11. Use the methods you learned in this section to draw a triangular prism.

(continued)

Study Guide: Practice & Application Exercises
For use with Section 1

Exploration 2

Find the volume of each prism built with centimeter cubes.

12.   **13.** 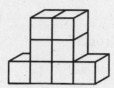   **14.**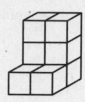

Find the volume of the prism you can build with centimeter cubes using each base plan and indicated height.

15. 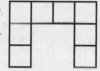   **16.** 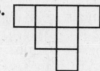   **17.**

height = 3 cm   height = 5 cm   height = 4 cm

Find the volume of each right prism.

18. 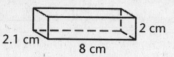   **19.** 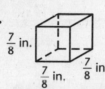   **20.**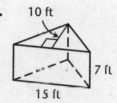

2.1 cm   2 cm
8 cm

$\frac{7}{8}$ in. $\frac{7}{8}$ in. $\frac{7}{8}$ in.

10 ft   7 ft   15 ft

For Exercises 21–23, replace each __?__ with the missing measurement for a prism with base of area *B*, height *h*, and volume *V*.

21. $B = 35$ in.^{2}

$h = 4$ in.

$V = $ __?__

22. $B = $ __?__

$h = 6$ ft

$V = 301.2$ ft^3

23. $B = 14.8$ cm^2

$h = $ __?__

$V = 79.92$ cm^3

24. An Olympic-sized swimming pool measures 50 m long, 25 m wide, and 2 m deep. If 1 cubic meter holds 1000 liters of water, how many liters of water can an Olympic-sized swimming pool hold?

25. A cardboard shipping box is 100 cm tall and has a volume of 42,000 cm^3. List three possible pairs of lengths and widths for its base plan.

Name ______________________ Date ______________

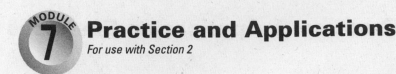

MODULE 7

Practice and Applications

For use with Section 2

For use with Exploration 1

1. Choose the best customary unit (*ounce*, *pound*, or *ton*) to express the weight of each object.

a. pen **b.** couch **c.** dog

d. bus **e.** shovel **f.** box of cereal

g. bicycle **h.** soccer ball **i.** cup of milk

j. table **k.** airplane **l.** mouse

2. Replace each __?__ with the missing number.

a. $5\frac{1}{2}$ lb = __?__ oz **b.** 6 oz = __?__ lb **c.** 11 tons = __?__ lb

d. 9000 lb = __?__ tons **e.** 800 lb = __?__ ton **f.** 80 oz = __?__ lb

g. 136 oz = __?__ lb **h.** 4 tons = __?__ oz **i.** $2\frac{3}{4}$ lb = __?__ oz

j. $4\frac{1}{2}$ lb = __?__ oz **k.** 2.8 tons = __?__ lb **l.** $1\frac{5}{8}$ lb = __?__ oz

3. Replace each __?__ with >, <, or =.

a. 4.5 lb __?__ 36 oz **b.** 58 oz __?__ 4 lb **c.** 72 oz __?__ 5 lb

d. $3\frac{3}{4}$ lb __?__ 60 oz **e.** 64,000 oz __?__ 2 tons **f.** $5\frac{1}{4}$ lb __?__ 95 oz

g. 1500 lb __?__ $\frac{3}{4}$ ton **h.** 5000 lb __?__ 3 tons **i.** 90 oz __?__ 6 lb

j. 1 ton __?__ 10,000 oz **k.** 3.2 tons __?__ 6500 lb **l.** $2\frac{3}{8}$ lb __?__ 38 oz

4. The weight limit for a delivery truck is 3 tons. The truck loads items from four locations for delivery. The first load weighs 1.2 tons. The second load weighs $\frac{3}{4}$ ton. The third load weighs 500 lb and the last load weighs 0.4 tons.

a. What is the total load?

b. How much more weight can the truck support before exceeding its limit?

Name _____ Date _____

 Study Guide
For use with Section 2

The Great Pyramid Weight in the Customary System

GOAL **LEARN HOW TO:** • measure weight in customary units
• convert customary units of weight
AS YOU: • explore the construction of the Great Pyramid

Exploration 1: Customary Units of Weight

Pyramids

A **pyramid** is a polyhedron that has one base, which is a polygon.
All the other faces of a pyramid are triangles that meet at a single vertex.

A pyramid is named by the shape of its base. The pyramid shown at the
right is a pentagonal pyramid since its base is a pentagon.

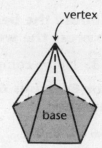

Customary Units of Weight

Some commonly used customary units of weight are:

• **ounce (oz)**, about the weight of 12 pennies

• **pound (lb)**, about the weight of 4 sticks of butter

• **ton**, about the weight of a compact car

The customary units of weight are related in the following ways.

1 lb = 16 oz   1 ton = 2000 lb

As with other units of measure, you multiply to convert to a smaller unit
and divide to convert to a larger unit.

Example

A car transport is carrying 8 cars, each weighing $2\frac{1}{4}$ tons, for delivery to a car dealer.

What is the total number of pounds the transport is carrying?

Sample Response

Step 1 Multiply to find the number of tons for 8 cars. $8 \cdot 2\frac{1}{4} = 18$ tons

Step 2 Multiply to find the number of pounds in 18 tons.

$$
\begin{array}{rcr}
1 \text{ ton} & = & 2000 \text{ lb} \\
\times\ 18 & = & \times\quad 18 \\
\hline
18 \text{ tons} & = & 36{,}000 \text{ lb}
\end{array}
$$

So, the transport is carrying 36,000 lb.

Study Guide: Practice & Application Exercises
For use with Section 2

Exploration 1

1. Choose the letter of the three-dimensional object that is a pyramid.

A. 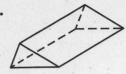   **B.** 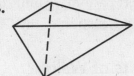   **C.**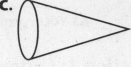

2. How is a triangular pyramid different from a triangular prism?

Choose the best customary unit (*ounce, pound, or ton*) to express the weight of each object.

3. laptop computer   **4.** computer disk   **5.** armored truck

For Exercises 6–8, replace each __?__ with the missing number.

6. 288 oz = __?__ lb   **7.** 0.25 lb = __?__ oz   **8.** 750 lb = __?__ ton

9. $4\frac{1}{2}$ tons = __?__ lb   **10.** 8 oz = __?__ lb   **11.** $\frac{1}{4}$ lb = __?__ oz

12. A buffet-style restaurant charges $5.99 per pound for hot items and $3.99 per pound for cold items. Lucy gets 0.33 lb of lasagna, 0.17 lb of steamed broccoli, 7 oz of split pea soup, and 5 oz of fruit salad. About how much will she pay for her meal?

13. **Archeology** Among the civilizations that built pyramids were the ancient Aztecs. Archeologists have found a stone that shows the Aztec calendar system. The Sun Stone is on view in a museum in Mexico City. The Sun Stone weighs almost 25 tons. About how many pounds does this stone weigh?

14. On November 19, 1997, in Des Moines, Iowa, the second known set of septuplets to be born alive was comprised of 4 boys and 3 girls. In the order of their birth, the McCaughey septuplets of Carlisle, Iowa, are Kenneth Robert, weighing 3 lb 4 oz; Alexis May, weighing 2 lb 11 oz; Natalie Sue, weighing 2 lb 10 oz; Kelsey Ann, weighing 2 lb 5 oz; Brandon James, weighing 3 lb 3 oz; Nathanial Roy, weighing 2 lb 14 oz; and Joel Steven, weighing 2 lb 15 oz. What was the total birth weight of the McCaughey septuplets?

MODULE 7   **LABSHEET 3A**

Data Table (Use with Questions 13 and 14 on page 464 and Question 16 on page 465.)

Directions Use string and a meter stick to measure your group's objects to the nearest tenth of a centimeter. Record the data for your group. Then record data from another group.

	Your Group				Another Group			
Object								
Circumference (C)								
Diameter (d)								

Scatter Plot (Use with Question 13 on page 464.)

Directions Plot the circumference and diameter for each object in your *Data Table*. Use a clear ruler to draw a fitted line for your scatter plot.

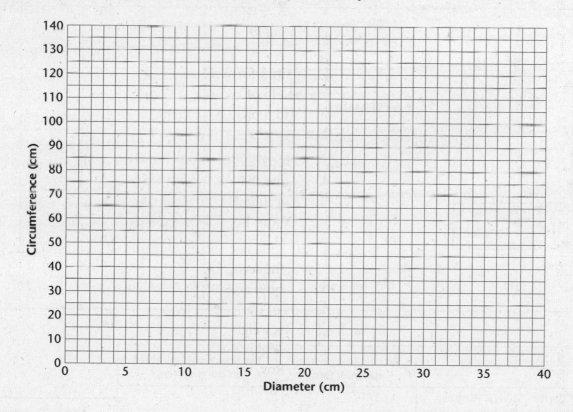

MODULE 7   LABSHEET **3B**

Epicenter Map (Use with Exercise 7 on page 467.)

Directions Complete the table to determine the distance on the map that each seismograph location is from the epicenter. Round your answers to the nearest tenth of a centimeter. Use a compass. Draw a circle for each seismograph location using the map distance you found as the radius.
Then mark an "X" at the point on the map where the three circles intersect.

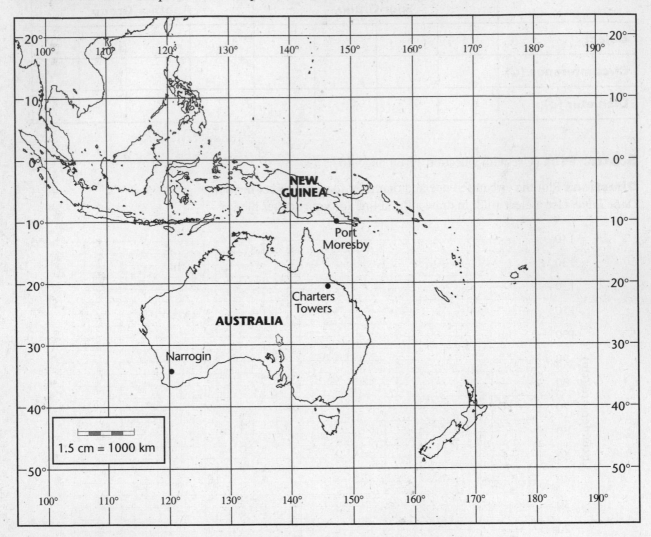

Seismograph location	Actual distance from epicenter (km)	Distance from epicenter on the map (cm)
#1: Charters Towers, Australia	3710	
#2: Port Moresby, New Guinea	2899	
#3: Narrogin, Australia	4633	

Use each answer as the radius for a circle you draw.

Name _____   Date _____

Practice and Applications
For use with Section 3

For use with Exploration 1

1. Name all the segments of each type shown on the circle with center O.

   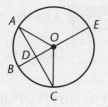

   a. radii   **b.** diameters

   c. chords

2. Use a compass to draw a circle with each radius or diameter.

   a. radius = 2.5 cm   **b.** diameter = 6 cm   **c.** diameter = 3 in.

For use with Exploration 2

In Exercises 3–5, use 3.14 for π.

3. Find the approximate circumference of each circle. Round to the nearest hundredth.

   a. $d = 15$ in.   **b.** $d = 9$ cm   **c.** $r = 8$ ft

   d. $d = 7$ in.   **e.** $r = 2.5$ cm   **f.** $r = 5$ cm

4. For the circle with each given circumference (C), approximate the missing radius or diameter. Replace each ___?___ with the missing length. Round to the nearest hundredth.

   a. $C = 75.36$ cm
   diameter ≈ ___?___ cm

   b. $C = 40.82$ in.
   radius ≈ ___?___ in.

   c. $C = 18.84$ mm
   diameter ≈ ___?___ mm

   d. $C = 12.56$ cm
   radius ≈ ___?___ cm

   e. $C = 109.9$ in.
   diameter ≈ ___?___ in.

   f. $C = 62.8$ cm
   radius ≈ ___?___ cm

5. A circular track has a radius of 18 ft.

   a. Erin runs across the track along the diameter to the other side of the track. Then she turns and runs back the same way to where she started. How far does Erin run?

   b. After running across the track, Erin runs around the track one time. How far is one time around the track?

   c. How far does Erin run altogether if she runs around the track two more times?

Name _____   Date _____

 **Study Guide**
For use with Section 3

The Circus Maximus   Circles and Circumference

GOAL   **LEARN HOW TO:** • identify and draw the parts of a circle
                                        • find the circumference of a circle
            AS YOU: • investigate the Roman Empire and gather data about circles

Exploration 1: Parts of a Circle

A **circle** is the set of points in a plane that are all the same distance
from a given point, called the **center**. A *compass* is an instrument
used to draw a circle.

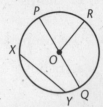

A **radius** is a segment from the center of a circle to any point on the
circle. All radii of a circle have the same length. A **chord** is a segment
that connects two points on a circle. A **diameter** is a chord that passes
through the center of a circle. It is the longest chord of the circle.

Point O is the center
of the circle.

$\overline{OR}$ is a radius.

All diameters of a circle have the same length. The terms *radius* and
diameter are used for lengths as well as segments. The length of any
radius of the circle is called *the radius* of the circle. The length of
any diameter of the circle is called *the diameter* of the circle.

$\overline{XY}$ is a chord.

$\overline{PQ}$ is a diameter.

Exploration 2: Distance Around a Circle

The distance around a circle is its **circumference**. The ratio of the
circumference C of any circle to its diameter d is always the same
number, which is called **pi**. Its symbol is π.

$$\frac{C}{d} = \pi$$

To express the exact circumference C, simply write: $C = \pi d$. To estimate
the circumference, use the value 3.14 for π or use the π key on a calculator.

Example

Find the circumference of a circle whose radius is 2.4 in.

Sample Response

$C = \pi d$

$\quad = \pi \cdot 4.8 \qquad$ ← Since $d = 2r$ and $r = 2.4$, $d = 2 \cdot 2.4$, or 4.8.

$\quad \approx 3.14 \cdot 4.8 \qquad$ ← Use 3.14 for π. (The symbol $\approx$ is read "is about equal to.")

$\quad \approx 15.07$

So, the circumference of the circle is 4.8π in., or about 15.1 in.

Math Thematics, Book 1
Student Workbook

Study Guide: Practice & Application Exercises

For use with Section 3

Exploration 1

For Exercises 1–3, name all the segments of each type shown on the circle with center *X*.

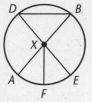

1. radii   **2.** diameters   **3.** chords

4. a. Use a compass to draw a circle with radius 10 cm. Then use a protractor and ruler to draw a diameter and chord that are perpendicular to each other. In addition to intersecting at right angles, make a prediction about how the diameter intersects the chord. Use a ruler to verify your prediction.

     b. Draw other diameters and chords that are perpendicular. Is the result the same? Draw a diameter and a chord that intersect but are not perpendicular. Is the previous result still true? Generalize your result.

Exploration 2

Find the approximate circumference of each circle. Round to the nearest hundredth.

5. $d = 17$ cm   **6.** $d = 24$ in.   **7.** $r = 9$ ft   **8.** $r = 10.6$ cm

For the circle with each given circumference (*C*), approximate the missing radius or diameter. Replace each ___?___ with the missing length. Round to the nearest hundredth.

9. $C = 76.34$ in.   **10.** $C = 32.59$ cm   **11.** $C = 107.65$ ft   **12.** $C = 1239.23$ mm
     diameter = __?__   radius = __?__   radius = __?__   diameter = __?__

13. The wheels of Leah's motorcycle are 20 in. in diameter. About how many revolutions (turns) would each wheel make if Leah rode her motorcycle from New York City to Los Angeles, a distance of 2794 mi? Explain your process.

14. The round tables in Mel's restaurant each have a circumference of 130 in. Mel wants the tablecloths to hang about 2 ft over the edge of each table all the way around. Tablecloths are sold in 72 in., 90 in., 108 in., and 120 in. diameters. Which size tablecloth should Mel buy? Explain.

15. A landscaper wants to install decorative tile around the circumference of a client's circular fish pond. The fish pond has a radius of 3 m, and each decorative tile is 12 cm long. How many tiles does the landscaper need to complete the job? Explain.

MODULE 7

Estimating the Area of a Circle (Use with Question 3 on page 472.)

Directions Complete parts (a)–(e) to estimate the area of the circle in the figure. Each grid square is 1 cm by 1 cm, or 1 cm^2.

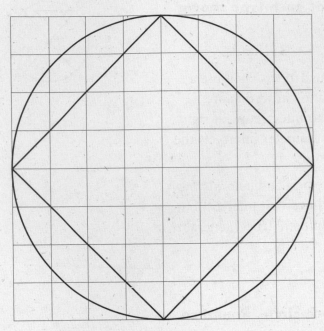

a. Is the area of the circle *greater than, less than,* or *equal to* the area of the outer square?

b. Is the area of the circle *greater than, less than,* or *equal to* the area of the inner square?

c. Find the area of the outer square. Describe the method you used.

d. Find the area of the inner square. Describe the method you used.

e. Use your results from parts (c) and (d) to estimate the area of the circle. Explain how you made your estimate.

MODULE 7 | **LABSHEET** **4B**

Prism A (Use with Questions 13–18 on pages 475–476.)

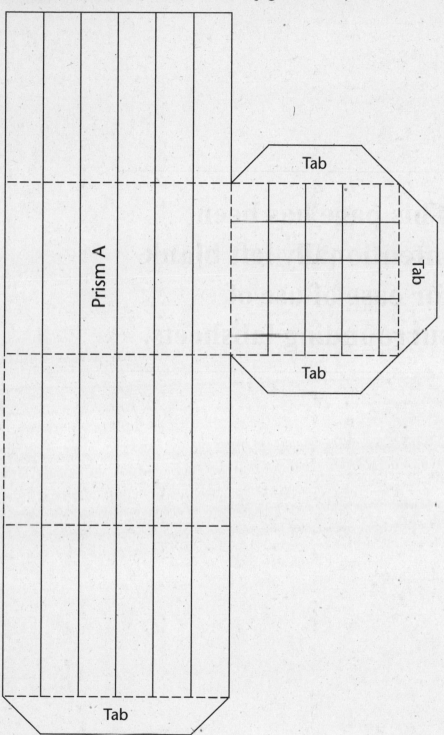

Prism A

Tab

Tab

Tab

Tab

This page has been
intentionally left blank
for ease of use of
surrounding labsheets.

Prism B and Cylinder 1 (Use with Questions 13–18 on pages 475–476.)

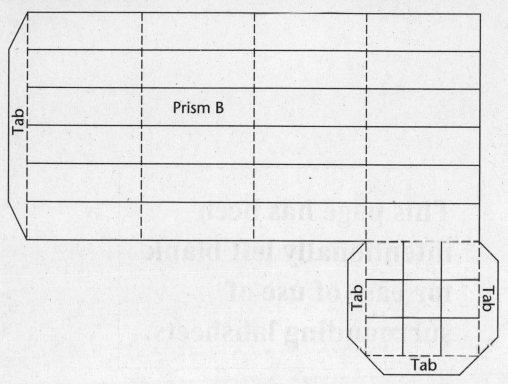

Prism B

Tab

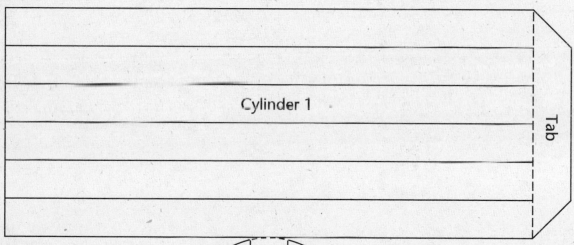

Cylinder 1

Tab

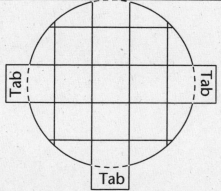

Tab

This page has been intentionally left blank for ease of use of surrounding labsheets.

MODULE 7   LABSHEET **4D**

Cylinder 2 (Use with Questions 13–18 on pages 475–476.)

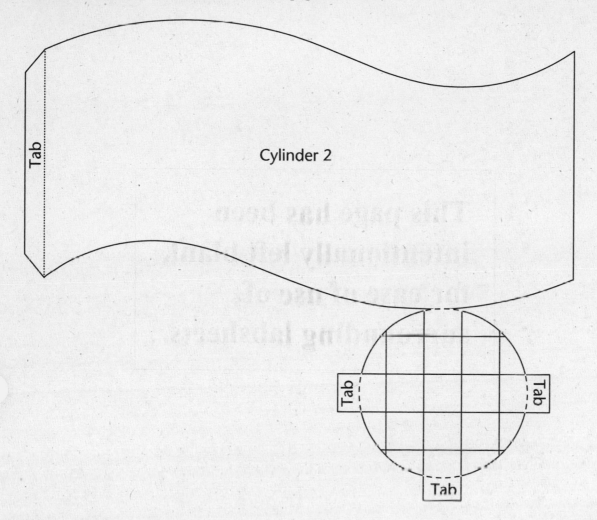

Cylinder 2

This page has been
intentionally left blank
for ease of use of
surrounding labsheets.

MODULE 7   **LABSHEET** **4E**

Cone and Cylinder Nets (Use with Exercises 34 and 35 on page 480.)

Directions Follow the instructions in your book. You will notice that one circular base has been left off of each net. This is so that the open figures can be filled with rice.

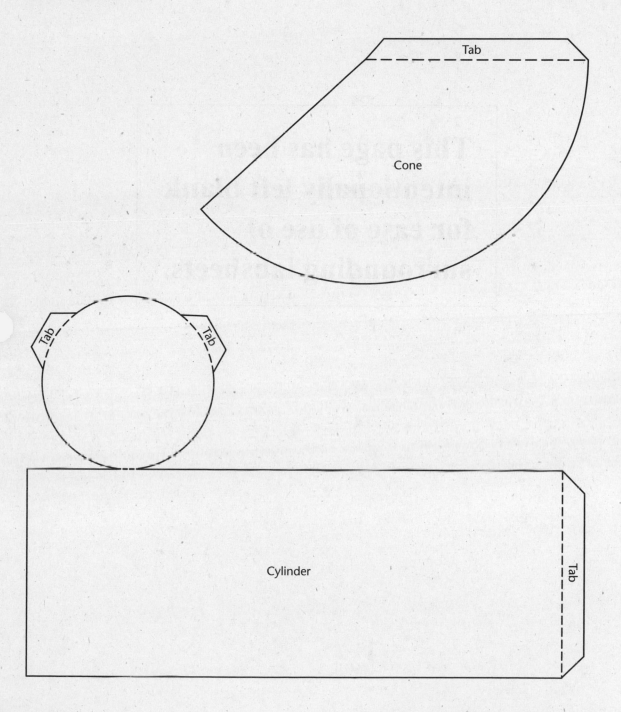

This page has been intentionally left blank for ease of use of surrounding labsheets.

Name _____   Date _____

Practice and Applications
For use with Section 4

For use with Exploration 1

1. Find the area of the circle with the given radius (*r*) or diameter (*d*).
Use the $\boxed{\pi}$ key on a calculator or 3.14 for π. Round to the nearest hundredth.

a. $r = \dfrac{3}{4}$ ft

b. $r = 54$ in.

c. $d = 5.6$ m

d.

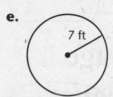

2.4 cm

e.

7 ft

f.

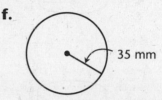

35 mm

2. Find the exact area of the circle with the given radius (*r*) or diameter (*d*).

a. $r = 18$ in.

b. $d = 75$ cm

c. $r = 5\dfrac{1}{4}$ ft

d.

43 mm

e.

32 yd

f.

3.8 m

3. The circumference of a circle is about 37.68 m. Find the approximate area of the circle.

4. The groundskeeper at Orange Field must mow a circular field. The diameter of the field is 250 yd. What is the area of the field that the groundskeeper must mow? Use the $\boxed{\pi}$ key on a calculator or 3.14 for π. Round to the nearest hundredth.

5. An artist wants to paint a circular picture. He puts the canvas 1 in. beyond the circular stretcher to make the painting surface, as shown in the diagram. What is the area of the canvas? Use the $\boxed{\pi}$ key on a calculator or 3.14 for π. Round to the nearest hundredth.

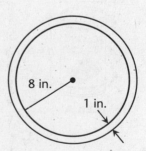

8 in.

1 in.

(continued)

Practice and Applications

For use with Section 4

For use with Exploration 2

6. Find the volume of each right cylinder. Round to the nearest hundredth.

a.

5 m
9 m

b.
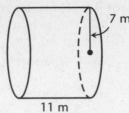
7 m
11 m

c.
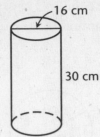
16 cm
30 cm

d.
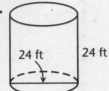
24 ft   24 ft

e.
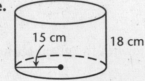
15 cm   18 cm

f.
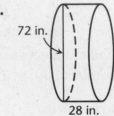
72 in.
28 in.

7. For each right cylinder, replace the ___?___ with the missing measurement. Round to the nearest hundredth.

a. $r = 3.2$ m
$h \approx$ ___?___
$V \approx 148$ m^3

b. $d = 9$ ft
$h = 7.1$ ft
$V \approx$ ___?___

c. $d = 2.8$ m
$h \approx$ ___?___
$V \approx 18$ m^3

d. $r = 4$ in.
$h = 16$ in.
$V \approx$ ___?___

e. $r = 11$ cm
$h = 6.3$ cm
$V \approx$ ___?___

f. $r \approx$ ___?___
$h = 8$ m
$V \approx 904$ m^3

8. Which can below holds more tomato sauce? Explain.

$d = 3$ in.
TOMATO SAUCE
$h = 5$ in.
Can A

$d = 4$ in.
TOMATO SAUCE
$h = 4$ in.
Can B

9. A water tank shaped like a cylinder has a diameter of 5 ft and is 7 ft long. What is the volume of the water tank?

Study Guide
For use with Section 4

The Mystery of Mesa Verde   Circles and Cylinders

GOAL **LEARN HOW TO:** • find the area of a circle
• recognize a cylinder
• find the volume of a cylinder

AS YOU: • determine how many people could fit in a kiva
• explore the size and shape of a kiva

Exploration 1: Area of a Circle

As shown in the figure at the right, a reasonable approximation for the area A of a circle with radius r is the sum of the areas of the three squares, with side lengths r.

To find the area A of a circle with radius r, multiply the square of the radius by the number π: $A = \pi r^2$. You can use this formula to determine both the exact value of the area of a circle as well as an approximate value.

$A \approx 3r^2$

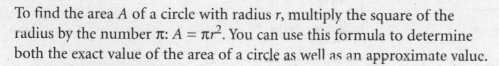

Example

Find the area of a circle with diameter 12 cm.

Sample Response

Use the area formula.

Since $d = 12$, then $r = d \div 2 = 12 \div 2$, or 6.

$$A = \pi r^2$$
$$A = \pi \cdot 6^2$$
$$= \pi \cdot 36$$

So, the exact area of the circle is 36π cm^2.

To estimate the area, substitute 3.14 for π.

$$A \approx 3.14 \cdot 36$$
$$\approx 113.04$$

So, the area of the circle is about 113 cm^2.

Using π

As shown in the Example above, when you write the area of a circle using the number π, you are giving the exact value of the area. When you substitute 3.14 for π or use the π key on a calculator, the result is only an approximation of the area. Usually, an approximation of the area is given to a specified place value.

Study Guide
For use with Section 4

Exploration 2: Volume of a Cylinder

Cylinders

A **cylinder** is a 3-dimensional figure that has a curved surface and two parallel, congruent bases. In this book, all the cylinders have circular bases.

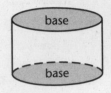

In a **right cylinder**, the curved surface is perpendicular to the bases. In an **oblique cylinder**, the curved surface is not perpendicular to the bases.

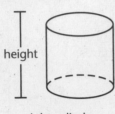 

right cylinder   oblique cylinder

Volume of a Cylinder

As with a prism, to find the volume V of a cylinder, you multiply the area of the base B of the cylinder by the height h of the cylinder. Since the bases of all cylinders in this book are circles, $B = \pi r^2$.

$V = Bh$
$V = \pi r^2 h$

Example

A cylinder has a diameter of 6.5 cm and a height of 8 cm. Find the volume of the cylinder. Round the result to the nearest hundredth.

■ Sample Response ■

Use the volume formula for a cylinder.

Since $d = 6.5$, then $r = d \div 2 = 6.5 \div 2$, or 3.25.

$V = \pi r^2 h$
$V = \pi \cdot 3.25^2 \cdot 8$
$= \pi \cdot 84.5$

So, the exact volume of the cylinder is 84.5π cm^3.

To estimate the volume, substitute 3.14 for π.

$V = 3.14 \cdot 84.5$
$= 265.33$

So, the volume of the cylinder is about 265 cm^3.

Study Guide: Practice & Application Exercises
For use with Section 4

Exploration 1

Unless you are asked to find exact areas or volumes, use the π key on a calculator or 3.14 for the value of π. Round to the nearest hundredth.

Find the area of the circle with the given radius (r) or diameter (d).

1. $r = 14$ cm

2. $d = 28\frac{1}{2}$ ft

3. 17 m

4. 6.8 in.

For Exercises 5–8, find the exact area of the circle with the given radius (r) or diameter (d).

5. $r = 19$ m   **6.** $d = 8.8$ cm   **7.** $d = 39$ in.   **8.** $r = 15$ ft

9. Find the approximate area of a circle whose circumference is 32.32 in.

Exploration 2

Find the volume of each right cylinder.

10. 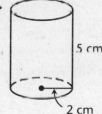 5 cm 2 cm

11. 3 ft 4.7 ft

12. 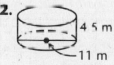 4.5 m 11 m

13. 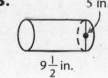 5 in. $9\frac{1}{2}$ in.

For each right cylinder in Exercises 14–17, replace the ____?____ with the missing measurement.

14. $r = 7$ ft
   $h = 12$ ft
   $V = $ ____?____

15. $d = 12.4$ cm
   $h = $ ____?____
   $V = 495.4$ cm^3

16. $r = 6$ in.
   $h = 6$ in.
   $V = $ ____?____

17. $r = 9.1$ m
   $h = $ ____?____ m
   $V = 4682.8$ m^3

18. Challenge The diagram at the right shows a section of a concrete drainage pipe, which has the shape of a hollowed-out cylinder. To the nearest cubic inch, how much concrete was used to make this section of pipe? (*Hint*: The hollowed-out portion is also a cylinder. Use subtraction.)

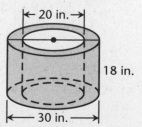
← 20 in. →
18 in.
← 30 in. →

Math Thematics, Book 1
Student Workbook   **297**

MODULE 7   **LABSHEET** **5A**

On the Trail of Marco Polo (Use with Question 21 on page 488.)

Game Board 1

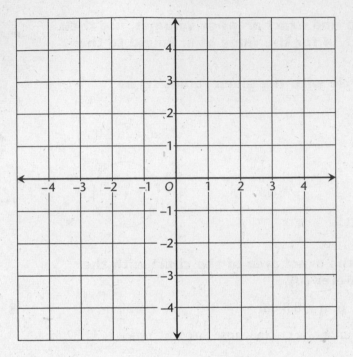

Game Board 2

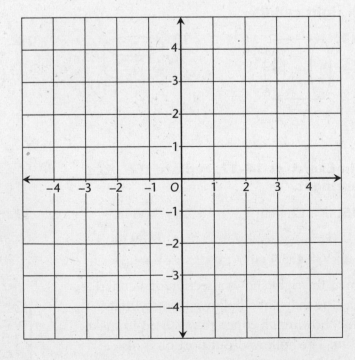

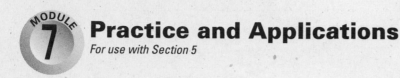

Practice and Applications
For use with Section 5

For use with Exploration 1

1. Select the warmer temperature in each pair.

a. 8°F, 10°F **b.** −2°C, 2°C **c.** −25°F, −14°F

2. a. List the next three integers to the right of −4 on a number line. Are they *positive* or *negative* integers?

b. List the next three integers to the left of −4 on a number line. Are they *positive* or *negative* integers?

3. Write an integer to represent each measurement.

a. 5° above zero **b.** 30 ft below sea level

c. a credit of $32 **d.** a gain of 15 yards in football

e. a loss of $50 **f.** a debt of $18

4. List three integers that are greater than each number.

a. −8 **b.** −1 **c.** −3

5. Draw a number line and use a dot to locate each integer on the number line. Then list the integers from least to greatest.

5, −3, 2, −6, 0, −1, 4,

6. Replace each ___?___ with > or <.

a. 2 __?__ −5 **b.** −12 __?__ −3 **c.** 0 __?__ 8

d. 6 __?__ −1 **e.** 0 __?__ −2 **f.** 6 __?__ −6

g. −7 __?__ 14 **h.** −2 __?__ 2 **i.** −3 __?__ 0

7. The low temperature for the day recorded at Yellowstone was −15°F. The next day the low temperature was −20°F. How many degrees less was the low temperature the next day?

8. At 5 A.M., the temperature was −12°F. At 8 A.M., the temperature was −2°F. At 1 P.M., the temperature was 24°F. At 5 P.M., the temperature was 0°F. What was the low temperature for the 12 hour period between 5 A.M. and 5 P.M.?

(continued)

Practice and Applications

For use with Section 5

For use with Exploration 2

Use the coordinate grid for Exercises 9–11.

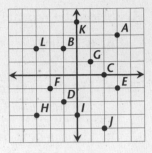

9. **a.** In which quadrant is the graph of point *L* located?

   b. In which quadrant is the graph of point *E* located?

   c. In which quadrant is the graph of point *H* located?

   d. In which quadrant is the graph of point *G* located?

10. Write the coordinates of the point.

   a. *G*   **b.** *K*   **c.** *H*

   d. *D*   **e.** *A*   **f.** *L*

   g. *J*   **h.** *E*   **i.** *B*

   j. *C*   **k.** *F*   **l.** *I*

11. If you were to plot the point with the coordinates $(-2, 0)$ on the coordinate grid, which labeled point would it be closest to?

12. Make a coordinate grid on graph paper. The integers on each axis should range from -10 to 10. Then plot each point on your grid.

   a. $(2, -4)$ **b.** $(-1, -5)$ **c.** $(8, -3)$

   d. $(-7, 1)$ **e.** $(6, 0)$ **f.** $(-6, -7)$

   g. $(-3, 0)$ **h.** $(-5, 1)$ **i.** $(0, -4)$

13. Paula plotted points on a coordinate grid and drew line segments connecting them in the following order: $(-3, -5)$, $(0, 5)$, $(3, -5)$, $(-5, 0)$, $(5, 0)$. She then connected the last point she plotted to the first point she plotted. What shape did Paula draw?

14. Draw a coordinate grid on graph paper. Plot points and draw segments connecting these points to create the first letter of your last name. List the ordered pairs for your design in the order they need to be connected.

Name _____ Date _____

Study Guide
For use with Section 5

World Traveler   Temperature, Integers, and Coordinate Graphs

GOAL **LEARN HOW TO:** • measure temperature
• compare integers
• graph points with integer coordinates on a coordinate grid

AS YOU: • explore Marco Polo's route and play *On the Trail of Marco Polo*

Exploration 1: Temperature and Integers

The units used to measure temperatures are degrees **Celsius** (°C) and degrees **Fahrenheit** (°F). In both systems, temperatures that are *above zero* are **positive** numbers and temperatures that are *below zero* are **negative** numbers. The number zero is neither positive nor negative. The numbers used most often to describe temperatures are called **integers**. The integers are the numbers ..., –3, –2, –1, 0, 1, 2, 3, ...

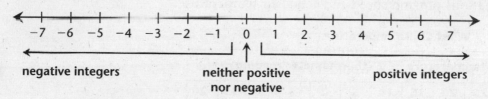

negative integers   neither positive   positive integers
                              nor negative

Comparing Integers

When you want to compare temperatures, think about comparing integers on a number line. Of two integers, the one that is to the right of the other on a number line is greater.

Exploration 2: Graphing Ordered Pairs

Coordinate grids were used previously in Module 4. When you extend the coordinate grid to include points with coordinates that are negative integers, the axes divide the grid into four parts, called **quadrants**. Recall that the point at which the axes meet is called the *origin*. Often labeled *O*, the coordinates of the origin are (0, 0).

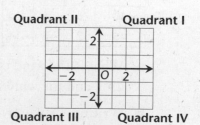

> ### Example
>
> To graph the point *P*(4, –3), start at the origin.
>
> The first coordinate tells you how many units to move left or right from the origin: 4 means go *right* 4 units.
>
> The second coordinate then tells you how many units to move up or down: –3 means to go *down* 3 units.
>
>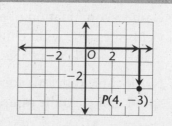

Study Guide: Practice & Application Exercises

For use with Section 5

Exploration 1

Match each geographic region with the letter of the mean temperature that might represent its warmest month.

A. 120°F   **B.** −5°C   **C.** 32°C   **D.** 32°F

1. the Arctic region   **2.** a tropical rain forest   **3.** the Sahara Desert

For Exercises 4–6, write an integer to represent each measurement.

4. a deposit of $50   **5.** a debt of $20   **6.** 40 ft above sea level

7. Draw a number line, and use a dot to locate each of the integers 8, −3, 0, −9, 7, 5, and 3 on the number line. Then list the integers from least to greatest.

8. **Writing** Use a number line to compare −7 to −5.

9. **Interpreting Data** The chart below gives the wind chill temperatures for various combinations of wind speed and actual air temperature.

Wind Chill Temperature

Wind speed (mi/hr)	Air temperature in °F (thermometer reading)										
	35	30	25	20	15	10	5	0	−5	−10	−15	−20
5	33	27	21	19	12	7	0	−5	−10	−15	−21	−26
10	22	16	10	3	−3	−9	−15	−22	−27	−34	−40	−46
15	16	9	2	−5	−11	−18	−25	−31	−38	−45	−51	−58
20	12	4	−3	−10	−17	−24	−31	−39	−46	−53	−60	−67
25	8	1	−7	−15	−22	−29	−36	−44	−51	−59	−66	−74
30	6	−2	−10	−18	−25	−33	−41	−49	−56	−64	−71	−79
35	4	−4	−12	−20	−27	−35	−43	−52	−58	−67	−74	−82
40	3	−5	−13	−21	−29	−37	−45	−53	−60	−69	−76	−84
45	2	−6	−14	−22	−30	−38	−46	−54	−62	−70	−78	−85

a. What is the wind chill temperature when the air temperature is 25°F and the wind is blowing at 15 mi/hr?

b. **Writing** Explain what is meant by the weather term *wind chill temperature.*

c. Name a combination of air temperature and wind speed that yields the same wind chill temperature as when the air temperature is 15°F and the wind speed is 5 mi/hr.

d. Name three different combinations of air temperature and wind speed that yield the same wind chill temperature.

(continued)

Study Guide: Practice & Application Exercises

For use with Section 5

Algebra Connection **The formula $F = \frac{9}{5}C + 32$ relates Fahrenheit temperatures and Celsius temperatures.**

10. Use the formula to convert 20°C to its equivalent Fahrenheit value.

11. Challenge Use the formula to convert 77°F to its equivalent Celsius temperature. Check your answer by using the formula to convert your Celsius temperature back to its equivalent Fahrenheit temperature.

12. a. In 1870, Jules Verne wrote a novel entitled *Twenty Thousand Leagues Under the Sea*. Using the modern conversion of 1 league = 3.452 mi, write an integer that could represent the depth in miles of 20,000 leagues.

b. A *bathyscaph* is a deepwater submarine with an observation room projecting from its bottom. In 1960, the bathyscaph *Trieste* carried two men to a depth of 35,810 ft. Using the conversion of 1 mi = 5280 ft, write an integer to represent the depth, to the nearest mile, that the *Trieste* descended.

c. Write an inequality to compare the two integers from parts (a) and (b).

Exploration 2

For Exercise 13, use the coordinate grid.

13. Write the coordinates of each labeled point *A–F*.

14. Make a coordinate grid on graph paper. The integers on each axis should range from −10 to 10. Then plot each point on your grid.

a. (10, 0) **b.** (−9, −2) **c.** (2, −7)

d. (−4, −5) **e.** (−6, 7) **f.** (−1, 5)

g. (6, 8) **h.** (4, 3) **i.** (3, −2)

15. Geometry Connection On a coordinate grid, plot the points *A*(−4, 0), *B*(4, 0), *C*(8, 7), and *D*(0, 7). Connect the points to form quadrilateral *ABCD*. What kind of quadrilateral is *ABCD*? Find the area of *ABCD*.

Name _____   Date _____

Practice and Applications

For use after Sections 1–5

For use with Section 1

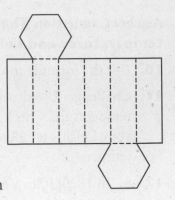

1. Will this net form a prism? If so, what kind of prism? Explain.

2. Describe the shapes of the faces.

3. Show that the number of faces, vertices, and edges of the polyhedron satisfies the formula $F + V - 2 = E$.

4. Replace each ___?___ with the missing measurement for a prism with a base area B, height h, and volume V.

   a. $B = 32$ ft^2
   $h = $ ___?___
   $V = 288$ ft^3

   b. $B = $ ___?___
   $h = 35$ cm
   $V = 1015$ cm^3

   c. $B = 342$ mm^2
   $h = 18$ mm
   $V = $ ___?___

For use with Section 2

5. Replace each ___?___ with the missing number.

   a. $3\frac{1}{4}$ lb = ___?___ oz

   b. 12 oz = ___?___ lb

   c. 7 tons = ___?___ lb

   d. 11,000 lb = ___?___ tons

   e. 3200 lb = ___?___ tons

   f. 64 oz = ___?___ lb

6. A baker has $8\frac{7}{8}$ lb of dough. He divides the dough into 4 oz pieces to make rolls. How many rolls can he make? Is there any dough left over? If so, how much?

For use with Section 3

7. Find the approximate circumference of each circle. Round to the nearest hundredth.

   a. $d = 14$ in.

   b. $d = 17$ cm

   c. $r = 20$ ft

8. For the circle with each given circumference (C), approximate the missing radius or diameter. Replace each ___?___ with the missing length. Round to the nearest hundredth.

   a. $C = 56.39$ cm
   diameter ≈ ___?___ cm

   b. $C = 14.13$ in.
   radius ≈ ___?___ in.

   c. $C = 87.92$ mm
   diameter ≈ ___?___ mm

(continued)

Name _____   Date _____

MODULE 7 Practice and Applications
For use after Sections 1–5

For use with Section 4

9. Find the area of the circle with the given radius (*r*) or diameter (*d*). Use the $\boxed{\pi}$ key on a calculator or 3.14 for π. Round to the nearest hundredth.

   a. *r* = 2.5 ft   **b.** *r* = 15 in.   **c.** *d* = 24 m

10. A circular sandbox has a diameter of 8 ft. What is the minimum area of a tarp that would cover the sandbox?

11. Find the volume of each right cylinder. Round to the nearest hundredth.

   a.   **b.**   **c.**

 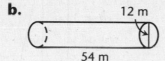 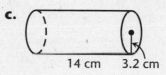

For use with Section 5

12. Write an integer to represent each measurement.

   a. 12° below zero   **b.** a loss of 10 yards

   c. 400 ft above sea level   **d.** a credit of $25

13. Replace each _?_ with > or <.

   a. −4 _?_ −5   **b.** −1 _?_ 0   **c.** −8 _?_ −2

   d. 2 _?_ −3   **e.** 0 _?_ −9   **f.** 3 _?_ −2

14. Plot each point on a coordinate grid.

   a. (0, −5)   **b.** (1, −1)   **c.** (−6, 3)

   d. (2, 3)   **e.** (−5, −7)   **f.** (8, 0)

MODULE 7   **PROJECT LABSHEET** Ⓐ

Model of the Great Pyramid at Giza (Use with Project Question 4 on page 495.)

Directions Follow the steps below to make and fold a net for a model of the Great Pyramid at Giza.

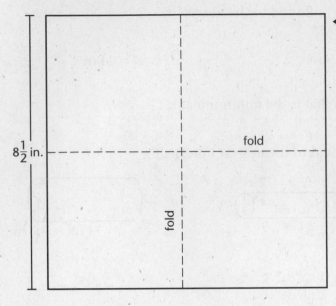

$8\frac{1}{2}$ in.

fold

fold

◀ **Step 1** First cut a sheet of paper to make a square with sides $8\frac{1}{2}$ in. long. Next fold the square in half and in half again. Then press down the square so it lies flat.

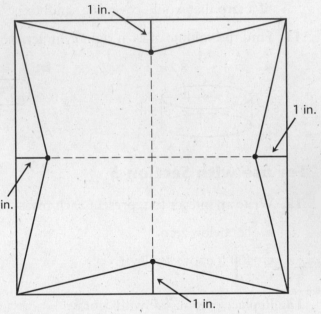

1 in.

1 in.

1 in.

1 in.

Step 2 Mark points 1 in. from the sides of ▶ the square along the folds. Then draw segments connecting these points with the vertices of the square, as shown.

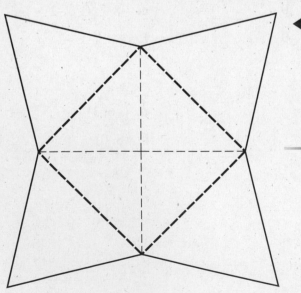

◀ **Step 3** Cut along the segments you drew in Step 2. Next draw dashed segments as shown. Then fold along the dashed segments and tape the triangles together.

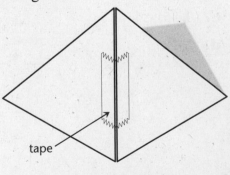

tape

Math Thematics, Book 1
Student Workbook

306

Name _____   Problem _____

Teacher Assessment Scales

For use with Module 8

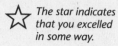 The star indicates that you excelled in some way.

Problem Solving

①   ②   ③   ④   ⑤

① You did not understand the problem well enough to get started or you did not show any work.

③ You understood the problem well enough to make a plan and to work toward a solution.

⑤ You made a plan, you used it to solve the problem, and you verified your solution.

Mathematical Language

①   ②   ③   ④   ⑤

① You did not use any mathematical vocabulary or symbols, or you did not use them correctly, or your use was not appropriate.

③ You used appropriate mathematical language, but the way it was used was not always correct or other terms and symbols were needed.

⑤ You used mathematical language that was correct and appropriate to make your meaning clear.

Representations

①   ②   ③   ④   ⑤

① You did not use any representations such as equations, tables, graphs, or diagrams to help solve the problem or explain your solution.

③ You made appropriate representations to help solve the problem or help you explain your solution, but they were not always correct or other representations were needed.

⑤ You used appropriate and correct representations to solve the problem or explain your solution.

Connections

①   ②   ③   ④   ⑤

① You attempted or solved the problem and then stopped.

③ You found patterns and used them to extend the solution to other cases, or you recognized that this problem relates to other problems, mathematical ideas, or applications.

⑤ You extended the ideas in the solution to the general case, or you showed how this problem relates to other problems, mathematical ideas, or applications.

Presentation

①   ②   ③   ④   ⑤

① The presentation of your solution and reasoning is unclear to others.

③ The presentation of your solution and reasoning is clear in most places, but others may have trouble understanding parts of it.

⑤ The presentation of your solution and reasoning is clear and can be understood by others.

Content Used: _____   Computational Errors: Yes ☐ No ☐

Notes on Errors: _____

Name _____   Problem _____

 Student Self-Assessment Scales
For use with Module 8

▬▬ *If your score is in the shaded area, explain why on the back of this sheet and stop.*

☆ *The star indicates that you excelled in some way.*

 Problem Solving

❶   ❷   ❸   ❹   ❺ ☆→

I did not understand the problem well enough to get started or I did not show any work.

I understood the problem well enough to make a plan and to work toward a solution.

I made a plan, I used it to solve the problem, and I verified my solution.

 Mathematical Language

❶   ❷   ❸   ❹   ❺ ☆→

I did not use any mathematical vocabulary or symbols, or I did not use them correctly, or my use was not appropriate.

I used appropriate mathematical language, but the way it was used was not always correct or other terms and symbols were needed.

I used mathematical language that was correct and appropriate to make my meaning clear.

 Representations

❶   ❷   ❸   ❹   ❺ ☆→

I did not use any representations such as equations, tables, graphs, or diagrams to help solve the problem or explain my solution.

I made appropriate representations to help solve the problem or help me explain my solution, but they were not always correct or other representations were needed.

I used appropriate and correct representations to solve the problem or explain my solution.

 Connections

❶   ❷   ❸   ❹   ❺ ☆→

I attempted or solved the problem and then stopped.

I found patterns and used them to extend the solution to other cases, or I recognized that this problem relates to other problems, mathematical ideas, or applications.

I extended the ideas in the solution to the general case, or I showed how this problem relates to other problems, mathematical ideas, or applications.

 Presentation

❶   ❷   ❸   ❹   ❺ ☆→

The presentation of my solution and reasoning is unclear to others.

The presentation of my solution and reasoning is clear in most places, but others may have trouble understanding parts of it.

The presentation of my solution and reasoning is clear and can be understood by others.

MODULE 8

Cubic Centimeter (Use with Question 12 on page 503.)

Directions Follow the steps to construct a cubic centimeter.

Step 1 Before you cut out one of the cube nets, place a layer of tape on both sides to reinforce the paper.

Step 2 Cut out the cube net.

Step 3 Fold the net along the dashed lines and tape the tabs to the faces to form a cube that is open on one face.

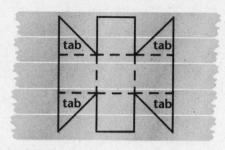

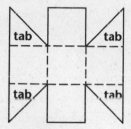 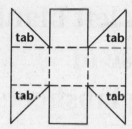 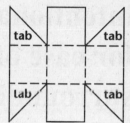

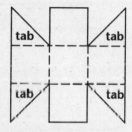 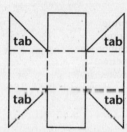 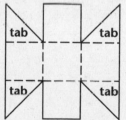

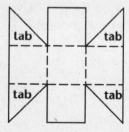 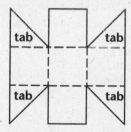 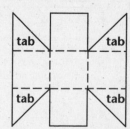

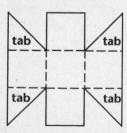 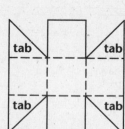

This page has been
intentionally left blank
for ease of use of
surrounding labsheets.

Name _____ Date _____

 Practice and Applications
For use with Section 1

For use with Exploration 1

1. Replace each ___?___ with the number that makes the statement true.

a. ___?___ qt = 64 fl oz **b.** ___?___ qt = 12 pt **c.** $3\frac{1}{2}$ c = ___?___ fl oz

d. ___?___ pt = 3 gal **e.** 2 gal = ___?___ fl oz **f.** ___?___ qt = 1 pt

g. 40 fl oz = ___?___ pt **h.** $\frac{1}{2}$ gal = ___?___ c **i.** 20 c = ___?___ pt

2. Students in a sixth grade class drink 18 pt of milk for lunch.
How many gallons of milk do they drink?

For use with Exploration 2

3. Find the capacity, in milliliters and in liters, of the rectangular container
with the given dimensions.

a. 25 cm × 4 cm × 10 cm **b.** 6 cm × 5 cm × 2 cm **c.** 4.5 cm × 10 cm × 15 cm

4. Replace each ___?___ with the number that makes the statement true.

a. 4300 L = ___?___ kL **b.** 7 kL = ___?___ L **c.** 371 mL = ___?___ L

d. 0.96 kL = ___?___ L **e.** 5.8 L = ___?___ mL **f.** 70 L = ___?___ mL

g. 850 mL = ___?___ L **h.** 2600 L = ___?___ kL **i.** 16 kL = ___?___ L

j. 3900 mL = ___?___ L **k.** 19 L = ___?___ mL **l.** 812 L = ___?___ kL

5. Choose the best estimate for each capacity.

a. capacity of a bath tub: 2000 mL   90 L   900 L

b. amount of soup in a restaurant soup pot: 400 mL   4 L   40 L

c. capacity of a water bottle: 300 mL   300 L   300 kL

d. amount of soup in a can of soup: 150 mL   1 L   10 L

6. Christopher drinks about 200 mL of water every time he gets thirsty.
If he gets thirsty and has a drink about 8 times a day, how many
liters of water will he drink in one week? Would one kL of water last
Christopher one week?

Name _____ Date _____

Patterns and Problem Solving Customary and Metric Capacity

GOAL **LEARN HOW TO:** • convert between customary units of capacity
• relate volume and metric capacity
• estimate capacity in metric units

AS YOU: • examine a visual pattern for capacity
• create benchmarks

Exploration 1: Customary Units of Capacity

The **capacity** of a container is the amount of liquid it can hold. In the customary system, capacity is measured in **gallons (gal)**, **quarts (qt)**, **pints (pt)**, **cups (c)**, or **fluid ounces (fl oz)**. These units are related in the following ways.

1 cup (c) = 8 fluid ounces (fl oz)   1 pint (pt) = 2 c
1 quart (qt) = 2 pt   1 gallon (gal) = 4 qt

To convert from a larger unit of capacity to
a smaller unit, you multiply. The conversion
of 6 gal to quarts is shown at the right.

$$\begin{array}{rcl} 1 \text{ gal} &=& 4 \text{ qt} \\ \times 6 &=& \times 6 \\ \hline 6 \text{ gal} &=& 24 \text{ qt} \end{array}$$

Exploration 2: Metric Capacity

In the metric system, there is a relation between volume and capacity:

1 cubic centimeter of water has
a capacity of 1 **milliliter (mL)**.

In the metric system, the basic unit of measure for capacity
is the **liter (L)**. Since 1 liter is just a little more than 1 quart,
a benchmark for 1 L is a 1-qt milk container. 1000 L are in
1 **kiloliter (kL)**.

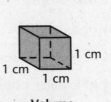
Volume

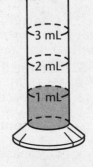
Capacity

Unit of measure	Abbreviation	Relationship to other metric units
milliliter	mL	$1 \text{ mL} = \frac{1}{1000} \text{ L} = 0.001 \text{ L}$
liter	L	$1 \text{ L} = 1000 \text{ mL}$ $1 \text{ L} = \frac{1}{1000} \text{ kL} = 0.001 \text{ kL}$
kiloliter	kL	$1 \text{ kL} = 1000 \text{ L}$

Also, 1 cubic meter (m^3) has a capacity of 1 kiloliter.

Study Guide: Practice & Application Exercises

For use with Section 1

Exploration 1

Which customary unit would be the most convenient for measuring the capacity of each item?

1. a can of soup   **2.** a tank of gasoline   **3.** a single-serving milk container

For Exercises 4–6, replace each __?__ with the number that makes the statement true.

4. $1\frac{1}{2}$ gal = __?__ pt   **5.** 288 fl oz = __?__ qt   **6.** 160 c = __?__ gal

7. Get Well Pharmacy pays $7.99 for 1 gal of cough syrup. The syrup is then repackaged into 8 fl oz bottles and sold for $1.39 each. How much profit does the pharmacy make on 1 gal of the syrup?

8. Sung and his brother are going on a hike. They each want to have 2 pt of water with them on the hike, but their water bottles are labeled in fluid ounces. If each water bottle can hold 14 fl oz of water, how many water bottles do Sung and his brother need to bring?

Exploration 2

Find the capacity, in milliliters and in liters, of the rectangular container with the given dimensions.

9. 4 cm × 25 cm × 10 cm   **10.** 8 cm × 5 cm × $2\frac{1}{2}$ cm   **11.** 7.3 cm × 10 cm × 4.2 cm

Find the capacity, in kiloliters, of the rectangular container with the given dimensions.

12. 5 m × 20 m × 8 m   **13.** 3 m × 20 m × $2\frac{2}{3}$ m   **14.** 8.6 m × 20 m × 5.3 m

Replace each __?__ with the number that makes the statement true.

15. 2400 L = __?__ kL   **16.** 4 kL = __?__ L   **17.** 745 mL = __?__ L

18. 3.4 L = __?__ mL   **19.** 3 kL = __?__ mL   **20.** 2000 mL = __?__ kL

Tell which metric unit (*milliliter, liter,* or *kiloliter*) would be most appropriate for measuring each capacity.

21. the amount of water in a bathtub   **22.** the amount of water in a coffee mug

23. the amount of water in a full kitchen sink   **24.** the amount of water in a swimming pool

25. the amount of water in a soup bowl   **26.** the amount of water in a lake

Name _____ Date _____

Practice and Applications
For use with Section 2

For use with Exploration 1

1. Use trading off to find each sum.

   a. 79 + 24

   b. 0.36 + 0.42

   c. 68 + 47

   d. 6.3 + 2.9

   e. 27 + 34 + 16

   f. $1.48 + $3.29

   g. 69 + 27

   h. 0.34 + 0.75

   i. 74 + 308

   j. 4.8 + 3.6

   k. 87 + 31 + 59

   l. 2.3 + 1.6 + 3.7

2. Use front-end estimation to estimate each sum.

   a. 7235 + 2148

   b. 18.6 + 12.3 + 31.8

   c. 216 + 680 + 106

   d. 14 + 92 + 61 + 72

   e. 3215 + 1145 + 2320

   f. 5.8 + 2.6 + 3.1 + 6.2

   g. 2.8 + 3.4 + 6.1 + 0.3

   h. 88 + 27 + 31 + 42 + 21

   i. 220 + 160 + 130 + 309

   j. 3412 + 2335 + 1210

   k. 14.28 + 11.86 + 6.41

   l. 43 + 18 + 59 + 84

3. **Estimation** Use front-end estimation to decide whether each sum or difference is *greater than* or *less than* 600.

   a. 765 − 172

   b. 278 + 197 + 283

   c. 855 − 212

4. Rebecca buys some markers for $4.37 and some construction paper for $1.48. How much does she spend altogether?

5. **Estimation** *Clustering* is another strategy for estimating a sum. The number of items sold by each grade at the yard sale on Saturday all *cluster* around 100.

Number of Items Sold	5th Grade	6th Grade	7th Grade	8th Grade
Saturday's Sale	94	105	89	101
Sunday's Sale	74	68	66	72

   a. Use clustering to estimate the total number of items sold on Saturday.

   b. What number do the items sold on Sunday cluster around?

   c. Estimate the total number of items sold on Sunday. Explain your method.

Math Thematics, Book 1
Student Workbook

Name _____ Date _____

 **Study Guide**
For use with Section 2

Math Detectives Estimation and Mental Math

 GOAL **LEARN HOW TO:** • use estimation and mental math strategies
AS YOU: • investigate the *Magic Sum* trick

Exploration 1: Estimation and Mental Math Strategies

Trading Off

Trading off is a technique that uses addition and subtraction to help find
the sum of a group of numbers mentally. In this technique, you add an
amount to one of the numbers so that the new number is easy to compute
with mentally and then subtract the same amount from the other number.

> **Example**
>
> Use trading off to find the sum: 3.87 + 1.38.
>
> **Sample Response**
>
> $\begin{array}{c} 3.87 \\ + 1.38 \end{array} \rightarrow \begin{array}{c} 3.87 + 0.13 \rightarrow \\ + 1.38 - 0.13 \rightarrow \end{array} \left.\begin{array}{c} 4.00 \\ + 1.25 \end{array}\right\} 5.25$ ← Use mental math.

Front-End Estimation

One way to estimate a sum is **front-end estimation**, a technique that
focuses on the leftmost digits, since they have the greatest value. Then
you can use the other digits to help you adjust the estimate.

> **Example**
>
> Use front-end estimation to estimate the sum: 3.45 + 2.57 + 4.04.
>
> **Sample Response**
>
> **1.** For a first estimate, focus
> on the leftmost digits.
>
> $\left.\begin{array}{r} 3.45 \\ 2.57 \\ +4.04 \end{array}\right\} 3 + 2 + 4 = 9$
>
> **2.** Look at the decimal
> parts separately.
>
> $\left.\begin{array}{r} 0.45 \\ 0.57 \\ +0.04 \end{array}\right\}$ about 1
>
> **3.** Adjust your estimate: 9 + 1 = 10. → The sum is about 10.

Study Guide: Practice & Application Exercises
For use with Section 2

Exploration 1

Mental Math Use trading off to find each sum.

1. $27 + 39$ **2.** $0.16 + 0.78$ **3.** $697 + 898 + 207$

4. $76 + 24 + 18$ **5.** $34.6 + 21.5$ **6.** $397 + 203$

7. $76 + 95 + 32$ **8.** $0.58 + 0.32$ **9.** $\$5.33 + \$2.48$

Estimation Use front-end estimation to estimate each sum.

10. $2689 + 4328$ **11.** $16.5 + 18.3$ **12.** $32 + 46 + 78 + 93$

13. $1202 + 396 + 421$ **14.** $12.8 + 10.7$ **15.** $16 + 67 + 22 + 80$

Estimation Use front-end estimation to decide whether each sum or difference is *greater than* or *less than* 300.

16. $258 + 72$ **17.** $965 - 687$ **18.** $421 - 98$

Estimation *Clustering* is another strategy for estimating a sum. The numbers of male commissioned officers on active duty in the U.S. Army in the years shown in the table *cluster* around 77,000.

U.S. Army Personnel on Active Duty: Commissioned Officers		
Year	**Male**	**Female**
1990	79,520	11,810
1991	77,489	11,959
1992	74,326	11,627

19. Use clustering to estimate the total number of male commissioned officers during the 3-year period.

20. Explain how you could use clustering to estimate the total number of female commissioned officers during the 3-year period.

MODULE 8   **LABSHEET** **3A**

Charge-O-Meter (Use with the *Setting the Stage* on page 520.)

Directions Read the rules below. Then play the game two times.

Game Rules:

- Both players start with their game pieces at 0 on the **Charge-O-Meter.**

- Players alternate turns. On your turn, place 7 beans in a cup, shake the cup, and pour out the beans.

- For each "+" (positive) bean that appears, move 1 unit to the right.

- For each "–" (negative) bean that appears, move 1 unit to the left.

- If you are 10 or more units away from your opponent at the end of your turn, **ZAP!** You **WIN!**

- If a player is off the **Charge-O-Meter** at the end of a turn or if there is no **ZAP** after 10 turns, the game ends in a tie.

Charge-O-Meter

+15 +14 +13 +12 +11 +10 +9 +8 +7 +6 +5 +4 +3 +2 +1 0 −1 −2 −3 −4 −5 −6 −7 −8 −9 −10 −11 −12 −13 −14 −15

Practice and Applications
For use with Section 3

For use with Exploration 1

1. Write the integer represented by each combination of algebra tiles.

    a. + − − +
        + + − −

    b. + − − + +
        − + − − − +

    c. + + − +

2. Draw a model that represents 3 and uses exactly three negative tiles.

3. Draw a model that represents −2 and uses a total of eight tiles.

4. Draw a model that represents 0 and uses a total of ten tiles.

5. Find each sum.

    a. $15 + (-17)$ **b.** $-4 + (-23)$ **c.** $-9 + 18$

    d. $0 + (-42)$ **e.** $-15 + 11$ **f.** $-6 + (-30)$

    g. $10 + (-25)$ **h.** $0 + (-52)$ **i.** $35 + (-23)$

    j. $-16 + (50)$ **k.** $28 + (-28)$ **l.** $-16 + (-14)$

    m. $12 + 73$ **n.** $-14 + (-31)$ **o.** $-23 + 16$

6. For each expression, describe the possible values for x.

    a. The sum $7 + x$ is a negative integer.

    b. The sum $-6 + x$ is a negative integer.

    c. The sum $x + 4$ is zero.

7. At 5 P.M. the temperature was −6°F. By midnight the temperature had fallen another 12°F. Write an addition expression to find the temperature at midnight. What was the temperature at midnight?

(continued)

Practice and Applications

For use with Section 3

For use with Exploration 2

8. Write an equivalent addition expression for each subtraction expression. Then find the sum.

   a. $14 - (-23)$ **b.** $-25 - 8$ **c.** $-16 - (-5)$

   d. $0 - (-12)$ **e.** $3 - 11$ **f.** $28 - 18$

9. Find each difference.

   a. $8 - (-14)$ **b.** $0 - 23$ **c.** $-7 - 14$

   d. $0 - (-35)$ **e.** $-14 - 6$ **f.** $-2 - (-12)$

   g. $16 - (-21)$ **h.** $3 - (-72)$ **i.** $42 - 21$

   j. $-38 - 30$ **k.** $18 - (-18)$ **l.** $-16 - 14$

10. For each expression, describe the possible values for x.

   a. The difference $x - 8$ is a negative integer.

   b. The difference $-3 - x$ is a positive integer.

   c. The sum $x - (-9)$ is zero.

   d. The difference $x - 14$ is a positive integer.

   e. The difference $2 - x$ is a negative integer.

11. Find each sum or difference.

   a. $32 + (-15)$ **b.** $-9 + (-54)$ **c.** $-16 + 25$

   d. $5 - 48$ **e.** $-17 - 13$ **f.** $14 - (-20)$

   g. $9 + (-22)$ **h.** $0 - (-48)$ **i.** $-29 - 13$

   j. $-43 + 18$ **k.** $53 - (-46)$ **l.** $-26 + (-19)$

12. The highest temperature recorded in Valley City last year was 98°F. The lowest temperature was –23°F. Write a subtraction expression to find the difference between the high and low temperatures. What is the difference?

Study Guide
For use with Section 3

Mind Games   Adding and Subtracting Integers

GOAL **LEARN HOW TO:** • add integers
                                    • subtract integers

    AS YOU: • analyze the game *Charge-O-Meter*
                      • model thundercloud charges with bean models

Exploration 1: Adding Integers

Integer Addition

- The sum of two positive integers
  is a positive integer. $6 + 4 = 10$

- The sum of two negative
  integers is a negative integer. $-6 + (-4) = -10$

- The sum of a positive integer and a negative integer can be:

    a positive integer, $6 + (-4) = 2$
    a negative integer, $4 + (-6) = -2$
    or zero. $6 + (-6) = 0$

- Two integers whose sum is zero
  are **opposites**.   6 and –6 are opposites.

- The sum of an integer and 0 is
  that integer. $-6 + 0 = -6$

Exploration 2: Subtracting Integers

Integer Subtraction

To subtract an integer, rewrite the subtraction as the addition of the
opposite of the integer.

Example		
	Subtracting a negative.	Subtracting a positive.
	$-6 - (-4)$	$-6 - 4$
Rewrite the subtraction	↕ opposites	↕ opposites
as the addition of the	$-6 + 4$	$-6 + (-4)$
opposite of the integer.		
	$= -2$	$= -10$

Name _____   Date _____

 Study Guide: Practice & Application Exercises
MODULE 8
For use with Section 3

Exploration 1

For Exercises 1–3, write the integer represented by each combination of algebra tiles.

1. ⊞ ⊞
⊟ ⊟

2. ⊞ ⊟ ⊞ ⊞
⊞ ⊟ ⊞

3. ⊟ ⊞ ⊟ ⊞
⊟ ⊟ ⊟

4. Draw a model that represents 5 and uses exactly three negative tiles.

For Exercises 5–12, find each sum.

5. $5 + (-7)$ **6.** $-11 + (-15)$ **7.** $-12 + 5$ **8.** $28 + (-30)$

9. $18 + (-12)$ **10.** $-15 + (-23)$ **11.** $-45 + 17$ **12.** $33 + (-11)$

13. Roller coasters are designed as loops so that riders return to the starting point. Suppose the design for a roller coaster calls for changes in the altitude of the cars as represented by the following sum:

$$50 + (\ 10) + 30 + (-40) + 15 + \underline{\quad ? \quad}$$

Replace the ___?___ with an integer so that the roller coaster completes a loop.

Exploration 2

Write the subtraction equation shown by each model.

14. ⊞ ⊞ ⊞ ⟨⊟⟩
⊞ ⊞ ⊞

15. ⊟ ⊟ ⊟ ⊟
⊟ ⊟ ⊟ ⊟
⟨⊞ ⊞ ⊞⟩→

16. ⊞ ⊞ ⊞ ⊞
⊞ ⊞ ⊞ ⟨⊟⟩↗

17. Draw a model of 7 that can be used to show the subtraction $7 - (-3)$.

For Exercises 18–25, write an equivalent addition expression for each subtraction expression. Then find the sum.

18. $23 - (-14)$ **19.** $-14 - 8$ **20.** $0 - (-13)$ **21.** $-6 - (-5)$

22. $9 - (-13)$ **23.** $-17 - (-31)$ **24.** $-14 - 20$ **25.** $19 - (-19)$

26. The lowest point in the Western Hemisphere, located in California's Death Valley, is 282 ft below sea level. Less than 100 mi away towers Mount Whitney, whose summit is the highest point in the lower 48 states of the U.S. at 14,495 ft above sea level. Find the difference in altitude between these two points.

Math Thematics, Book 1
Student Workbook   **321**

MODULE 8

Practice and Applications

For use with Section 4

For use with Exploration 1

1. Suppose an object falls at random onto each target shown below. For each target, find the probability that the object will land in a shaded region.

a.

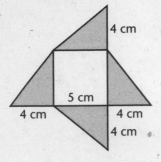

4 cm

5 cm

4 cm   4 cm

4 cm

b.

c.

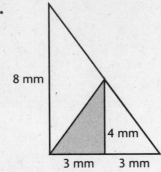

8 mm

4 mm

3 mm   3 mm

d.

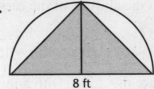

8 ft

e.

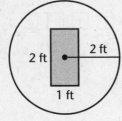

2 ft   2 ft

1 ft

f.

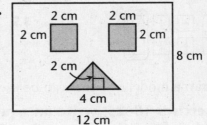

2 cm   2 cm

2 cm   2 cm

2 cm   8 cm

4 cm

12 cm

2. Paul throws a dart and hits the target shown. Each white area is a quarter of a circle.

a. What is the probability that Paul hits the white region?

b. How many times would you expect the white region to be hit if a dart is thrown at and hits the target randomly 50 times?

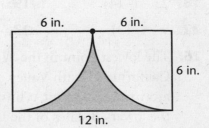

6 in.   6 in.

6 in.

12 in.

Name _____   Date _____

 **Study Guide**
For use with Section 4

Statistical Safari   Geometric Probability

GOAL   **LEARN HOW TO:** • find gemoetric probabilities
   • use probability to make predictions
   AS YOU: • describe the chance of an object falling in a particular area

Exploration 1: Predicting with Geometric Probability

Two events are **complementary events** if one or the other must occur, but they cannot both happen at the same time. Probabilities that are based on lengths, areas, or volumes are called **geometric probabilities.**

Example

A dart that hits the target shown is equally likely to hit any point on the target. Suppose Sue Ellen throws a dart at the target. What is the probability that when the dart hits the target, it will

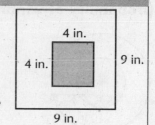

a. land in the shaded region?   **b.** land in the unshaded region?

Sample Response

a. Calculate the area of the shaded region and the total area of the target. Then write a ratio to represent the probability.

$$\text{Probability that the dart lands in the shaded area} = \frac{\text{Area of shaded region}}{\text{Total area of target}} = \frac{4 \cdot 4}{9 \cdot 9} = \frac{16}{81}$$

The probability the dart will land in the shaded region is $\frac{16}{81}$ or about 20%.

b. The sum of the chances that an event will happen and that it will not happen is 1, or 100%.

$$\text{Probability dart lands in the shaded region} + \text{Probability dart lands in the unshaded region} = 1$$

$$\frac{16}{81} + \text{Probability dart lands in the unshaded region} = 1$$

$$\text{Probability dart lands in the unshaded region} = 1 - \frac{16}{81}$$

$$= \frac{81}{81} - \frac{16}{81}, \text{ or } \frac{65}{81}$$

The probability that the dart will land in the unshaded area is $\frac{65}{81}$ or about 80%.

Study Guide: Practice & Application Exercises

For use with Section 4

Exploration 1

Suppose an object falls at random onto each target shown below. For each target, find the probability that the object will land in a shaded region.

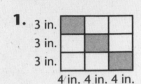

1. 3 in. 3 in. 3 in. / 4 in. 4 in. 4 in.

2. 6 cm 6 cm / 6 cm 6 cm

3. 9 in. / 9 in.

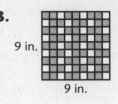

For Exercises 4–6, suppose a dart randomly hits each target. The player is a winner if the dart lands in the shaded region. Write dimensions for the shaded region of each target so that the probability of winning with one dart is 25%.

4.

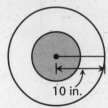

10 in.

5.

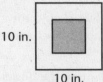

10 in. / 10 in.

6.

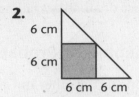

10 in. / 10 in.

7. Challenge In a game at a fair, you toss a penny onto a board that has been divided into 1-in. squares. If the penny lands without touching any line, you win. Otherwise, you lose your penny. If the radius of a penny is about $\frac{3}{8}$ in., what is the probability that in one toss of a penny, you will win? Explain your reasoning.

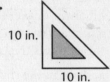

8. A bag holds 8 red balls and 2 yellow balls. Marco closes his eyes and reaches into the bag to pull out a ball.

  a. Estimate the probability that he pulls out a red ball.

  b. Estimate the probability that he pulls out a yellow ball.

  c. What is the probability that he chooses either a red or a yellow ball?

9. Caitlin is kicking a soccer ball at the net at right. She kicks the ball into the net 40 times. She does not aim at any specific area. How many times would you expect the ball to hit one of the shaded areas?

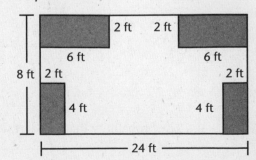

2 ft   2 ft / 6 ft   6 ft / 8 ft   2 ft   2 ft / 4 ft   4 ft / 24 ft

MODULE 8   LABSHEET **5A**

Translation Patch
(Use with Question 5 on page 544.)

Directions Complete parts (a)–(d).

a. Place your triangle on the shaded triangle. Slide your triangle to the right so that Side B of your triangle is on Line 1. Trace around your triangle.

b. From its new position, slide your triangle along Line 1 until Side A touches the bottom of the patch. Trace around your triangle.

c. Now slide your triangle all the way to the left and trace it.

d. Shade in all of your triangle outlines.

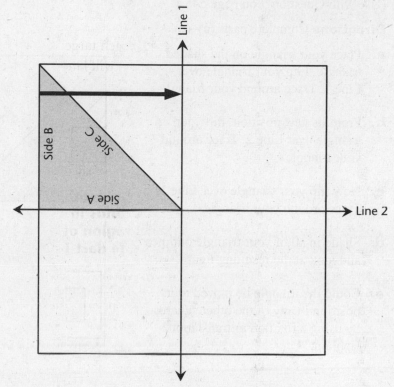

Rotation Patch
(Use with Question 7 on page 544.)

Directions Complete parts (a)–(d).

a. Place your triangle on the shaded triangle. Using the point of rotation shown, turn your triangle clockwise so that Side A is on Line 1. Trace around your triangle.

b. Turn your triangle clockwise from its new position so that Side A is on Line 2. Trace around your triangle.

c. Now turn your triangle clockwise so that Side A is on Line 1. Trace around your triangle.

d. Shade in all of your triangle outlines.

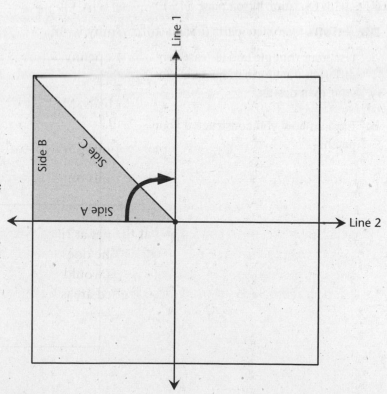

MODULE 8   **LABSHEET** **5B**

Reflection Patch

(Use with Question 9 on page 545.)

Directions Complete parts (a)–(e).

a. Place your triangle on the shaded triangle. Flip your triangle over Line 1. Trace around your triangle.

b. From its new position, flip your triangle over Line 2. Trace around your triangle.

c. Now flip your triangle over Line 1. Trace around your triangle.

d. Shade in all of your triangle outlines and look at the resulting figure.

e. Could the triangle be moved to its position in any of the other squares by using a rotation or translation? Explain.

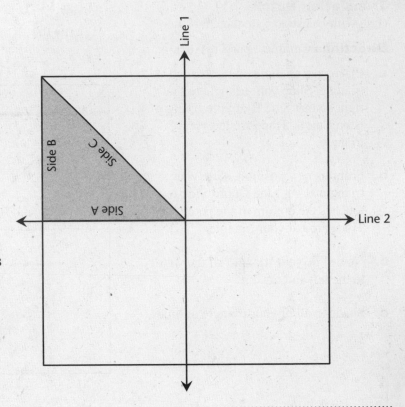

Create Your Own Patch

(Use with Question 11 on page 545.)

Directions Complete parts (a) and (b).

a. Use your triangle and at least two different transformations to make your own design.

b. Explain how you constructed your patch.

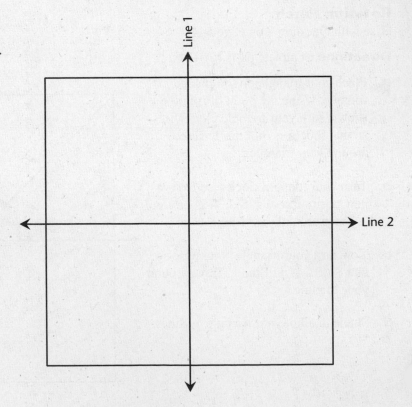

Math Thematics, Book 1
Student Workbook

326

MODULE 8 LABSHEET **5C**

Zigzag Design (Use with Questions 13–17 on page 547.)

Directions Follow the directions in your book to create the zigzag design by using square patches and transformations.

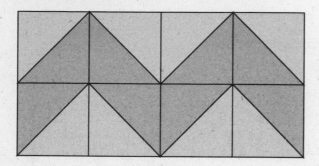

B	C	F	G
A	D	E	H

MODULE 8   **LABSHEET** **5D**

Grid for Transformations (Use with Exercise 11 on page 550.)

Directions Make a sketch of each transformation.

a. a reflection of the boat across the line

b. a 90° counterclockwise rotation of the flag

c. a translation of the stairs the distance and direction shown by the arrow

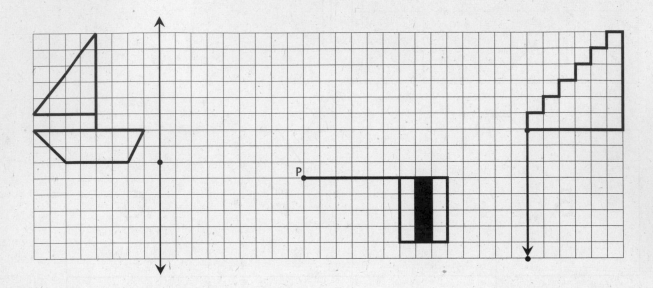

Double Reflection Grid (Use with Exercise 19 on page 551.)

Directions Draw the reflection of the trapezoid over $\overleftrightarrow{AB}$. Then draw the reflection of your drawing over $\overleftrightarrow{AC}$.

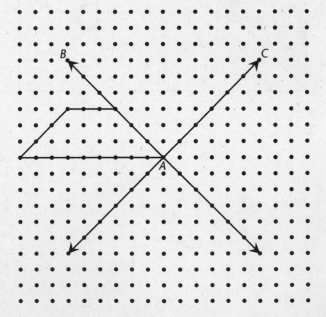

Practice and Applications

For use with Section 5

For use with Exploration 1

1. Name the transformation that will move each shaded figure onto the unshaded figure.

   a. 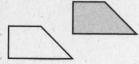   **b.**   **c.**

   d. 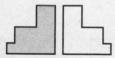   **e.**    **f.**

2. Decide if a *translation*, a *rotation*, or a *reflection* best describes the situation.

   a. Inserting a dollar bill into a change machine

   b. Winding a timer to set it

   c. Folding a letter in half for mailing

For use with Exploration 2

3. Name the transformations that will move each shaded figure onto the unshaded figure.

   a. 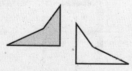   **b.** 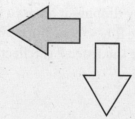   **c.**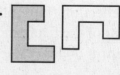

4. Beth successively reflects the following shape to create 4 sections of a quilt square. Draw a 16-square section of Beth's quilt.

Study Guide
For use with Section 5

Creating Things   Transformations

GOAL   **LEARN HOW TO:** • perform a translation, a rotation, and a reflection
• use transformations to make designs

AS YOU: • create quilt patch designs
• create a zigzag quilt

Exploration 1: Translations, Rotations, and Reflections

Transformations

A **transformation** is a change made to a figure or its position.
The following types of transformations change the position of a figure
but not its size or shape.

A **translation** (slide) moves a figure by sliding it. In the figure at
the right, every point of the figure moves the same distance in the
same direction along a flat surface. Here the letter **F** is translated
4 units right and 1 unit up.

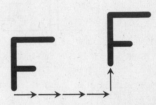

A **rotation** (turn) moves a figure by turning it. Every point of the
figure moves around a fixed point in either a clockwise or
counterclockwise direction. Here the letter **F** is rotated
90° clockwise around point *O*.

A **reflection** (flip) moves a figure by flipping it across a line. Every
point of the figure moves across the line so that the new figure is
a *mirror image* of the original. Here the letter **F** is reflected across
line ℓ.

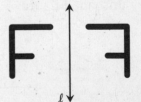

Exploration 2: Transformations in Quilting

Geometric patterns involving transformations are popular designs.
The basic design shown at the right, which might be repeated so
that it can be used for the border of a quilt, is made from a triangle
that is reflected across a line.

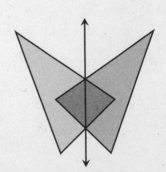

Study Guide: Practice & Application Exercises

MODULE **8**

For use with Section 5

Exploration 1

Name the transformation shown in each figure.

1.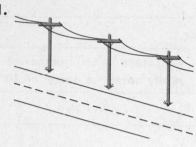

2.

Name the transformation that will move each shaded figure onto the unshaded figure.

3.

4.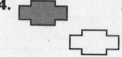

5.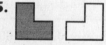

In Exercises 6–8, A changes to B in the same way that C changes to D. Sketch figure D.

6. ☆ | ☆ | ✿ | ?
   A   B   C   D

7. ◁ | ▷ | ◁ | ?
   A   B   C   D

8. ⊔ | ⊏ | ⊏ | ?
   A   B   C   D

Sketch the next three terms in each sequence.

9. □   □
   , □, , □, ?, ?, ?, ...

10. ◺, ◹, ◺, ◹, ?, ?, ?, ...

11. ⊥, ⊢, ⊤, ⊣, ?, ?, ?, ...

Exploration 2

12. **Visual Thinking** Attorney Kamul is having the wallpaper at the right hung on one wall of his office. The top row of the sheet just hung is shown below. Explain how they should position the next sheet to the right of this sheet.

Math Thematics, Book 1
Student Workbook   **331**

MODULE 8   **LABSHEET 6A**

Planet Distance Model (Use with the *Setting the Stage* on page 553 and
Question 10 on page 555.)

Directions You will use sticky notes to represent the distance of each planet
from the sun. One sticky note will represent 100,000,000 km. Complete the
table below.

Planet	Distance from the sun		
	in km	expressed as the number of sticky notes • 100,000,000	expressed as the number of sticky notes • a power of 10
Earth	149,600,000	1.496 • 100,000,000	$1.496 \cdot 10^8$
Jupiter	778,330,000		
Mars	227,940,000		
Mercury	57,910,000		
Neptune	4,504,000,000		
Saturn	1,429,400,000		
Uranus	2,870,990,000		
Venus	108,200,000		

As a class, build the model of the planet distances by:

- marking index cards with the names of the planets, one for each planet
  and one for the sun.

- clearing an open space on the floor and placing the sun card at one end of
  the space.

- rounding the number of sticky notes for each planet to the nearest
  half note.

- placing a line of sticky notes on the floor to represent each planet's
  distance from the sun.

- placing the corresponding planet card at the end of the line of sticky notes.

Name _____   Date _____

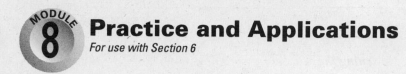

Practice and Applications
For use with Section 6

For use with Exploration 1

1. Tell whether each number is written in scientific notation. If a number is not in scientific notation, explain why not.

   a. $0.4 \cdot 10^5$ **b.** $4 \cdot 10^5$ **c.** $40 \cdot 10^5$

   d. $3.29 \cdot 10^3$ **e.** $6.3 \cdot 5^2$ **f.** $6.03 \cdot 10^4$

2. Write each number in scientific notation.

   a. 70,000,000   **b.** 82,300   **c.** 4,050,000

   d. 2,000   **e.** 6 billion   **f.** 380,000

   g. 1,372,000,000   **h.** 98,000,000   **i.** 15,300

3. Write each number in standard form.

   a. $3 \cdot 10^8$ **b.** $1.05 \cdot 10^3$ **c.** $6.12 \cdot 10^5$

   d. $5.8 \cdot 10^4$ **e.** $8 \cdot 10^6$ **f.** $9.3 \cdot 10^5$

   g. $7.0 \cdot 10^1$ **h.** $5.639 \cdot 10^7$ **i.** $4.76 \cdot 10^4$

4. Use scientific notation to express each distance.

   a. The planet Venus is 67,240,000 miles from the Sun.

   b. The diameter of the planet Neptune is 30,200 miles.

5. Without changing the numbers to standard form, order the numbers from least to greatest.

   a. $1.34 \cdot 10^3, 2.8 \cdot 10^3, 3.2 \cdot 10^2$ **b.** $3.5 \cdot 10^5, 3.5 \cdot 10^6, 3.5 \cdot 10^4$

   c. $5.684 \cdot 10^8, 5.2 \cdot 10^7, 5.2 \cdot 10^8$ **d.** $7.3 \cdot 10^7, 7.1 \cdot 10^7, 6.9 \cdot 10^7$

   e. $9.34 \cdot 10^2, 9.33 \cdot 10^3, 9.35 \cdot 10^2$ **f.** $6.7 \cdot 10^4, 7.6 \cdot 10^4, 6.67 \cdot 10^4$

   g. $8.3 \cdot 10^1, 8.1 \cdot 10^2, 8.4 \cdot 10^1$ **h.** $3.98 \cdot 10^9, 4.98 \cdot 10^8, 3.7 \cdot 10^9$

6. The Andromeda Galaxy is one of the closest galaxies to the Milky Way Galaxy. It is 2.2 million light years away. Write the number of light years in standard form.

Study Guide
For use with Section 6

Comparisons and Predictions   Scientific Notation

GOAL   **LEARN HOW TO:** • write large numbers in scientific notation
AS YOU: • work with statistics about the planets

Exploration 1: Writing Numbers in Scientific Notation

To make reading and writing large numbers easier, they are often written in a form called **scientific notation**. Scientific notation uses powers of 10 to express the value of a number. In scientific notation, a number is expressed as a product where:

- the first part of the product is a number greater than or equal to 1 but less than 10, and

- the second part of the product is a power of 10.

Example

In scientific notation, $6{,}340{,}000{,}000 = 6.34 \cdot 10^9$

a number greater than   a power of 10
or equal to 1 but less than 10

Example

In standard form, $4.06 \cdot 10^8 = 4.06 \cdot 100{,}000{,}000$
$= 406{,}000{,}000$ ←   To multiply by 100,000,000, move the decimal point 8 places to the right.

Study Guide: Practice & Application Exercises
For use with Section 6

Exploration 1

Write each number in scientific notation.

1. 168,000

2. 18,000

3. 47,000,000

4. 7 billion

5. 3,760,000

6. 98 thousand

Write each number in standard form.

7. $6.3 \cdot 10^5$

8. $1.2 \cdot 10^3$

9. $7.94 \cdot 10^7$

10. $9.13 \cdot 10^{10}$

11. $7.7 \cdot 10^4$

12. $9.34 \cdot 10^8$

Use scientific notation to express each fact.

13. The diameter of Earth at the equator is about 7930 mi.

14. The distance from Earth to the sun when they are closest is about 91,400,000 mi.

15. The distance from Neptune to Earth when they are closest is about 2,678,000,000 mi.

16. The population of the United States is about 302,000,000.

17. The population of Canada is about 33,300,000.

18. The population of Mexico is about 108,700,000.

19. In New York City, about 1,070,000,000 gallons of water are consumed every day.

Without changing the numbers to standard form, order the numbers from least to greatest.

20. $5.6 \cdot 10^7, 5.6 \cdot 10^8, 5.6 \cdot 10^6$

21. $8.55 \cdot 10^4, 8.53 \cdot 10^4, 8.54 \cdot 10^4$

22. $2.39 \cdot 10^6, 3.29 \cdot 10^6, 9.23 \cdot 10^6$

23. $2.3 \cdot 10^4, 2.5 \cdot 10^6, 2.4 \cdot 10^4$

24. $1.4 \cdot 10^1, 1.3 \cdot 10^1, 1.2 \cdot 10^2$

25. $4.44 \cdot 10^5, 2.22 \cdot 10^4, 3.33 \cdot 10^5$

Practice and Applications
For use after Sections 1–6

For use with Section 1

1. Replace each ___?___ with the number that makes the statement true.

   a. ___?___ qt = 96 fl oz   **b.** ___?___ qt = 18 pt   **c.** $3\frac{1}{2}$ c = ___?___ fl oz

   d. ___?___ pt = 5 gal   **e.** $1\frac{1}{2}$ gal = ___?___ fl oz   **f.** ___?___ qt = 5 pt

2. Replace each ___?___ with the number that makes the statement true.

   a. 1900 L = ___?___ kL   **b.** 3 kL = ___?___ L   **c.** 175 mL = ___?___ L

   d. 0.27 kL = ___?___ L   **e.** 0.6 L = ___?___ mL   **f.** 20 L = ___?___ mL

For use with Section 2

3. Use front-end estimation to estimate each sum.

   a. 6122 + 1873   **b.** 13.8 + 11.9 + 27.5

   c. 411 + 390 + 120   **d.** 12 + 62 + 51 + 49

4. Use trading off to find each sum.

   a. 3.45 + 6.55   **b.** 22 + 48

   c. 12.3 + 32.4   **d.** 2998 + 7429

For use with Section 3

5. For each expression, describe the possible values for x.

   a. The sum 8 + x is a positive integer.

   b. The sum −5 + x is a negative integer.

   c. The sum x + 2 is zero.

6. Find each sum or difference.

   a. 11 + (−48)   **b.** −13 + 19   **c.** −58 + 39

   d. 16 − 58   **e.** −24 − 60   **f.** 16 − (−47)

7. The highest point in Louisiana is 535 ft above sea level. The lowest
   point is 8 ft below sea level. Write a subtraction expression to find the
   difference between the high and low elevations in Louisiana. What is
   the difference of the elevations?

(continued)

Math Thematics, Book 1
336 Student Workbook

MODULE 8

Practice and Applications
For use after Sections 1–6

For use with Section 4

8. Suppose an object falls at random onto each target shown below. For each target, find the probability that the object will land in a shaded region.

a.

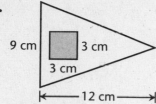

9 cm   3 cm

3 cm

⟵ 12 cm ⟶

b.

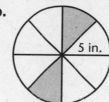

5 in.

For use with Section 5

9. Name the transformation that will move each shaded figure onto the unshaded figure.

a.

b.

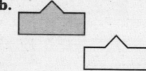

c.

For use with Section 6

10. Write each number in scientific notation.

   a. 8,900,000   **b.** 407,000   **c.** 500,000,000

11. Write each number in standard form.

   a. $6 \cdot 10^7$ **b.** $1.3 \cdot 10^4$ **c.** $7.02 \cdot 10^3$

12. Without changing the numbers to standard form, order the numbers from least to greatest.

   a. $1.45 \cdot 10^3, 1.3 \cdot 10^3, 1.5 \cdot 10^3$

   b. $4.3 \cdot 10^4, 4.3 \cdot 10^5, 4.3 \cdot 10^3$

   c. $8.7 \cdot 10^7, 7.8 \cdot 10^7, 8.8 \cdot 10^9$